# Palgrave Studies in Classical Liberalism

**Series Editors**
David F. Hardwick
Department of Pathology and Laboratory Medicine
The University of British Columbia
Vancouver, BC, Canada

Leslie Marsh
Department of Pathology and Laboratory Medicine
The University of British Columbia
Vancouver, BC, Canada

This series offers a forum to writers concerned that the central presuppositions of the liberal tradition have been severely corroded, neglected, or misappropriated by overly rationalistic and constructivist approaches.

The hardest-won achievement of the liberal tradition has been the wrestling of epistemic independence from overwhelming concentrations of power, monopolies and capricious zealotries. The very precondition of knowledge is the exploitation of the epistemic virtues accorded by society's situated and distributed manifold of spontaneous orders, the DNA of the modern civil condition.

With the confluence of interest in situated and distributed liberalism emanating from the Scottish tradition, Austrian and behavioral economics, non-Cartesian philosophy and moral psychology, the editors are soliciting proposals that speak to this multidisciplinary constituency. Sole or joint authorship submissions are welcome as are edited collections, broadly theoretical or topical in nature.

More information about this series at
http://www.palgrave.com/gp/series/15722

David F. Hardwick • Leslie Marsh
Editors

# Reclaiming Liberalism

palgrave
macmillan

*Editors*
David F. Hardwick
Department of Pathology and Laboratory Medicine
The University of British Columbia
Vancouver, BC, Canada

Leslie Marsh
Department of Pathology and Laboratory Medicine
The University of British Columbia
Vancouver, BC, Canada

ISSN 2662-6470 ISSN 2662-6489 (electronic)
Palgrave Studies in Classical Liberalism
ISBN 978-3-030-28759-7 ISBN 978-3-030-28760-3 (eBook)
https://doi.org/10.1007/978-3-030-28760-3



This Palgrave Macmillan imprint is published by the registered company Springer Nature Switzerland AG.
The registered company address is: Gewerbestrasse 11, 6330 Cham, Switzerland

**Francisco Goya: Plate 43 from 'Los Caprichos': The sleep of reason produces monsters (El sueño de la razon produce monstruos), 1799**

*To Virginia Baldwin: in appreciation of decades of interest and support (DH)*

*In memory of my grandparents, Sara and Samuel Fine, whose families the Bolsheviks wanted to banish and the Nazis wanted to snuff out (LM)*

# Preface

Each passing decade of the twentieth and twenty-first centuries has been accompanied by proclamations of liberalism's decline. Despite this, it is not at all clear whether the Owl of Minerva can be said to have taken flight. The "reclaiming" of the title of this collection is perhaps more a timely *re-excavation* of classical liberalism from the accumulated conceptual hubris and downright illiteracy that has come to obscure its central presupposition, which is, the wresting of epistemic independence from overwhelming concentrations of power, monopolies, and capricious zealotries, whether they be of a state, religious, or corporate in character. Unfortunately, much of what goes by the label of "liberal" is overly rationalistic and constructivist and, as such, stirs an authoritarian impulse in its implementation.

This collection offers a variety of disciplinary perspectives on liberalism, from a contemporary focus and some with a distinctly historical hue. Collectively these chapters will, in all probability, be deemed contentious. Classical liberals are a fractious lot, and though there will be internecine squabbles, no one viewpoint seeks to inhibit another's perspective.

Hayek's profound and paradoxical insight that knowledge becomes less incomplete only if it becomes more dispersed has informed our institutional design and operational management within the International Academy of Pathology and The University of British Columbia

Department of Pathology and Laboratory Medicine. Since we subscribe to Hayek's adage that "exclusive concentration on a specialty has a peculiarly baneful effect: it will not merely prevent us from being attractive company or good citizens but may impair our competence in our proper field", we make no apology for not staying within our academic silos.

Epistemic humility and open inquiry are central virtues for the classical liberal and this has proved the most successful way to approach the truth for the greater good. We thus thought that Aldous Huxley's comment[1] on Goya's caption "El sueño de la razon produce monstrous", as per the frontispiece, resonates deeply with the spirit of this project:

> It is a caption that admits of more than one interpretation. When reason sleeps, the absurd and loathsome creatures of superstition wake and are active, goading their victim to an ignoble frenzy. But this is not all. Reason may also dream without sleeping, may intoxicate itself, as it did during the French Revolution, with the daydreams of inevitable progress, of liberty, equality, and fraternity imposed by violence, of human self-sufficiency and the ending of sorrow ... by political rearrangements and a better technology.

Vancouver, BC, Canada

David F. Hardwick
Leslie Marsh

## Note

1. Aldous Huxley, "Variations on Goya," *On Art and Artists*, Morris Philipson, ed. (London: Chatto and Windus, 1960), pp. 218–19.

# Acknowledgments

We wish to thank the following for their community service: Corey Abel, Peter Barnes, Eugene Callahan, Gilles Campagnolo, Nicholas Capaldi, Lars Feld, Steven Gerencser, Ignacio Herrera-Anchustegui, Stefan Kolev, Peter Lewin, Drew Maciag, Terry Nardin, Noel O'Sullivan, and Viktor Vanberg.

We'd also like to thank the Palgrave team for their diligent and friendly support: Ruth Noble, Clara Heathcock, and last, but by no means least, Laura Pacey, who so carefully and enthusiastically gestated this series. Project Manager, Sarulatha Krishnamurthy's patient technical support, is also much appreciated.

Nothing we do could be done without the unwavering support of Charles Ramey and Shannon Selin.

# Contents

# Notes on Contributors

**Sarah M. Burns** is Assistant Professor of Political Science at Rochester Institute of Technology. Her research examines the intersection of political liberalization and American constitutional development, with an eye toward policy implications for democratization across the globe. She has written on war powers, American foreign policy, elections, and constitutionalism. Her latest book project examines the theoretical and historical development of war powers. She demonstrates how the constitutional system creates an invitation to struggle that the political branches increasingly ignore.

**Chor-yung Cheung** teaches politics in the Department of Public Policy of the City University of Hong Kong. His research interests are in the fields of Western political theory, modern Chinese political thought, and Hong Kong politics. His published books include《弗雷德里希·海耶克》(*Friedich Hayek*), 台北:聯經出版公司, 2018; *The Poetic Character of Human Activity: Collected Essays on the Thought of Michael Oakeshott*, co-authored with Wendell John Coats, Jr., 2012; and *The Quest for Civil Order: Politics, Rules and Individuality*, 2007.

**David D. Corey** is Professor of Political Science in the Honors College at Baylor University in Waco, Texas, USA. He is the author of *The Sophists* *in Plato's Dialogues* and (with J. Daryl Charles) *The Just War Tradition*. He is working on a book about the history and philosophy of liberalism.

**Gus diZerega** is a retired American political scientist, now working as an independent scholar. He has written extensively on liberalism, democratic theory, comparative politics, environmental theory, and F. A. Hayek in *The Review of Politics, The Western Political Quarterly, Cosmos + Taxis, The Independent Review, Studies in Emergent Order, Critical Review, Social Theory and Practice, Environmental Ethics, PEGS (Political Economy and the Good Society), Ideazione, Elites, Telos, The Trumpeter,* the *Journal of Ecosophy, Wirtschafts-Politische Blatter*, and many chapters in books. His own book on democracy is *Persuasion, Power and Polity: A Theory of Democratic Self-Organization.*

**David P. Ellerman** is a retired economist, mathematician, and philosopher affiliated as a visiting scholar at the University of California Riverside, visiting researcher at the University of Ljubljana, Slovenia, and fellow at the Stellenbosch Institute for Advanced Study. He taught economics for 20 years in the Boston area, founded several non-profit and for-profit consulting firms in the US and Eastern Europe focusing on worker ownership, and worked for ten years at the World Bank, including as senior advisor and speechwriter for Joseph Stiglitz. He has written five books and numerous articles in academic journals. Website: www.ellerman.org.

**Lauren K. Hall** is Associate Professor of Political Science at Rochester Institute of Technology. She is the author of *The Medicalization of Birth and Death*, 2019, and *Family and the Politics of Moderation*, 2014, and the co-editor of a volume on the political philosophy of French political thinker Chantal Delsol. She has written extensively on the classical liberal tradition, including articles on Edmund Burke, Adam Smith, and Montesquieu. She serves on the executive board of the interdisciplinary journal *Cosmos + Taxis*. Her current research deals with the politics of women and the family in classical liberalism as well as issues in bioethics and healthcare regulation.

**David F. Hardwick** is Professor Emeritus of Pathology and Paediatrics and is Special Advisor on Planning at the Faculty of Medicine at The University of British Columbia. He has also been Secretary of the International Academy of Pathology, the world's oldest and largest pathology organization. He is a founding co-editor of the *Palgrave Studies in Classical Liberalism* and is a prime mover behind the open-access journal *Cosmos + Taxis*. He also co-edited *Propriety and Prosperity: New Studies on the Philosophy of Adam Smith,* 2014.

**Andrew David Irvine** is Professor of Philosophy and Professor of Mathematics at The University of British Columbia (UBC), Okanagan. He is a past head of the Department of Economics, Philosophy and Political Science; a past senior advisor to the UBC president; and a past vice-chair of The University of British Columbia Board of Governors. He is also a past president of the British Columbia Civil Liberties Association and a member of the board of directors of the Society for Academic Freedom and Scholarship. An advocate of traditional democratic civil liberties, he has written about the importance of the rule of law for both modern and ancient democracies. He has held visiting positions at several Canadian and American universities.

**Leslie Marsh** is a senior researcher in Department of Pathology and Laboratory Medicine at The University of British Columbia. He is a prime mover behind the journals *EPISTEME* and *Cosmos + Taxis* and the Michael Oakeshott Association. He is a founding co-editor of the *Palgrave Studies in Classical Liberalism* and has written on social complexity, social epistemology, philosophical psychology, and the philosophy of literature—specializing in Michael Oakeshott, Friedrich Hayek, Adam Smith, Herbert Simon, Walker Percy, and John Kennedy Toole.

**Mikayla Novak** is in the School of Sociology at The Australian National University. Her research interests include political economy, inequality and living standards, economics of gender and race, economic and fiscal sociology, public choice, and constitutional political economy. Novak is the author of *Inequality: An Entangled Political Economy Perspective* (Palgrave Studies in Classical Liberalism series).

**Stephen Turner** is a Distinguished University Professor at the Department of Philosophy, University of South Florida. His books include *Liberal Democracy 3.0: Civil Society in an Age of Experts*, 2003, and essays collected in *The Politics of Expertise*, 2013. He has also written extensively on Max Weber, especially on politics, in *Max Weber and the Dispute Over Reason and Value: A Study in Philosophy, Ethics, and Politics*, 1984, and *Max Weber: The Lawyer as Social Thinker.*

**Chad Van Schoelandt** is an Assistant Professor in Tulane University's Department of Philosophy and also affiliated with Tulane's City, Culture, and Community PhD program; Tulane's Program in Medical Ethics and Human Values; and George Mason University's F. A. Hayek Program for Advanced Study in Philosophy, Politics, and Economics. He works on social and political philosophy, particularly in the public reason and social contract traditions, and his articles appear in journals including *Ethics*, *Social Philosophy & Policy*, and *Philosophical Studies.*

# List of Figures

## Reclaiming Democratic Classical Liberalism

# Reclaiming Democratic Classical Liberalism

David P. Ellerman

## Helping Others Versus Self-Help: Implications of Classical Liberalism

Classical liberalism expresses a skepticism about governmental organizations being able to "do good" for people. Instead an important role of government is to set up and maintain the conditions for people to be empowered and enabled to do good for themselves, for example, in establishing and enforcing the private property prerequisites for the functioning of a market economy as emphasized in the economic way of thinking (e.g., Heyne et al. 2006, pp. 36–38).

The reasons for the general ineffectiveness of the government to directly do good for people are not unique to government; the reasons apply as well to other external organizations that are also tasked to "do good" such

D. P. Ellerman (✉)
University of California, Riverside, Riverside, CA, USA

University of Ljubljana, Ljubljana, Slovenia
e-mail: david@ellerman.org



D. F. Hardwick, L. Marsh (eds.), *Reclaiming Liberalism*, Palgrave Studies in Classical Liberalism, https://doi.org/10.1007/978-3-030-28760-3_1

as philanthropic, development aid, or other helping organizations in general.[1] As John Dewey (1859–1952) put it:

> The best kind of help to others, whenever possible, is indirect, and consists in such modifications of the conditions of life, of the general level of subsistence, as enables them independently to help themselves (Dewey and Tufts 1908, p. 390).

The aim of a helping organization (including government) should not be to "do good" in any direct sense. The goal should be to increase people's autonomy, organizational efficacy, and effective social agency so they can do good for themselves—individually or, more likely, jointly in their *own organizations*. That is how the virtues of individual self-regarding activity in the marketplace generalize to the virtues of collective activity by people in their own organizations.

The classical liberal normative framework that emphasizes this autonomy and self-efficacy is perhaps best stated by James M. Buchanan (1919–2013):

> The justificatory foundation for a liberal social order lies, in my understanding, in the normative premise that individuals are the ultimate *sovereigns* in matters of social organization, that individuals are the beings who are entitled to choose the organizational-institutional structures under which they will live. In accordance with this premise, the legitimacy of social-organizational structures is to be judged against the voluntary agreement of those who are to live or are living under the arrangements that are judged. The central premise of *individuals as sovereigns* does allow for delegation of decision-making authority to agents, so long as it remains understood that individuals remain as *principals*. The premise denies legitimacy to all social-organizational arrangements that negate the role of individuals as either sovereigns or as principals (Buchanan 1999, p. 288).

It should be particularly noted that Buchanan goes beyond the common image of the sovereign individual acting in the marketplace to the individual acting in an organization which allows "for delegation of decision-making authority." Then the legitimacy of the "social-organizational arrangements" depends on the individuals being principals in their organizations.

## What Is Denied Legitimacy in the Classical Liberal Social Order?

### Coercive Institutions

The first broad category of institutions ruled out in the liberal social order are those that are involuntarily imposed without "the voluntary agreement of those who are to live" under the arrangements. The examples are standard fare in liberal thought such as (involuntary) slavery or (involuntary) non-democratic government (Fig. 1).

> Fundamentally, there are only two ways of co-ordinating the economic activities of millions. One is central direction involving the use of coercion—the technique of the army and of the modern totalitarian state. The other is voluntary co-operation of individuals—the technique of the market place (Friedman 1962, p. 13).

But Buchanan's strictures go beyond these war-horse examples to rule out the legitimacy of voluntary arrangements where the individuals do not remain principals. Since that institutional territory is little explored, if not little known, I will explore the intellectual history of such arrangements in some detail. The voluntary contractual arrangements where individuals do not remain principals are those that alienate (rather than

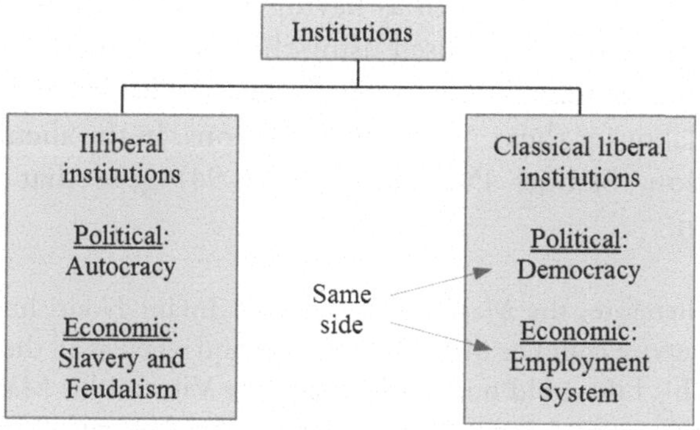


**Fig. 1** The conventional framing of coercion versus consent

delegate) decision-making authority. The contractually established decision-making ruler or ruling body rules in its own name and is not empowered only as a delegate or representative of the individuals under its authority. These alienation contracts can be divided into the individual and the collective cases.

## Individual Alienation Contracts: The Voluntary Slavery Contract

Today "slavery" is usually discussed as if it were intrinsically involuntary so that "'[v]oluntary slavery' is impossible, much as a spherical cube or a living corpse is impossible" (Palmer 2009, p. 457). But in fact from Antiquity onward, the sophisticated defense of slavery have always been based on implicit or explicit voluntary contracts. For western jurisprudence, the story starts with Roman law as codified in the *Institutes* of Justinian:

> Slaves either are born or become so. They are born so when their mother is a slave; they become so either by the law of nations, that is, by captivity, or by the civil law, as when a free person, above the age of twenty, suffers himself to be sold, that he may share the price given for him (*Institutes* Lib. I, Tit. III, sec. 4).

In addition to the third means of outright contractual slavery, the other two means were also seen as having aspects of contract. A person born of a slave mother and raised using the master's food, clothing, and shelter was considered as being in a perpetual servitude contract to trade a lifetime of labor for these and future provisions. In the alienable natural rights tradition, Samuel Pufendorf (1632–94) gave that contractual interpretation:

> Whereas, therefore, the Master afforded such Infant Nourishment, long before his Service could be of any Use to him; and whereas all the following Services of his Life could not much exceed the Value of his Maintenance, he is not to leave his Master's Service without his Consent. But 'tis manifest, That since these Bondmen came into a State of Servitude not by any

> Fault of their own, there can be no Pretence that they should be otherwise dealt withal, than as if they were in the Condition of perpetual hired Servants. (Pufendorf 2003 (1673), pp. 186–87).

Manumission was an early repayment or cancellation of that debt. And Thomas Hobbes (1588–1679), for example, clearly saw a "covenant" in the ancient practice of enslaving prisoners of war:

> And this dominion is then acquired to the victor when the vanquished, to avoid the present stroke of death, covenants either in express words or by other sufficient signs of the will that, so long as his life and the liberty of his body is allowed him, the victor shall have the use thereof at his pleasure. ... It is not, therefore, the victory that gives the right of dominion over the vanquished but his own covenant (Hobbes 1958 (1651), Bk. II, chapter 20).

Thus *all* of the three legal means of becoming a slave in Roman law had explicit or implicit contractual interpretations.

John Locke's (1632–1704) *Two Treatises of Government* (1690) is one of the classics of liberal thought. Locke would not condone a contract which gave the master the power of life or death over the slave:

> For a Man, not having the Power of his own Life, *cannot*, by Compact or his own Consent, *enslave* himself to any one, nor put himself under the Absolute, Arbitrary Power of another, to take away his Life, when he pleases (Second Treatise, §23).

This is the fount and source of what is sometimes taken as a "liberal doctrine of inalienable rights" (Tomasi 2012, p. 51). But after taking this edifying stand, Locke pirouettes in the next section and accepts a slavery contract that has some rights on both sides. Locke is only ruling out a voluntary version of the old Roman slavery where the master could take the life of the slave with impunity. But once the contract was put on a more civilized footing, Locke accepted the contract and renamed it "drudgery":

> For, if once *Compact* enter between them, and make an agreement for a limited Power on the one side, and Obedience on the other, the State of

> War and *Slavery* ceases, as long as the Compact endures.... I confess, we find among the *Jews*, as well as other Nations, that Men did sell themselves; but, 'tis plain, this was only to *Drudgery, not to Slavery*. For, it is evident, the Person sold was not under an Absolute, Arbitrary, Despotical Power (Second Treatise, §24).

Locke is here setting an intellectual pattern, repeated many times later, of taking a high moral stand against an extreme form of contractual slavery, but then turning around and accepting a civilized form on contractual slavery (e.g., rights on both sides at least in the law books) usually with some more palatable linguistic designation such as drudgery, perpetual servitude, or perpetual hired servant.

Moreover, Locke agreed with Hobbes on the practice of enslaving the war captives as a quid pro quo plea-bargained exchange of slavery instead of death and based on the ongoing consent of the captive:

> Indeed having, by his fault, forfeited his own Life, by some Act that deserves Death; he, to whom he has forfeited it, may (when he has him in his Power) delay to take it, and make use of him to his own Service, and he does him no injury by it. For, whenever he finds the hardship of his Slavery out-weigh the value of his Life, 'tis in his Power, by resisting the Will of his Master, to draw on himself the Death he desires (Second Treatise, §23).

In Locke's constitution for the Carolinas, he seemed to have justified slavery by interpreting the slaves purchased by the slave traders on the African coast as the captives in internal wars who had accepted the plea bargain of a lifetime of slavery instead of death.[2] Thereafter, the title was transferred by commercial contracts. If the slave later decides to renege on the plea-bargain contract and to take the other option, then "by resisting the Will of his Master, (he may) draw on himself the Death he desires."

Another basis for liberal jurisprudence is English common law. William Blackstone (1723–1780), in his codification of English common law, stuck to Locke's choreography. Blackstone rules out a slavery where "an absolute and unlimited power is given to the master over the life and fortune of the slave." Such a slave would be free "the instant he lands in

England." After such an edifying stand on high moral ground, Blackstone pirouettes and adds:

> Yet, with regard to any right which the master may have lawfully acquired to the perpetual service of John or Thomas, this will remain exactly in the same state as before: for this is no more than the same state of subjection for life, which every apprentice submits to for the space of seven years, or sometimes for a longer term (Blackstone 1959, section on "Master and Servant").

Another source of liberal thought is Montesquieu (1689–1755). On the question of voluntary slavery, he employed the same Lockean choreography in his treatment of inalienability and that treatment was paraphrased in modern times by the dean of high liberalism, John Rawls (1921–2002). Montesquieu begins with the usual repudiation of the self-sale contract in an extreme form:

> To sell one's freedom is so repugnant to all reason as can scarcely be supposed in any man. If liberty may be rated with respect to the buyer, it is beyond all price to the seller (Montesquieu 1912 (1748), Vol. I, Bk. XV, Chap. II).

Rawls paraphrases this argument from Montesquieu to argue that in the original position, the

> grounds upon which the parties are moved to guarantee these liberties, together with the constraints of the reasonable, explain why the basic liberties are, so to speak, beyond all price to persons so conceived. (Rawls 1996, p. 366)

After the "beyond all price" passage paraphrased by Rawls, Montesquieu goes on to note: "I mean slavery in a strict sense, as it formerly existed among the Romans, and exists at present in our colonies" (Montesquieu 1912 (1748), Vol. I, Bk. XV, Chap. II). Then Montesquieu performs his *volte-face* by noting that this would not exclude a civilized or "mild" form of the contract.

> This is the true and rational origin of that mild law of slavery which obtains in some countries; and mild it ought to be, as founded on the free choice a man makes of a master, for his own benefit; which forms a mutual convention between two parties (Montesquieu 1912 (1748), Vol. I, Bk. XV, Chap. V).

And then Rawls goes on to follow the same choreography in his treatment of inalienability:

> This explanation of why the basic liberties are inalienable does not exclude the possibility that even in a well-ordered society some citizens may want to circumscribe or alienate one or more of their basic liberties. …
>
> Unless these possibilities affect the agreement of the parties in the original position (and I hold that they do not), they are irrelevant to the inalienability of the basic liberties (Rawls 1996, pp. 366–67 and fn. 82).

Of course, no one thinks that John Rawls would personally endorse a voluntary slavery contract, but the question is his theories, not his personal views. And in his treatment of inalienability, he repeated the pattern and even some of the language ("beyond all price") of a "liberal doctrine of inalienable rights" descending from Locke, Blackstone, and Montesquieu that *did* explicitly endorse a civilized form of voluntary contractual slavery, drudgery, or perpetual servitude.[3] Below we will outline the *genuine* theory of inalienable rights that descends from the Reformation inalienability of conscience through the Scottish and German Enlightenments and English Dissenters, and that was transferred "from a religious on to a juridical plane" (Lincoln 1971, p. 2) by the abolitionist and democratic movements.[4]

Rawls' Harvard colleague, Robert Nozick (1938–2002), was notoriously explicit in accepting the (re)validation of the voluntary slavery contract.[5] He accepted that a free society should allow people to jointly alienate their political sovereignty to a "dominant protective association" (Nozick 1974, p. 15):

> The comparable question about an individual is whether a free system will allow him to sell himself into slavery. I believe that it would (Nozick 1974, p. 331).

Nozick is reported to have had second thoughts in his later life precisely on the question of inalienability, but Nozick never developed a *theory* of inalienability that would overturn his earlier position.[6]

The contractual defense of slavery was also used in the debate over slavery in ante-bellum America. The proslavery position is usually presented as being based on illiberal racist or paternalistic arguments. Considerable attention is lavished on illiberal paternalistic writers such as George Fitzhugh,[7] while consent-based contractarian defenders of slavery are passed over in silence. For example, Rev. Samuel Seabury (1801–1872) gave a sophisticated liberal-contractarian defense of ante-bellum slavery in the tradition of alienable natural rights theory:

> From all which it appears that, wherever slavery exists as a settled condition or institution of society, the bond which unites master and servant is of a moral nature; founded in right, not in might; .... Let the origin of the relation have been what it may, yet when once it can plead such prescription of time as to have received a fixed and determinate character, it must be assumed to be founded in the consent of the parties, and to be, to all intents and purposes, a compact or covenant, of the same kind with that which lies at the foundation of all human society (Seabury 1969 (1861), p. 144).

> "Contract!" methinks I hear them exclaim; "look at the poor fugitive from his master's service! He bound by contract! A good joke, truly." But ask these same men what binds them to society? Are they slaves to their rulers? O no! They are bound together by the COMPACT on which society is founded. Very good; but did you ever sign this compact? Did your fathers every sign it? "No; it is a tacit and implied contract." (Seabury 1969 (1861), p. 153).

Yet this voluntary contractual defense of slavery has largely gone down the memory hole in the liberal intellectual history of the slavery debates. For instance, McKitrick (1963) collects essays of fifteen proslavery writers, Faust (1981) collects seven proslavery essays, and Finkelman (2003) collects seventeen proslavery writers, but *none* of them include a single writer who argues to allow slavery on a contractual basis such as Seabury—not to mention Grotius, Pufendorf, Hobbes, Locke, Blackstone, Molina, Suarez, Montesquieu, and a host of others.[8]

The intellectual history of civilized voluntary slavery contracts concludes with modern economic theory. Often the discussion of slavery is colored with excesses and attributes that were unnecessary to slavery as an economic institution. The economic essence of the contract is the lifetime ownership of labor services by the master, not the ownership of persons or souls or the like. Even the Stoic philosopher Chrysippus noted that "a slave should be treated as a 'laborer hired for life'" (Sabine 1958, p. 150). James Mill explained:

> The only difference is, in the mode of purchasing. The owner of the slave purchases, at once, the whole of the labour, which the man can ever perform: he, who pays wages, purchases only so much of a man's labour as he can perform in a day, or any other stipulated time (Mill 1826, Chapter I, section II).

And ante-bellum slavery apologists made a similar point:

> Our property in man is a right and title to human labor. And where is it that this right and title does not exist on the part of those who have money to buy it? The only difference in any two cases is the tenure (Bryan 1858, p. 10; quoted in Philmore 1982, p. 43).

One of the most elementary points in the solely economic way of thinking is that the prohibition of a voluntary exchange between a willing buyer and willing seller (in the absence of externalities) precludes allocative efficiency. For instance, efficiency requires full futures markets in all goods and services including human labor. Any attempt to truncate future labor contracts at, say, T years could violate market efficiency since there might today be willing buyers and sellers of labor to be performed T + 1 years in the future. Hence market efficiency requires full future markets in labor—which allows the perpetual servitude contract. One will not find this point in the textbooks on the economic way of thinking, but the Johns Hopkins University economist Carl Christ made the point quite explicit in no less a forum than Congressional testimony:

> Now it is time to state the conditions under which private property and free contract will lead to an optimal allocation of resources .... The institution of private property and free contract as we know it is modified to

> permit individuals to sell or mortgage their persons in return for present and/or future benefits (Christ 1975, p. 334).

In spite of the efficiency losses, the voluntary contract to capitalize all of one's labor is now abolished:

> Since slavery was abolished, human earning power is forbidden by law to be capitalized. A man is not even free to sell himself; he must *rent* himself at a wage (Samuelson 1976, p. 52). [9]

## Individual Alienation Contracts: The Coverture Marriage Contract

Another historical example of a personal alienation contract is the *coverture marriage contract* that "identified" the legal personality of the wife with that of the husband:

> By marriage, the husband and wife are one person in law: that is, the very being or legal existence of the woman is suspended during the marriage, or at least is incorporated and consolidated into that of the husband; under whose wing, protection, and cover, she performs everything; and is therefore called in our law-French, a feme covert, and is said to be under the protection and influence of her husband, her baron, or lord; and her condition during her marriage is called her coverture (Blackstone 1959 (1765), section on husband and wife).

The baron–femme relationship established by the coverture marriage contract exemplified the identity fiction in past domestic law. A female was to pass from the cover of her father to the cover of her husband (the origin of today's vestiges where the bride's father "gives away" the bride to the groom and the bride takes the groom's family name)—always a "femme covert" instead of the anomalous "femme sole." The identity fiction for the baron–femme relation was that "the husband and wife are one person in law" with the implicit or explicit rider, "and that one person is the husband." A wife could own property and make contracts, but only in the name of her husband. Obedience counted as "fulfilling" the contract to have the wife's legal personality subsumed under and identified with that of the husband.

## Collective Alienation Contracts: The Hobbesian *Pactum Subjectionis*

Democracy is not merely "government based on the consent of the governed," since that consent might be to a pact of subjection or *pactum subjectionis*, wherein people alienate (not delegate) their decision-making sovereignty to a ruler. The political constitution of subjection (which turns a citizen into a subject) finds its classic expression in Hobbes, but the idea of an implicit or explicit non-democratic constitution again goes back to Antiquity.

Again we may begin the intellectual history with Roman law. The sovereignty of the Roman emperor was usually seen as being founded on a contract of rulership enacted by the Roman people. The Roman jurist Ulpian gave the classic and oft-quoted statement of this view in the *Institutes* of Justinian (1948):

> Whatever has pleased the prince has the force of law, since the Roman people by the *lex regia* enacted concerning his *imperium*, have yielded up to him all their power and authority.[10]

The American constitutional scholar Edward S. Corwin noted the questions that arose in the Middle Ages about the nature of this pact:

> During the Middle Ages the question was much debated whether the *lex regia* effected an absolute alienation (*translatio*) of the legislative power to the Emperor, or was a revocable delegation (*cessio*). The champions of popular sovereignty at the end of this period, like Marsiglio of Padua in his *Defensor Pacis*, took the latter view (Corwin 1955, p. 4, fn. 8).

It is precisely this question of *translatio* or *concessio*—alienation or delegation of the right of government in the contract—that is the key question, not consent versus coercion. Consent is on both sides of that alienation (*translatio*) versus delegation (*concessio*) framing of the question—and thus the later Buchanan moved beyond the calculus of consent (1962) to the additional requirement that people remain the principals who only delegate their decision-making authority. The alienation version of the contract became a sophisticated tacit contract defense of non-democratic government wherever the latter existed as a settled condition. And the delegation version of the contract became the foundation for democratic theory.

The German legal thinker Otto von Gierke (1841–1921) was quite clear about the alienation-versus-delegation question:

> This dispute also reaches far back into the Middle Ages. It first took a strictly juristic form in the dispute ... as to the legal nature of the ancient "*translatio imperii*" from the Roman people to the Princeps. One school explained this as a definitive and irrevocable alienation of power, the other as a mere concession of its use and exercise. ... On the one hand from the people's abdication the most absolute sovereignty of the prince might be deduced, .... On the other hand the assumption of a mere "*concessio imperii*" led to the doctrine of popular sovereignty (Gierke 1966, pp. 93–94).

A state of government which had been settled for many years was seen as being legitimated by the tacit consent of the people. Thomas Aquinas (1225–74) expressed the canonical medieval view:

> Aquinas had laid it down in his *Summary of Theology* that, although the consent of the people is essential in order to establish a legitimate political society, the act of instituting a ruler always involves the citizens in alienating—rather than merely delegating—their original sovereign authority (Skinner 1978, Vol. I, p. 62).

In about 1310, according to Gierke, "Engelbert of Volkersdorf is the first to declare in a general way that all *regna et principatus* originated in a *pactum subjectionis* which satisfied a natural want and instinct" (1958, p. 146). Indeed, at least by the late Middle Ages,

> there was developed a doctrine which taught that the State had a rightful beginning in a Contract of Subjection to which the People was party ....

> Indeed that the legal title to all Rulership lies in the voluntary and contractual submission of the Ruled could therefore be propounded as a philosophic axiom (Gierke 1958, pp. 38–40).

That idea passed over into the alienable natural law tradition. After noting that an individual could sell himself into slavery under Hebrew and Roman law, Hugo Grotius (1583–1645) extends the possibility to the political level:

> Now if an individual may do so, why may not a whole people, for the benefit of better government and more certain protection, completely transfer their sovereign rights to one or more persons, without reserving any portion to themselves? (Grotius 1901 (1625), p. 63).

Thomas Hobbes made the best-known attempt to found non-democratic government on the consent of the governed. Without an overarching power to hold people in awe, life would be a constant war of all against all. To prevent this state of chaos and strife, men should join together and voluntarily alienate and transfer the right of self-government to a person or body of persons as the sovereign. This *pactum subjectionis* would be a

> covenant of every man with every man, in such manner as if every man should say to every man, I authorize and give up my right of governing myself to this man, or to this assembly of men, on this condition, that you give up your right to him and authorize all his actions in like manner (Hobbes 1958 (1651), p. 142).

The consent-based contractarian tradition is brought fully up to date in Robert Nozick's contemporary libertarian defense of the contract to alienate one's right of self-determination to a "dominant protective association."

In view of this history of apologetics for autocracy based on consent, the conventional distinction between coercion and government based on the "consent of the governed" was *not* the key to democratic theory. The real debate was within the sphere of consent and was between the alienation (*translatio*) and delegation (*concessio*) versions of the basic social or political constitution. Late medieval thinkers such as Marsilius of Padua (1275–1342) and Bartolus of Saxoferrato (1314–57) laid some of the foundations for democratic theory in the distinction between consent that establishes a relation of delegation versus consent to an alienation of authority:

> The theory of popular sovereignty developed by Marsiglio (Marsilius) and Bartolus was destined to play a major role in shaping the most radical version of early modern constitutionalism. Already they are prepared to argue that sovereignty lies with the people, that they only delegate and never alienate it, and thus that no legitimate ruler can ever enjoy a higher status than that of an official appointed by, and capable of being dismissed by, his own subjects (Skinner 1978, Vol. I, p. 65).

As Marsilius put it:

> The aforesaid whole body of citizens or the weightier part thereof is the legislator regardless of whether it makes the law directly by itself or entrusts the making of it to some person or persons, who are not and cannot be the legislator in the absolute sense, but only in a relative sense and for a particular time and in accordance with the authority of the primary legislator (Marsilius 1980 (1324), p. 45).

According to Bartolus, the citizens "constitute their own *princeps*," so any authority held by their rulers and magistrates "is only delegated to them (*concessum est*) by the sovereign body of the people" (Skinner 1978, Vol. I, p. 62).

Quentin Skinner, writing in the civic republican tradition, continually emphasized the alienation-versus-delegation theme in his two volumes, *The Foundations of Modern Political Thought* (1978). Yet other modern intellectual historians, such as Jonathan Israel (e.g., 2010) writing in more the conventional liberal tradition, have covered the same history of democratic thought and yet ignore the alienation-versus-delegation theme[11] in favor of the emphasis on the consent of the governed as if that were sufficient to entail democratic government.[12] This is in spite of Gierke pointing out that at least by the late Middle Ages, it was "propounded as a philosophic axiom" that "the legal title to all Rulership lies in the voluntary and contractual submission of the Ruled."

This highlights the importance of James Buchanan, in his mature work, of seeing classical liberalism as requiring social-organizational arrangements that are not only voluntary but have people remaining as sovereigns or as principals only delegating their decision-making authority. That establishes a theoretical bond between classical liberalism and democracy:

> To Plato there are natural slaves and natural masters, with the consequences that follow for social organization, be it economic or political. To Adam Smith, by contrast, who is in this as in other aspects the archetype classical liberal, the philosopher and the porter are natural equals with observed differences readily explainable by culture and choice (Buchanan 2005, p. 67).

This natural equality means the sovereigns-or-principals principle would apply to all and thus would rule out governance arrangements based on a voluntary contract of alienation of governance rights:

> The postulate of natural equality carries with it the requirement that genuine classical liberals adhere to democratic principles of governance; political equality as a necessary norm makes us all small 'd' democrats (Buchanan 2005, p. 69).

This implication of Buchanan's version of *democratic* classical liberalism exposes a fault line that runs through today's classical liberal and libertarian thinkers. For instance, it would rule out the non-democratic governance contract to be agreed to "for the benefit of better government and more certain protection" by voluntarily moving to a charter city, a startup city, a shareholder state, or a seastead city—all of which are widely supported by free-market thinkers along classical liberal, libertarian, or Austrian lines:

> (I)f one starts a private town, on land whose acquisition did not and does not violate the Lockean proviso (of non-aggression), persons who chose to move there or later remain there would have no right to a say in how the town was run, unless it was granted to them by the decision procedures for the town which the owner had established (Nozick 1974, p. 270).

The libertarian bottom line is that government must be based on consent which includes the possibility of exit when consent is withdrawn. Libertarianism is, of course, not against democratic government; the point is that democracy is only one choice among other consent-based rule-of-law governments. The point is that there should be a "democratizing choice of law, governance, and regulation"[13] which includes well-regulated non-democratic enclaves like old Hong Kong and new Dubai. Libertarian models of consent-based non-democratic municipal or state governments include the notion of "free cities" or "startup cities," proprietary cities, Patri Friedman's floating seastead cities, Paul Romer's charter cities, or "shareholder states" (Tyler Cowen's phrase) all of which see the resident-subjects as having agreed to a *pactum subjectionis* as evidenced by their voluntary decision to move to and remain in the city or state (assuming free exit).

The philosophical defense of charter/startup cities (e.g., Freiman 2013) also applies the solely economic way of thinking to the piecemeal voluntary alienation of decision-making in the selling of votes:

> Under normal conditions voluntary economic exchange is *ex ante* mutually beneficial. A trade is not consummated unless both parties expect to benefit. I will exchange a quarter for an apple only if I value the apple more than the quarter and an apple seller will exchange an apple for my quarter only if she values the quarter more than the apple. The same analysis applies to votes. I'll sell my vote for *n* dollars only if I value *n* dollars more than my vote and the buyer will buy my vote for *n* dollars only if she values my vote more than *n* dollars. All things equal, vote markets leave both buyers and sellers better off (Freiman 2014, p. 3).[14]

## Inalienable Rights: Minimum Constraints on the Economic Way of Thinking

### The Self-Sale Contract and the *Pactum Subjectionis*

We have seen that the debate about slavery and non-democratic government was not a simple consent-versus-coercion debate. From Antiquity down to the present, there were consent-based arguments for slavery and autocracy as being founded on certain explicit or implicit contracts. The abolitionist and democratic movements needed to answer not just the worst but the "best" arguments based on explicit or implicit voluntary contracts.

In contrast to the faux "liberal doctrine of inalienable rights" developed by Locke, Blackstone, and Montesquieu, the abolitionist and democratic movements developed arguments that there was something inherently invalid in the voluntary alienation contracts—even there might be mutual benefits, and thus that the rights which these contracts pretended to alienate were in fact inalienable. The theory of inalienable rights gives minimum constraints on the economic-way-of-thinking arguments applied to personal alienation contracts such as the voluntary self-sale contract and the collective pact of subjection (and, one might add, the coverture marriage contract) which are already abolished.

The key is that in consenting to such an alienation contract, a person is agreeing to, in effect, take on the legal role of a non-adult, indeed, a non-person or thing. Yet all the consent in the world would not in fact turn an adult into a minor or person of diminished capacity, not to mention, turn a person into a thing. The most the person could do was obey the master, sovereign, or employer—and the authorities would "count" *that* as fulfilling the contract. Then all the legal rights and obligations would be assigned according to the "contract" (as if the person in fact had diminished or no capacity). But since the person remained a de facto fully capacitated adult person with only the legal-contractual role of a non-person, the contract was impossible and invalid. A system of positive law that accepted such contracts was only a legalized fraud on an institutional scale.

Applying this argument requires prior analysis to tell when a contract puts a person in the legal role of a non-person. Having the role of a non-person is not necessarily explicit in the contract and it has nothing to do with the payment in the contract, the incompleteness of the contract, or the like. Persons and things can be distinguished on the basis of decision-making and responsibility. For instance, a genuine thing such as a tool like a shovel can be alienated or transferred from person A to B. Person A, the owner of the tool, can indeed give up making decisions about the use of the tool and person B can take over making those decisions. Person A does not have the responsibility for the consequences of the employment of the tool by person B. Person B makes the decisions about using the tool and has the de facto responsibility for the results of that use. Thus a contract to sell or rent a tool such as a shovel from A to B can actually be fulfilled. The decision-making and responsibility for employing the tool can *in fact* be transferred or alienated from A to B.

But now replace the tool by person A himself or herself. Suppose that the contract was for person A to sell or rent himself or herself to person B—as if a person was a transferable or alienable instrument that could be "employed" by another person like a shovel might be employed by others. The *pactum subjectionis* is a collective version of such a contract but it is easier to understand the individualistic version. The contract could be perfectly voluntary. For whatever reason and compensation, person A is willing to take on the legal role of a talking instrument (to use Aristotle's phrase). But the person A cannot in fact transfer decision-making or responsibility over his or her own actions to B. The point is not that a person should not or ought not do it or that the person is not paid enough; the point is that a person *cannot* in fact make such a voluntary transfer. At most, person A can agree to cooperate with B by doing what B says—even if B's instructions are quite complete. But that is no alienation or transference of decision-making or responsibility. Person A is still inexorably involved in ratifying B's decisions and person A inextricably shares the de facto responsibility for the results of A's and B's joint activity—as everyone recognizes in the case of a hired criminal.

Yet a legal system could "validate" such a (non-criminous) contract and could "count" obedience to the master or sovereign as "fulfilling" the contract and then rights are structured *as if* it were actually fulfilled, that is, as if the person were actually of diminished or no capacity. But such an institutionalized fraud always has one revealing moment when anyone can see the legal fiction behind the system. That is when the legalized "thing" would commit a crime. Then the "thing" would be suddenly metamorphosed—in the eyes of the law—back into being a person to be held legally responsible for the crime. For instance, an ante-bellum Alabama court asserted that slaves

> are rational beings, they are capable of committing crimes; and in reference to acts which are crimes, are regarded as persons. Because they are slaves, they are … incapable of performing civil acts, and, in reference to all such, they are things, not persons (Catterall 1926, p. 247).

Since there was no legal theory that slaves *physically* became things in their "civil acts," the fiction involved in treating the slaves as "things" was clear. And this is a question of the facts about human nature, facts that are unchanged by consent or contract. If the slave had acquired that legal role in a voluntary contract, it would not change the fact that the contractual slave remained a de facto person with the law only "counting" the contractual slave's non-criminous obedience as "fulfilling" the contract to play the legal role of a non-responsible entity, a non-person or thing.

## The Self-Rental Contract

The surprising and controversial result is that the inalienability argument applies as well to the self-rental contract—that is, today's employment contract—as to the self-sale contract or pact of subjection.[15] I can certainly voluntarily agree to a contract to be "employed" by an "employer" on a long- or short-term basis, but I cannot in fact "transfer" my own actions for the long or short term. The factual inalienability of responsible human action and decision-making is independent of the duration of the contract. That factual inalienability is also independent of the compensation paid in the contract—which is why this inalienability analysis has *nothing* to do with exploitation theories of either the Marxian variety (extracting more labor time than is embodied in the wages) or neoclassical variety (paying wages less than the value of the marginal productivity of labor).

Where the legal system "validates" such contracts, it must fictitiously "count" one's inextricably co-responsible cooperation with the "employer" as fulfilling the employment contract—unless, of course, the employer and employee commit a crime together. The servant in work then morphs into the co-responsible partner in crime:

> All who participate in a crime with a guilty intent are liable to punishment. A master and servant who so participate in a crime are liable criminally, not because they are master and servant, but because they jointly carried out a criminal venture and are both criminous (Batt 1967, p. 612).

When the "venture" being "jointly carried out" by the employer and employee is not criminous, then the *facts* about human responsibility are unchanged. But then the fiction takes over. The joint venture or partnership is transformed into the employer's sole venture. The employee is legally transformed from being a co-responsible partner to being only an input supplier sharing no legal responsibility for either the input liabilities or the produced outputs of the employer's business.

## Some Intellectual History of Inalienable Rights

Where has this key insight—that a person cannot voluntarily fit the legal role of a non-person (e.g., the de facto inalienability of responsible agency)—erupted in the history of thought? The Ancients did not see this matter clearly. For Aristotle, slavery was based on "fact"; some adults were seen as being inherently of diminished capacity if not as "talking instruments" marked for slavery "from the hour of their birth." Treating them as slaves was no more inappropriate for Aristotle than treating a donkey as a non-person.

The Stoics held the radically different view that no one was a slave by their nature; slavery was an *external* condition juxtaposed to the internal freedom of the soul. After being essentially lost during the Middle Ages, the Stoic doctrine that the "inner part cannot be delivered into bondage" (Davis 1966, p. 77) re-emerged in the Reformation doctrine of liberty of conscience. Secular authorities who try to compel belief can only secure external conformity:

> Besides, the blind, wretched folk do not see how utterly hopeless and impossible a thing they are attempting. For no matter how much they fret and fume, they cannot do more than make people obey them by word or deed; the heart they cannot constrain, though they wear themselves out trying. For the proverb is true, "Thoughts are free." Why then would they constrain people to believe from the heart, when they see that it is impossible? (Luther 1942 (1523), p. 316).

Martin Luther was explicit about the de facto element; it was "impossible" to "constrain people to believe from the heart.":

> Furthermore, every man is responsible for his own faith, and he must see it for himself that he believes rightly. As little as another can go to hell or heaven for me, so little can he believe or disbelieve for me; and as little as he can open or shut heaven or hell for me, so little can he drive me to faith

> or unbelief. Since, then, belief or unbelief is a matter of every one's conscience, and since this is no lessening of the secular power, the latter should be content and attend to its own affairs and permit men to believe one thing or another, as they are able and willing, and constrain no one by force (ibid.).

Although an atheist and a Jew, it was perhaps Benedict de Spinoza (1632–1677) who first translated the Protestant doctrine of the inalienability of conscience into the political notion of a right that could not be ceded "even with consent." In Spinoza's 1670 *Theologico-Political Treatise*, he spelled out the essentials of the inalienable rights argument:

> However, we have shown already (Chapter XVII) that no man's mind can possibly lie wholly at the disposition of another, for no one can willingly transfer his natural right of free reason and judgment, or be compelled so to do. For this reason government which attempts to control minds is accounted tyrannical, and it is considered an abuse of sovereignty and a usurpation of the rights of subjects, to seek to prescribe what shall be accepted as true, or rejected as false, or what opinions should actuate men in their worship of God. All these questions fall within a man's natural right, which he cannot abdicate even with consent (Spinoza 1951, p. 257).

But it was Francis Hutcheson (1694–1746), the predecessor of Adam Smith in the chair in moral philosophy in Glasgow and one of the leading moral philosophers of the Scottish Enlightenment, who (independently?) arrived at the same idea in the form that was to later enter the political lexicon through the American Declaration of Independence. Although intimated in earlier works (1725), the inalienability argument is best developed in Hutcheson's influential *A System of Moral Philosophy*:

> Our rights are either *alienable*, or *unalienable*. The former are known by these two characters jointly, that the translation of them to others can be made effectually, and that some interest of society, or individuals consistently with it, may frequently require such translations. Thus our right to our goods and labours is naturally alienable. But where either the translation cannot be made with any effect, or where no good in human life requires it, the right is unalienable, and cannot be justly claimed by any other but the person originally possessing it (Hutcheson 1755, p. 261).

Hutcheson appeals to the inalienability argument in addition to utility. He contrasts de facto alienable goods where "the translation of them to others can be made effectually" (like the aforementioned shovel) with factually inalienable faculties where "the translation cannot be made with any effect." This was not just some outpouring of moral emotions that one should not alienate this or that basic right. Hutcheson actually set forth a *theory* which could have legs of its own far beyond Hutcheson's (not to mention Luther's) intent. He based the theory on what in fact could or could not be transferred or alienated from one person to another. Hutcheson goes on to show how the "right of private judgment" is inalienable:

> Thus no man can really change his sentiments, judgments, and inward affections, at the pleasure of another; nor can it tend to any good to make him profess what is contrary to his heart. The right of private judgment is therefore unalienable (Hutcheson 1755, pp. 261–62).

Democratic theory carried over this theory from the inalienability of conscience to a critique of the Hobbesian *pactum subjectionis*, the contract to alienate and transfer the right of self-determination as if it were a property right that could be transferred from a people to a sovereign:

> There is, at least, one right that cannot be ceded or abandoned: the right to personality. Arguing upon this principle the most influential writers on politics in the seventeenth century rejected the conclusions drawn by Hobbes. They charged the great logician with a contradiction in terms. If a man could give up his personality he would cease being a moral being. … This fundamental right, the right to personality, includes in a sense all the others. To maintain and to develop his personality is a universal right. It … cannot, therefore, be transferred from one individual to another. … There is no *pactum subjectionis*, no act of submission by which man can give up the state of a free agent and enslave himself (Cassirer 1963, p. 175).

Few have seen these connections as clearly as Staughton Lynd in his *Intellectual Origins of American Radicalism* (1969). When commenting on Hutcheson's theory, Lynd noted that when "rights were termed 'unalienable' in this sense, it did not mean that they could not be transferred without consent, but that their nature made them untransferrable"

(Lynd 1969, p. 45).[16] The crucial link was to go from the de facto inalienable liberty of conscience to a *theory* of inalienable rights based on the same idea:

> Like the mind's quest for religious truth from which it was derived, self-determination was not a claim to ownership which might be both acquired and surrendered, but an inextricable aspect of the activity of being human. (Lynd 1969, pp. 56–57)

In the American Declaration of Independence, "Jefferson took his division of rights into alienable and unalienable from Hutcheson, who made the distinction popular and important" (Wills 1979, p. 213). But the theory behind the notion of inalienable rights was lost in the transition from the Scottish Enlightenment to the slave-holding society of ante-bellum America. The phraseology of "inalienable rights" is a staple in our political culture, for example, our 4th of July rhetoric, but the original theory of inalienability has been largely ignored or forgotten (Fig. 2).[17]

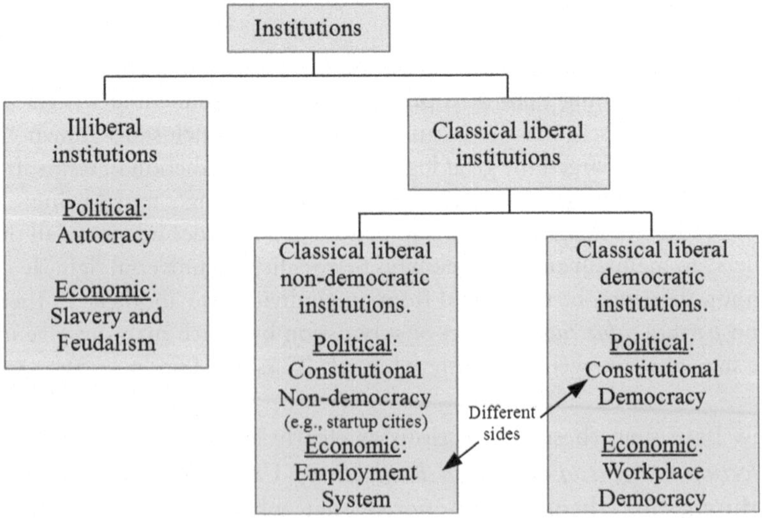


**Fig. 2** Reframing that separates non-democratic and democratic classical liberalism

## The Implications for Today's Social-Organizational Structures

After this long "detour" through intellectual history, we must return to the main theme of how the virtues of individual self-regarding activity in the marketplace might generalize to the virtues of collective activity by people in their own organizations. We have taken James M. Buchanan's description of the normative basis for classical liberalism as the framework to apply to the theme. We have also noted that Buchanan's mature thought moved beyond the mere calculus of consent in the solely economic way of thinking to the stronger requirement that people always remain sovereign or principals who only delegate decision-making authority. And we have noted how Buchanan's strictures implied democratic self-governance in contrast to the currents of right-libertarianism and Austrian thought that accept the consent of the governed to non-democratic governance, for example, startup cities.

In many modern discussions of associative and deliberative democracy (e.g., in the tradition of Tocqueville), there is a curious "dog that didn't bark." The emphasis is rightly on the associative activities of citizens who come together for discussion, dialogue, deliberation, and responsible action to address problems that they cannot resolve at the level of the individual or the family. People create many associations for collective action: church groups, charities, issue-oriented non-profits, unions, social clubs, hobby groups, political parties, and ad hoc special-purpose groups. People might participate after-hours in these various Tocquevillean associations to try to accomplish together what they cannot accomplish individually.

But that list of non-governmental associations leaves out the one organization that dominates most people's lives outside the family, namely, the workplace.[18] That lacuna corresponds to the curious classification of non-governmental organizations into the second sector of private workplace organizations and the third sector of "non-profit" organizations.

Of course, some people work for themselves or in small family firms so those workplaces are only a marginal extension of family life. But most people work in larger organizations requiring the concerted associated activities of many non-family members. These work organizations provide the primary sites, outside the family, where people acquire mental habits and social skills and where they engage in effective collective activities.

Almost all workplaces are organized on the basis of the employment contract. In common usage, to have an income-producing job is to be "employed." Indeed, Ronald Coase (1910–2013) identifies the nature of the firm with the "legal relationship normally called that of 'master and servant' or 'employer and employee'" (1937, p. 403).[19]

In the employment contract, the employees are not Buchanan's principals; they do not delegate decision-making authority to the employer. The employer is not the representative or delegate of the employees; the employer does not manage the organization in the name of those who are managed. The employees are not directly or indirectly part of the decision-making group; the employees have alienated and transferred to the employer the discretionary decision-making rights over their activities within the scope of the employment contract. In short, the employment contract is the limited *pactum subjectionis* of the workplace.

The form of workplace organization that would satisfy the strictures of Buchanan's liberalism is one where all the people working in a firm are the members or workplace citizens. That requires re-constituting the corporation as a democratic organization; the workplace citizens are the principals who only delegate decision-making authority to the managers.

## Two Earlier Liberal Philosophers

### John Stuart Mill

To see the context and corroboration for Buchanan's normative framework, we might consider the work of two earlier liberal philosophers, John Stuart Mill (1806–1873) and John Dewey.

Mill argued that social institutions should be judged in large part by the degree to which they "promote the general mental advancement of the community, including under that phrase advancement in intellect, in virtue, and in practical activity and efficiency" (Mill 1972, Chapter 6).

Mill saw government by discussion as an "agency of national education" and mentioned "the practice of the dicastery and the ecclesia" in ancient Athens as institutions that developed the active political capabilities of the citizens.

In his *Principles of Political Economy*, Mill considered how the form of work would affect those capabilities and how the workplace association could become a school for the civic virtues if it progressed beyond the employment relation:

> But if public spirit, generous sentiments, or true justice and equality are desired, association, not isolation, of interests, is the school in which these excellences are nurtured. The aim of improvement should be not solely to place human beings in a condition in which they will be able to do without one another, but to enable them to work with or for one another in relations not involving dependence (Mill 1899, *Book IV*, Chapter VII).

Previously those who lived by labor and were not individually self-employed would have to work "for a master," that is, would not be a principal in their work activity:[20]

> But the civilizing and improving influences of association, ..., may be obtained without dividing the producers into two parties with hostile interests and feelings, the many who do the work being mere servants under the command of the one who supplies the funds, and having no interest of their own in the enterprise except to earn their wages with as little labor as possible (Mill 1899, *Book IV*, Chapter VII).

One halfway house in this direction would be various forms of association between capital and labor:

> The form of association, however, which if mankind continue to improve, must be expected in the end to predominate, is not that which can exist between a capitalist as chief, and workpeople without a voice in the management, but the association of the labourers themselves on terms of equality, collectively owning the capital with which they carry on their operations, and working under managers elected and removable by themselves (Mill 1899, *Book IV*, Chapter VII).

Under this form of cooperation, Mill sees an increase in the productivity of work since the workers then have the enterprise as "their principle and their interest.":

> It is scarcely possible to rate too highly this material benefit, which yet is as nothing compared with the moral revolution in society that would accompany it: the healing of the standing feud between capital and labour; the transformation of human life, from a conflict of classes struggling for opposite interests, to a friendly rivalry in the pursuit of a good common to all; the elevation of the dignity of labour; a new sense of security and independence in the labouring class; and the conversion of each human being's daily occupation into a school of the social sympathies and the practical intelligence (Mill 1899, *Book IV*, Chapter VII).

What Mill sees as happening in the democratic workplace echoes what he earlier found in Tocqueville's description of the educational effect of the New England township. In Tocqueville's words:

> Nevertheless local assemblies of citizens constitute the strength of free nations. Town-meetings are to liberty what primary schools are to science; they bring it within the people's reach, they teach men how to use and how to enjoy it. A nation may establish a system of free government, but without the spirit of municipal institutions it cannot have the spirit of liberty (Tocqueville 1961, Chap. V, p. 55).

As Mill expanded on the point:

> In this system of municipal self-government, coeval with the first settlement of the American colonies…our author (Tocqueville) beholds the principal instrument of that political education of the people, which alone enables a popular government to maintain itself, or renders it desirable that it should. It is a fundamental principle in his political philosophy, as it has long been in ours, that only by the habit of superintending their local interests can that diffusion of intelligence and mental activity, as applied to their joint concerns, take place among the mass of the people, which can qualify them to superintend with steadiness or consistency the proceedings of their government, or to exercise any power in national affairs except by fits, and as tools in the hands of others (Mill 1961 (1835), p. xvii).

## John Dewey

A century later, John Dewey emphasized the formative implications of people's daily activity in an industrial society:

> For illustration, I do not need to do more than point to the moral, emotional and intellectual effect upon both employers and laborers of the existing industrial system. … I suppose that every one who reflects upon the subject admits that it is impossible that the ways in which activities are carried on for the greater part of the waking hours of the day, and the way in which the share of individuals are involved in the management of affairs in such a matter as gaining a livelihood and attaining material and social security, can not but be a highly important factor in shaping personal dispositions; in short, forming character and intelligence (Dewey in: Ratner 1939, pp. 716–17).

Do these primary sites for outside-the-family socialization and development foster the virtues of associative democracy? While "democratic social organization make provision for this direct participation in control: in the economic region, control remains external and autocratic" (Dewey 1916, p. 260),

> [c]ontrol of industry is from the top downwards, not from the bottom upwards. The greater number of persons engaged in shops and factories are "subordinates." They are used to receiving orders from their superiors and acting as passive organs of transmission and execution. They have no active part in making plans or forming policies—the function comparable to the legislative in government—nor in adjudicating disputes which arise. In short their mental habits are unfit for accepting the intellectual responsibilities involved in political self-government (Dewey and Tufts 1932, pp. 392–393).

From his earliest writings in 1888 to his mature years, Dewey's liberalism saw democracy as a norm applicable to all spheres of human activity, not just to the political sphere:

> (Democracy) is but a name for the fact that human nature is developed only when its elements take part in directing things which are common,

things for the sake of which man and women form groups—families, industrial companies, governments, churches, scientific associations and so on. The principle holds as much of one form of association, say in industry and commerce, as it does in government (Dewey 1948, p. 209).

It should not be too much of a surprise that the normative framework of James M. Buchanan's classical liberalism has the same implications for Tocqueville's "science of associations" in this regard as Mill and Dewey[21] even though the full implications were not explicitly drawn.[22]

## Re-constitutionalizing the Corporation

People are involved in effective collective action all day long in their work associations. But today the structure of most companies of any size—namely, the employment relation with the "employer" being the absentee "owners" on the stock market—institutionalizes irresponsibility by disconnecting the far-flung shareholders from the social and environmental impact of their "corporate governance."[23] Or viewed the other way around, that employment structure prevents the local managers and staff in widely held companies from being the principals to use the main outside-the-family organizational involvement to address local problems. That institutionalized irresponsibility in turn increases the need for a stronger third sector to address the resulting social problems.

There have been a few social commentators who have pointed out the institutionalized irresponsibility of the *absentee-owned* joint stock corporation. In his 1961 book aptly entitled *The Responsible Company*, George Goyder quoted a striking passage from Lord Eustace Percy's *Riddell Lectures* in 1944:

Here is the most urgent challenge to political invention ever offered to the jurist and the statesman. The human association which in fact produces and distributes wealth, the association of workmen, managers, technicians and directors, is not an association recognised by the law. The association which the law does recognise—the association of shareholders, creditors and directors—is incapable of production and is not expected by the law to

> perform these functions. We have to give law to the real association, and to withdraw meaningless privilege from the imaginary one (Percy 1944, p. 38; quoted in Goyder 1961, p. 57).

This elemental solution re-constitutionalizes the corporation so that the "human association which in fact produces and distributes wealth" is recognized in law as the legal corporation where the ownership/membership in the company would be assigned to the "workmen, managers, technicians and directors" who work in the company.

## Conclusion

That would change everything—including essentially abolishing much of the distinction between the second sector and the third sector. The natural site of collective action for people to address their own community problems would be where people are involved in effective collective action all day long: their work organization. When firms are organized as workplace democracies, then *that* is the natural generalization of sovereign individuals acting in the marketplace—so ably described in the classical liberal economic way of thinking—to associated individuals acting *as the principals in their own organizations.*

## Notes

1. The phrase "external organization" does not apply to associations where people join together to apply their collective efficacy to address some problems of their own; it applies to organizations, particularly those with a paid staff, tasked to help others. The aim of a helping agency should be to do itself out of a job—which is rather difficult for a professionally staffed organization of any type. See Ellerman (2005) for a development of this theme along with a philosophical analysis of why it is so difficult for such external helping organizations to actually "help people help themselves."
2. See Laslett (1960), notes on §24, pp. 325–26.

3. Locke, Montesquieu, and Blackstone are not arbitrary choices. When discussing Adam Smith's classical liberalism, Frank Knight noted: "Interestingly enough, the political and legal theory had been stated in a series of classics, well in advance of the formulation of the economic theory by Smith. The leading names are, of course, Locke, Montesquieu, and Blackstone" (Knight 1947, p. 27, fn. 4).
4. For more of this development, see Ellerman (1992 or 2010).
5. It is a re-validation since in the decade prior to the Civil War, there was explicit legislation in six states "to permit a free Negro to become a slave voluntarily" (Gray 1958, p. 527; quoted in Philmore 1982, p. 47). For instance in Louisiana, legislation was passed in 1859 "which would enable free persons of color to voluntarily select masters and become slaves for life" (Sterkx 1972, p. 149).
6. David Boaz (2011) reports that Tom Palmer said that David Schmidtz said at a Cato Institute forum in 2002 that:

   > Nozick told him that his alleged "apostasy" was mainly about rejecting the idea that to have a right is necessarily to have the right to alienate it, a thesis that he had reconsidered, on the basis of which reconsideration he concluded that some rights had to be inalienable. That represents, not a movement away from libertarianism, but a shift toward the mainstream of libertarian thought.

   In his own book on libertarian theory, Palmer traces the "mainstream of libertarian thought" (2009, p. 457) about inalienable rights back to Locke's treatment.
7. See, for example, Genovese (1971), Wish (1960), or Fitzhugh (1960).
8. For a more complete story, see Philmore (1982) or Ellerman (2010).
9. This may seem an unusual use of "rent" but "hiring a car" in the U. K. and "renting a car" in the U.S. are the same thing. As Paul Samuelson (1915–2009) goes on to explain:

   > One can even say that wages are the rentals paid for the use of a man's personal services for a day or a week or a year. This may seem a strange use of terms, but on second thought, one recognizes that every agreement to hire labor is really for some limited period of time. By outright purchase, you might avoid ever renting any kind of land. But in our society, labor is one of the few productive factors that cannot legally be bought outright. Labor can only be rented, and the wage rate is really a rental (1976, p. 569).

10. *Institutes*, Lib. I, Tit. II, 6; Quoted in: Corwin (1955, p. 4).
11. Often the liberal literature just fudges or ignores the alienation-versus-delegation distinction by describing either type of contract as "giving up rights" to the government or as establishing "hierarchy."
12. Again, this follows the intellectual pattern set by Locke who had no genuine inalienable rights theory to counter Hobbes so he ignored Hobbes and took Robert Filmer (1588–1653) as his foil since Filmer's patriarchal theory (1680) did not require the consent of the governed anymore that the father's governance over his children requires the consent of the children.
13. This phrase was used without apparent irony in an earlier version of the free cities website. In the current version of the *startup cities site*, the phrase is "democratizing access to law and governance." Even though the subjects have no vote, the startup cities nevertheless have "democratic accountability by giving people the ability to raise their voice through the power of exit."
14. See also: http://bleedingheartlibertarians.com/2014/03/vote-markets/. As James Tobin grudgingly noted: "Any good second year graduate student in economics could write a short examination paper proving that voluntary transactions in votes would increase the welfare of the sellers as well as the buyers" (Tobin 1970, p. 269; quoted in: Ellerman 1992, p. 100).
15. This has generated a minor industry of thinkers who develop ad hoc arguments against the perpetual service contract (e.g., the rule against perpetuities supposedly rules out all "till death do us part" contracts) but not against the time-limited person rental contract. These arguments are dealt with from a Nozickian perspective by J. Philmore who concludes with what libertarians would take as a *reductio ad absurdum*: "Any thorough and decisive critique of voluntary slavery or constitutional non-democratic government would carry over to the employment contract—which is the voluntary contractual basis for the free market free enterprise system" (1982, p. 55).
16. The fact that the inalienability of conscience was rooted in the aspects of personhood that do not change with consent or contract was expressed with great clarity by the New Light minister Elisha Williams in 1744:

    No action is a religious action without understanding and choice in the agent. Whence it follows, the rights of conscience are sacred and equal in all, and strictly speaking unalienable. This *right of judging*

> *every one for himself in matters of religion* result from the nature of man, and is so inseperably connected therewith, that a man can no more part with it than he can with his power of thinking: and it is equally reasonable for him to attempt to strip himself of the power of reasoning, as to attempt the vesting of another with this right. And whoever invades this right of another, be he pope or Caesar, may with equal reason assume the other's power of thinking, and so level him with the brutal creation. A man may alienate some branches of his property and give up his right in them to others; but he cannot transfer the right of conscience, unless he could destroy his rational and moral powers (Williams 1998, p. 62).

See also Smith (2013, pp. 88–94) on inalienability which includes references to Williams.

17. These and related "forgotten" ideas are developed at book length with a focus on economic theory in Ellerman (1992) which was published in a series co-edited by the late neo-Austrian economist, Don Lavoie, who described the theory in his acceptance letter as follows:

> The book's radical re-interpretation of property and contract is, I think, among the most powerful critiques of mainstream economics ever developed. It undermines the neoclassical way of thinking about property by articulating a theory of inalienable rights, and constructs out of this perspective a 'labor theory of property' which is as different from Marx's labor theory of value as it is from neoclassicism. It traces roots of such ideas in some fascinating and largely forgotten strands of the history of economics. It draws attention to the question of 'responsibility' which neoclassicism has utterly lost sight of. …It constitutes a better case for its economic democracy viewpoint than anything else in the literature (Lavoie 1991, pp. 1–2).

18. Cornuelle (1991) is a welcome exception to the rule.
19. The older name of the relation was the "master-servant" relation but, aside from a few law books on agency law that use the "master-servant" language as technical terms (e.g., Batt 1967), that usage was slowly replaced in the late nineteenth century and early twentieth century with the Newspeak terms of "employer" and "employee."
20. Kant considered working for a master in the master-servant relation as being so subordinating as to disqualify one for a civic personality.

Apprentices to merchants or tradesmen, servants who are not employed by the state, minors (*naturaliter vel civiliter*), women in general and all those who are obligated to depend for their living (i.e., food and protection) on the offices of others (excluding the state)—all of these people have no civil personality,.... (Kant 1991 (1797), p. 126, Section 46).

21. Note how the implications of Buchanan's *principals principle* gives essentially the same results as Dewey's democratic "principle (that) holds as much of one form of association, say in industry and commerce, as it does in government."
22. This is much like Jefferson and the Founding Fathers who enunciated the principle of inalienable rights, but did not apply it to the peculiar institution of their time.
23. As was noted long ago (for example, Scitovsky 1951), there is no reason for the entrepreneur or family firm to take profits as the sole maximizing goal (although costs, of course, have to be covered for long-term sustainability). But with scattered absentee owners, profit seems to be the only thing that they can agree on in general. Hence profit maximization has been canonized as "the goal" of the firm when in fact it is only an artifact of a particular organizational form.

## References

Batt, Francis. 1967. *The Law of Master and Servant*. London: Pitman.

Blackstone, William. 1959 (1765). *Ehrlich's Blackstone*. New York: Capricorn Books.

Boaz, David. 2011. Misunderstanding Nozick, Again, *Cato at Liberty* (June 20, 2011). http://www.cato.org/blog/misunderstanding-nozick-again. Retrieved May 15, 2014.

Bryan, Edward B. 1858. *Letters to the Southern People*. Charleston: Press of Walker, Evans & Co.

Buchanan, James M. 1999. *The Logical Foundations of Constitutional Liberty: The Collected Works of James M. Buchanan Vol. 1*. Indianapolis: Liberty Fund.

______. 2005. *Why I, Too, Am Not a Conservative: The Normative Vision of Classical Liberalism*. Cheltenham: Edward Elgar.

Buchanan, James M. and Gordon Tullock. 1962. *The Calculus of Consent: Logical Foundations of Constitutional Democracy*. Ann Arbor: University of Michigan Press.

Cassirer, Ernst. 1963. *The Myth of the State*. New Haven: Yale University Press.
Catterall, Helen T. 1926. *Judicial Cases Concerning Slavery and the Negro*. Washington, DC: Carnegie Institute.
Christ, Carl F. 1975. The Competitive Market and Optimal Allocative Efficiency. In: *Competing Philosophies in American Political Economics*. John Elliott and John Cownie eds., pp. 332–338. Pacific Palisades: Goodyear.
Coase, R. H. 1937. The Nature of the Firm. *Economica* IV (Nov. 1937): 386–405.
Cornuelle, Richard C. 1991. New Work for Invisible Hands. *Times Literary Supplement* (5 April 1991): 1–4.
Corwin, Edward S. 1955. *The 'Higher Law' Background of American Constitutional Law*. Ithaca: Cornell University Press.
Davis, David Brion. 1966. *The Problem of Slavery in Western Culture*. Ithaca: Cornell University Press.
Dewey, John. 1916. *Democracy and Education*. New York: Free Press.
_____. 1948. *Reconstruction in Philosophy* (Enlarged edition). Boston: Beacon Press.
Dewey, John and James Tufts. 1908. *Ethics*. New York: Henry Holt.
_____. 1932. *Ethics*. Revised ed., New York: Henry Holt.
Ellerman, David. 1992. *Property & Contract in Economics: The Case for Economic Democracy*. Cambridge, MA: Blackwell.
_____. 2005. *Helping People Help Themselves: From the World Bank to an Alternative Philosophy of Development Assistance*. Ann Arbor: University of Michigan Press.
_____. 2010. Inalienable Rights: A Litmus Test for Liberal Theories of Justice. *Law and Philosophy*. 29 (5 September): 571–599.
Faust, Drew Gilpin, ed. 1981. *The Ideology of Slavery: Proslavery Thought in the Antebellum South, 1830–1860*. Baton Rouge: Louisiana State University Press.
Filmer, Robert. 1680. *Patriarcha; of the Natural Power of Kings*. London: Richard Chiswell.
Finkelman, Paul. 2003. *Defending Slavery: Proslavery Thought in the Old South: A Brief History with Documents*. Boston: Bedford/St. Martin's.
Fitzhugh, George. 1960 (1857). *Cannibals All! or, Slaves Without Masters*. Cambridge, MA: Harvard University Press.
Freiman, Christopher. 2013. Cosmopolitanism Within Borders: On Behalf of Charter Cities. *Journal of Applied Philosophy*. 30 (1): 40–52.
_____. 2014. Vote Markets. *Australasian Journal of Philosophy* 92 (4): 759–74.
Friedman, Milton. 1962. *Capitalism and Freedom*. Chicago: University of Chicago Press.

Genovese, Eugene. 1971. *The World the Slaveholders Made*. New York: Vintage Books.
Gierke, Otto von. 1958. *Political Theories of the Middle Age*. F. W. Maitland (trans.), Boston: Beacon Press.
_____. 1966. *The Development of Political Theory*. B. Freyd (trans.), New York: Howard Fertig.
Goyder, George. 1961. *The Responsible Company*. Oxford: Basil Blackwell.
Gray, Lewis Cecil. 1958. *History of Agriculture in the Southern United States to 1860*. Gloucester: Peter Smith.
Grotius, Hugo. 1901 (1625). *The Rights of War and Peace*. A. C. Campbell (trans.), Washington: M. Walter Dunne.
Heyne, Paul, Peter Boettke and David Prychitko. 2006. *The Economic Way of Thinking*. Eleventh edition. Upper Saddle River: Prentice Hall.
Hobbes, Thomas. 1958 (1651). *Leviathan*. Indianapolis: Bobbs-Merrill.
Hutcheson, Francis. 1725. *An Inquiry into the Original of Our Ideas of Beauty and Virtue*. London.
_____. 1755. *A System of Moral Philosophy*. London.
Israel, Jonathan. 2010. *A Revolution of the Mind: Radical Enlightenment and the Intellectual Origins of Modern Democracy*. Princeton: Princeton University Press.
Justinian. 1948. *The Institutes of Justinian*. T. C. Sandars (trans.), London: Longmans, Green & Co.
Kant, Immanuel. 1991 (1797). *The Metaphysics of Morals*. Mary Gregor (trans.), New York: Cambridge University Press.
Knight, Frank. 1947. *Freedom and Reform*. New York: Harper & Row.
Laslett, Peter. 1960. Introduction with Notes. In: *John Locke: Two Treatises of Government*. Peter Laslett (ed.), New York: New American Library.
Lavoie, Don. 1991. *Letter to Publishing Assistant Jane Betar* (Private Comm. April 24). 2 pages.
Lincoln, Anthony. 1971. *Some Political & Social Ideas of English Dissent 1763–1800*. New York: Octagon Books.
Locke, John. 1960 (1690). *Two Treatises of Government*. New York: New American Library.
Luther, Martin. 1942 (1523). Concerning Secular Authority. In *Readings in Political Philosophy*. Francis W. Coker ed., New York: Macmillan, pp. 306–329.
Lynd, Staughton. 1969. *Intellectual Origins of American Radicalism*. New York: Vintage Books.
Marsilius of Padua. 1980 (1324). *Defensor Pacis*. Alan Gewirth (trans.), Toronto: University of Toronto Press.

McKitrick, Eric. ed. 1963. *Slavery Defended: the views of the Old South.* Englewood Cliffs: Prentice-Hall.
Mill, James. 1826. *Elements of Political Economy.* London.
Mill, John Stuart. 1899. *Principles of Political Economy.* New York: Colonial Press.
______. 1961 (1835). Introduction: An appraisal of Volume I of *Democracy in America.* In: *Democracy in America,* New York: Schocken, pp. v–xlix.
______. 1972 (1861). Considerations of Representative Government. In: *J. S. Mill: Utilitarianism, On Liberty and Considerations on Representative Government.* H. B. Acton ed., London: J. M. Dent and Sons, pp. 187–428.
Montesquieu. 1912 (1748). *The Spirit of the Laws.* T. Nugent (trans.), New York: Appleton.
Nozick, Robert. 1974. *Anarchy, State, and Utopia.* New York: Basic Books.
Palmer, Tom G. 2009. *Realizing Freedom: Libertarian Theory, History, and Practice.* Washington DC: Cato Institute.
Percy, Eustace. 1944. *The Unknown State: 16th Riddell Memorial Lectures.* London: Oxford University Press.
Philmore, J. 1982. The Libertarian Case for Slavery: A Note on Nozick. *Philosophical Forum.* XIV (Fall 1982): 43–58.
Pufendorf, Samuel. 2003 (1673). *The Whole Duty of Man, According to the Law of Nature.* Indianapolis: Liberty Fund.
Ratner, Joseph, ed. 1939. *Intelligence in the Modern World: John Dewey's Philosophy.* New York: Modern Library.
Rawls, John. 1996. *Political Liberalism.* New York: Columbia University Press.
Sabine, George H. 1958. *A History of Political Theory.* New York: Henry Holt and Company.
Samuelson, Paul A. 1976. *Economics.* Tenth edition. New York: McGraw-Hill.
Scitovsky, Tibor. 1951. *Welfare and Competition.* Chicago: Irwin.
Seabury, Samuel. 1969 (1861). *American Slavery Justified by the Law of Nature.* Miami: Mnemosyne Publishing Company.
Skinner, Quentin. 1978. *The foundations of modern political thought.* Volumes I and II. Cambridge: Cambridge University Press.
Smith, George H. 2013. *The System of Liberty: Themes in the History of Classical Liberalism.* New York: Cato Institute, Cambridge University Press.
Spinoza, Benedict de. 1951 (1670). *Theologico-Political Treatise.* R. H. M. Elwes (trans.), New York: Dover Publications.
Sterkx, H. E. 1972. *The Free Negro in Ante-Bellum Louisiana.* Cranbury: Associated University Presses.

Tobin, James. 1970. On Limiting the Domain of Inequality. *Journal of Law and Economics.* 13 (2 October): 263–277.
Tocqueville, Alexis de. 1961. *Democracy in America Vol. I.* Henry Reeve (trans.), New York: Schocken.
Tomasi, John. 2012. *Free Market Fairness.* Princeton: Princeton University Press.
Williams, Elisha. 1998 (1744). The Essential Rights and Liberties of Protestants. In *Political Sermons of the American Founding Era, 1730–1805 Vol. I.* Ellis Sandoz ed., Indianapolis: Liberty Fund, pp. 55–118.
Wills, Garry. 1979. *Inventing America.* New York: Vintage Books.
Wish, Harvey, ed. 1960. *Ante-bellum.* New York: Capricorn Books.

# Democracy, Liberalism, and Discretion: The Political Puzzle of the Administrative State

Stephen Turner

"Democracy," in the classic sense, is a legal regime that operates with procedures that define the ways in which laws are made or changed through some form of majority rule. The procedures may specify a requirement for super-majorities to change certain fundamental, or constitutional, laws. For the purposes of discussions of liberal democracy as a functioning order, the relevant rights are those which are the conditions for democracy, understood as government by majority voting, normally with representation, based on discussion. Constraints on discussion, or interventions by the state to control or bias the discussion, that is to say violations of the political neutrality of the state, are violations of the relevant rights. This was, essentially, the notion of democracy that was the starting point for the literature that this chapter discusses, on the relationship between democracy and the administrative state. As one of the key figures put it, "the term refers to any form of government in which the policy making authorities are chosen on a broad and substantially

S. Turner (✉)
Department of Philosophy, University of South Florida, Tampa, FL, USA
e-mail: turner@usf.edu



D. F. Hardwick, L. Marsh (eds.), *Reclaiming Liberalism*, Palgrave Studies in Classical Liberalism, https://doi.org/10.1007/978-3-030-28760-3_2

equal suffrage basis in elections that are free from direct government coercion." The author adds that under modern conditions this "necessarily embodies the principle of responsibility to public opinion" (Millspaugh 1937, p. 64). But as we will see, this principle, as understood by the advocates of the administrative state, is not only different from the idea of democratic accountability, but hostile to it.

We can call this the narrow theory of liberal democracy. It does not involve notions like the will of the people, understood as something beyond and distinct from the expressions of that will through the procedures of the particular democracy, nor does it involve ends which are taken to be part of the full life or the full life of a community, such as social justice or economic equality. It leaves these to democratic decision. For the narrow theory, rights, social justice, and the like are the policy products or outcomes of the legal procedures, and are created by the choices made through these procedures, such as a law establishing a legal right. What counts as "just" from the point of view of the narrow theory is itself the product of political decision, not something that can be used as a standard to judge it. The narrow sense allows for making "health care" a "right" through these procedures. But for the narrow sense, this too is a matter for democratic decision.[1]

The narrow conception is law-centered: it treats law as the expression of democracy, and democracy as the product of legal procedures. It treats constitutional form as the product of legal democratic choice, rather than something to be measured against a philosophical standard of "genuine democracy." And, although the conception of democracy is narrow, it applies widely and equally to all legal orders that operate through legal procedures to express the choices of the people regardless of what those choices are. A "liberal" democracy is simply one in which the procedures reflect the freedom of individuals to choose, without state coercion or significant state limitations on the formation of opinion through discussion. A democratic choice to impose such restrictions is possible, but this would make the democracy an illiberal one. The critics of liberalism, such as Carl Schmitt, pointed out the inherent conflict between "democracy" and "liberalism" resulting from this possibility, and argued that this unstable compound had long since collapsed: the government by discussion and public opinion of the eighteenth century no longer existed, public opinion was mere acclamation, and no one any longer believed that losing the vaunted freedom of speech would make any difference to political outcomes. (Schmitt [1928] 2008, p. 275, 1985, pp. 48–50). And the fear of the failure of these institutions has been a pervasive part of the history of democracy. During the democratic revival of the nineteenth century, the negative example of Florence was more potent, especially for Central Europe, than the example of the United States.

Conventional accounts of liberal constitutions, especially "liberal" ones, tend to ignore or obscure one large fact: the administrative state. There are, however, some revealing exceptions. The basic account of the "rule of law" comes from Albert Venn Dicey (Dicey [1914] 1962), and is expressly concerned with the developing administrative state of his own time in Britain, the late nineteenth and early twentieth centuries, and the example of the Continental administrative states that were already fully developed. Dicey's fear was that the administrative state, if it was not constrained by the common courts, would degrade into arbitrariness. As one commentator explains him, the essence of doctrine of the "rule of law, of which Dicey has, of course, given us the classic expression," is the "absence of arbitrary power of government officers and subjection of every man, including government officers, to ordinary law administered by ordinary tribunals" (Thach 1935, p. 273). Others have noted the non-democratic character and origins of administrative law—in the royal prerogative (Hamburger 2014) and in the royal bureaucratic powers of continental states that continued after the abolition of monarchy. Carl Schmitt's thinking is particularly relevant here. Rather than attempting to derive the legality of administrative law from other forms of law, he points out that it is a separate constitutional principle, with its own distinctive form of legitimacy (Schmitt [1928] 2008, p. 93), and indeed argues that the modern bourgeois *Rechtsstaat*, what he calls the legislative state, presupposes the administrative state ([1932] 2004, pp. 12–13).

My concern in this chapter is with the administrative state, but from the point of view of liberal political theory. I provide a basic introduction to the legal issues, but my concern is with the place of administrative discretion in liberal political theory. To address this will require turning the clock back to the point at which the institutions in question were being established. For reasons that will become apparent, this was largely an American discussion: it took the form of a debate over the relation of democracy to the administrative state. In Europe, as Schmitt, and, before him, as we will see, Woodrow Wilson noted, there was no such discussion. The administrative state preceded the "democratizing" impulse and accommodated it, sufficiently for the regimes in question to ignore the problem.

## Administrative Law

Legal issues are critical to understanding the political problem of the administrative state, even if they are not sufficient. The distinction between law and administrative law works like this in the United States: "Under the U.S. Constitution, the government could bind its subjects only through the use of legislative or judicial power" (Hamburger 2014, p. 3). This meant that "binding" had to be the result of a vote or an act of a court that was part of the judicial branch itself. This is law, as it is normally understood. However, the executive had its own powers, among them the denial of government benefits, and the implementation of regulatory regimes created in legislation, but which involved quasi-judicial and quasi-legislative powers, normally based on some form of licensure. This was nominally different. It was not about binding, and it was an assumed power of the executive not rooted in the constitution. But this acknowledged power gradually was transformed into something else—the power not only to make regulations with the force of law loosely based on actual law, but to adjudicate on the basis of these regulations in administrative courts or proceedings, and to enforce the results of these judgments, usually through sanctions involving the refusal of benefits or exclusion from licensed activities. The benefits in question might be those of participation is government grant programs, or broadcasting, which was licensed.

The constitutional status of the "state" as distinct from the judiciary and legislature, is usually subsumed under the category of "the executive." But in practice the administrative state, the actual carriers-out of the legal instructions of the executive and the other branches, has a great deal of autonomy. The legal basis for this autonomy is complex. Kelsen explains the discretionary power of courts in the face of ambiguous legislation in this way (Kelsen 1955, pp. 77–80). The ambiguities are legally meaningful: they represent a delegation of authority to decide the meaning of the law to the courts. The same principle applies to administration, and this produces some remarkable results. The number of "rules" in the form of enforceable regulations which administrative agencies make in interpreting the laws produced in the United States is twenty-seven times the "laws" (Crews 2017). And this is just the published regulations, which are supposed to go through a process of public review (a requirement that is often ignored). There are also directives which say, essentially, what the regulated body must do in order to prevent the regulatory agency from taking action against them. Together with the various forms of legal insulation against political supervision of these administrative bodies, this produced a relatively autonomous branch of government.

These agencies are legally considered to be part of the executive, but they are protected from the elected "executive" as well as the courts, in various ways. Judicial review is rare and involves special constitutional courts that rarely act. In the United States, the situation differs, but the results are similar: judicial review is common, but agencies are deferred to under a doctrine enunciated in the Chevron case, and agencies are protected from suits by the legal interpretation of "standing," which limits accountability radically.[2] Agencies cannot be held to account by the public in court unless the plaintiff meets very rigorous tests of provable personal harm, tests that are rarely met. There is, in short, a high degree of autonomy in fact, and a high level of legal and procedural insulation that supports this autonomy.

An incidental consequence of the fact that administrative units in the executive can interpret their own regulations, adjudicate their own cases, and define their own procedures, is that there is a larger role for discretion in enforcing them, and a much more limited power of public contestation of them. Moreover, one major way of sanctioning institutions is the threat of denial of funds, which is both vague and difficult to adjudicate, if it is adjudicable in ordinary courts at all. The enforcement powers of the administrative state involve extraordinary discretion, allowing the state to threaten legal action to produce results that are not specified in regulations, and also permits vague regulation, such as letters of guidance which are not themselves regulations and therefore unchallengeable. In theory, these actions are subject to judicial supervision and legislative clarification, but the courts have generally "deferred" to executive agencies in the use of these powers, though on occasion have intervened, and legislative revision is fraught with the same issues of control of implementation as the original legislation, with the additional complication that regulation creates new interests by virtue of the fact that it creates an advantaged class of beneficiaries of the regulation, made up of people taking advantage of the opportunities created by it, which becomes a constituency for its continuation.

## The American Reception of the Administrative State

The administrative state, and administrative law, regardless of questions in legal theory about its legal foundation, is a reality. What led to it? Is there an alternative? And what were the arguments for it in the first place? This is a lacuna in present discussions of liberalism: the focus is on the law and on the idea of politically limiting the expansion of the state and state power. To face the issues we need to return to an earlier discussion, the discussion that took place during the birth of the American administrative state. As noted, there was no comparable discussion on the European continent: the administrative state was an institutional inheritance from monarchy and absolutism which theorists sought to control and curtail, but not to abolish. In the United States, in contrast, it needed to be invented, and it was, with the model of the European bureaucratic state in mind. It was these institutions that American reformers of the late nineteenth century admired and wished to create in the United States. The founders of the Columbia University School of Economics and Political Science travelled to Europe to observe the educational systems that supported these bureaucracies, in order to copy them (Hoxie 1955, pp. 21–3). John Burgess, the head and creator of this school, was a noted Germanophile. Albion Small, similarly, wrote his sole major work on the Cameralists, the German theorists of states administration whose writings started in the 1500s (Small 1909). It was a tradition he took as a model for what social science itself should become: an administrative science. And although sociology, his nominal field, did not become one, the debate over administrative science, which became the field of public administration, and its relation to social science, formed a significant part of the subsequent literature.

Ironically, this vast literature has been forgotten, and the term administrative state is now being treated as an invention of the paranoid Right and a misunderstanding of the nature of the state itself. The issues debated in the period between the 1870s and the 1946 passage of the Administrative Procedures Act have been submerged, and the topic is instead reframed as a perennial one between those who believe the expansive state is our best, and most democratic, means for caring for one another and those who wrongly see it as oppressive (Eckart 2017). The progenitors of this state, however, and the participants in the earlier debate, were under no illusions about its anti-democratic character, its reliance on discretion, the need to insulate officials from the law, and the conflict between this kind of state and the rule of law, and indeed they discussed it obsessively.

The discussion began in earnest in the 1880s under the heading "Democracy and Efficiency," as a classic paper by Woodrow Wilson put it (1901), and in a second paper, "The Study of Administration" (Wilson [1886] 1941). The argument was couched in terms of "saving democracy." The ills of democratic politics, were described in the most lurid manner by Wilson, in terms of decline from the early days of the Republic:

> Our later life has disclosed serious flaws, has even seemed ominous of pitiful failure, in some of the things we most prided ourselves upon having managed well: notably, in pure and efficient local government, in the successful organization of great cities, and in well-considered schemes of administration. The boss—a man elected by no votes, preferred by no open process of choice, occupying no office of responsibility—makes himself a veritable tyrant among us, and seems to cheat us of self-government; parties appear to hamper the movements of opinion rather than to give them form and means of expression; multitudinous voices of agitation, an infinite play of forces at cross-purpose, confuse us; and there seems to be no common counsel or definite union for action, after all (Wilson 1901, n.p.).

The reasons for this "pitiful failure" include a standard list, which reappears throughout the long literature that followed. The solution is administrative reform. The principle of democracy, he insists, is not the problem; execution is: "What we have blundered at is its new applications and details, its successful combination with efficiency and purity in governmental action." The evils of present administration are clear. "The poisonous atmosphere of city government, the crooked secrets of state administration, the confusion, the sinecurism, and corruption ever and again discovered in the bureau of Washington" (Wilson [1886] 1941, pp. 485–6). The solution is professionalization: "Our theory, in short, has paid as little heed to efficiency as our practice. It has been a theory of non-professionalism in public affairs; and in many great matters of public action non-professionalism is non-efficiency" (Wilson 1901, n.p.).

The reasons for non-professionalism are not hard to find, though Wilson is careful not to say this directly. The reason is that Americans elect too many officials.

> They give us so many elective offices that even the most conscientious voters have neither the time nor the opportunity to inform themselves with regard to every candidate on their ballots, and must vote for a great many men of whom they know nothing. They give us, consequently, the local machine and the local boss; and where population crowds, interests compete, work moves strenuously and at haste, life is many-sided and without unity, and voters of every blood and environment and social derivation mix and stare at one another at the same voting places, government miscarries, is confused, irresponsible, unintelligent, wasteful. Methods of electoral choice and administrative organization, which served us admirably well while the nation was homogeneous and rural; serve us oftentimes ill enough now that the nation is heterogeneous and crowded into cities (Wilson 1901, n.p.).

The solution, elaborated by many American professors over the next seventy years, was to replace the system by which most offices were elected and involved short terms of office with a professional administration, meaning officials with tenure, a system of examinations, and to create (or at least pretend the existence of) the science of administration.

The model was explicitly European—administration "is a foreign science…developed by French and German Professors" (Wilson [1886] 1941, p. 486). Wilson acknowledged that some modifications needed to be made to adapt the system to American tastes, and recognized the dangers of pure bureaucratic rule. And this set up the basic conflict in the system, recognized by all its commentators, between a class of bureaucrats, insulated from direct political accountability and believing in its own expertise, and the public which sought, with little success, to control it. As David Levitan put it, at the end of this period, "Unwise legislation may be mitigated somewhat by considerate and humane administration, but the citizen has no 'cushion' against arbitrary officialdom, often hidden behind the cloak of 'administrative necessity.'" And Levitan offers what was to become the standard solution, which often took the form of a lament: "The real protection of the citizen lies in the development of a high degree of democratic consciousness among the administrative hierarchy" (1943, p. 357). It is apparent from the extensive literature on the education of public administrators that democratic consciousness went against the grain both of the systems of education, which eschewed political theory, and the hiring habits of administrative agencies, which preferred technicians to generalists. The theoretical solution to the problem of arbitrary officialdom was for the officials to voluntarily accept public opinion as a guide and limit, and to cultivate public opinion.

Leonard White, a major thinker in the formative years of the discipline of public administration, put it thus:

> The problem, therefore, has gradually developed into that of finding means to ensure that the acts of administrative officers' shall be consistent not only with the law but equally with the purposes and temper of the mass of citizens. With the best of intentions, it is difficult for a conscientious administrator always to observe the limits placed either by law or by public opinion (White 1926, p. 419).

The reason for this problem with "observing limits" is that public opinion is backward: "The highest type of official will be in the advance guard of public opinion, and will concern himself to educate opinion to the standards which he knows should be applied" (Ibid.). The official is always, in this account, "Chafing at the discrepancies between the opportunities for accomplishment which science has put in his hands and prevailing standards" (Ibid.). One can see here, *in nuce*, the idea of a superior class directing the inferior masses both through administration and generating supportive public opinion.

With this we arrive at the nub of the problem: either the official is a leader who imposes enlightened opinions and practices on a backward democratic public through regulation and subsidies, or the official defers to public opinion and to its expression in the electoral process and respects the checks on behavior in the law. The solution to this problem, on the side of the administrative class, was *not* to find a way to keep administrators in check, but to both find a way to grant discretionary power for the officials to both lead and to "render justice." This was, straightforwardly and self-consciously, an appropriation of ruling power from politics and the people to administration and the administrative class, and a violation of the political neutrality of the liberal state. But it was done, then as now, in the name of "democracy." The key to this solution was discretion.

Wilson was unambiguous on this—the way to make the system of professional administration work was to combine accountability with discretion:

> And let me say that large powers and unhampered discretion seem to me the indispensable conditions of responsibility. Public attention must be easily directed, in each case of good or bad administration, to just the man deserving of praise or blame. There is no danger in power, if only it be not irresponsible. If it be divided, dealt out in shares to many, it is obscured; and if it be obscured, it is made irresponsible. But if it be centered in heads of the service and in heads of branches of the service, it is easily watched and brought to book. If to keep his office a man must achieve open and honest success, and if at the same time he feels himself intrusted with large freedom of discretion, the greater his power the less likely is he to abuse it, the more is he nerved and sobered and elevated by it. The less his power, the more safely obscure and unnoticed does he feel his position to be, and the more readily does he relapse into remissness (Wilson [1886] 1941, pp. 497–98).

This was an expression of faith: give an administrator discretion and it would not go to his head, but sober him up. It is difficult to imagine a more dubious psychological theory.

But Wilson, and many of the rest of the writers on this topic, had a fig leaf that allowed them to call this power democratic: to combine discretionary power with non-electoral legitimacy. While they worked to create a greater concentration of power, and more immunity from the courts and the law, they sought ways of legitimating their activities directly, for example by experts speaking directly to the public, and to legitimate the bureaucracy on its own, so that, in Wilson's own words, "trust" could be established ([1886] 1941, p. 494), and "docility" in acceptance of this new authority be generated among citizens ([1886] 1941, p. 506). Accountability remains as part of the sales pitch, along with the goal of efficiency. According to Wilson, public opinion will do this job, because public opinion exists in the Unites States and is undeveloped in the Continent:

> The right answer seems to be that public opinion shall play the part of authoritative critic. But the method by which its authority shall be made to tell? Our peculiar American difficulty in organizing administration is not the danger of losing liberty, but the danger of not being able or willing to separate its essentials from its accidents. Our success is made doubtful by that besetting error of ours, the error of trying to do too much by vote. Self-government does not consist in having a hand in everything, any more than housekeeping consists necessarily in cooking dinner with one's own hands. The cook must be trusted with a large discretion as to the management of the fires and the ovens (Wilson [1886] 1941, p. 498).

And his larger image of the legitimation of the administrative state shows why. But he does not explain how the administrator is to be held accountable or "brought to book."

There were many elements of this argument, and many corollaries. One corollary was a sustained assault on the concept of the rule of law, and a search for alternatives that would free the discretionary administrative state from the legal traditions of the Anglosphere. The service state, it was routinely claimed, makes the idea of "the rule of law, of that lawyer-made bit that was forced between the teeth of the sovereign state in order that there be no Bastille and no *lettres de cachet* on, at least, British and American soil" irrelevant (Thach 1935, p. 274). The "rule of law, and all that it infers, is no longer found an effective means for, on the one hand, the satisfactory accomplishment by government of its necessary duties, on the other for the prevention of arbitrary action particularly on the part of administrative underlings" (Ibid.). The reason for this is the necessity of discretion, which is a consequence of the necessity for "general" laws:

> It seems too patent to need elaboration that the laws which emanate from the representative assembly must be steadily more, not less, general in character. That is to say, the terms used in the underlying statute must of necessity be of the character of standards, of norms, whose detailed content must be subsequently somehow filled in. The impossibility of detailed legislation with respect to most of the matters concerning which modern statutes must deal is apparent enough. On the one hand, the information, the special knowledge of a representative body cannot extend to technical details. On the other, the attempt to govern minutiae by the statute would result in placing administration in a hopeless straitjacket (Ibid.)

The "hopeless straightjacket" would, of necessity, be loosened. And this led to a prophecy:

> at this juncture we come all too forcibly face to face with a major defect of the rule of law, old style. In the United States it is always possible to attack the grant of ordinance power as in fact a grant of legislative power itself. But, to all realistic intents and purposes, such an attack will prove fruitless save in most extreme cases, for the good and sufficient reason that most such grants are plainly a necessity (Thach 1935, pp. 274–5).

This was, in effect, the response to Dicey and the liberal tradition: the courts are simply incapable of dealing with the issues of administration, and will fail to do so. Thach, the author of these comments, acknowledges the legal point made by Hamburger, that the grant of legislative power is contrary to the rule of law. But he frankly states that the traditional concept of the rule of law, with its inevitable delay, is bankrupt:

> The ancient formulae of the common law frequently fail to submit to equitable application in an industrial age. More and more it is being realized that justice can be rendered only by investing administrative officers and tribunals with discretion to render justice in accordance with the needs of the situation, unbound by precedent and unfettered by technical legal procedure (Pfiffner 1935, p. 397).

The fetters of legal procedure were to be loosened in a variety of ways. One was to not be bound by precedent, nor to give justifications for their actions that could be picked apart by lawyers:

> For this reason administrative tribunals refuse to be bound by precedent. They publish no reasoned decisions upon which to predict future action. Such decisions as they do publish usually set forth a short statement of the facts supplemented by the decision reached (Ibid.).

This practice greatly limited the capacity of citizens to hold administrators accountable through the courts, even if they had access to them.

What discretion amounted to was impunity: officials, in the performance of their duties, were to be freed from personal liability for their actions, including criminal liability:

> If the duty, in the performance of which the act causing the damage was done, is discretionary in character, the general rule is that executive and administrative officers may not be held responsible since the courts do not like to interfere with the discretion of the administration. Such discretionary action being of a *judicial* character, the officer is exempt from all responsibility by action for the motives which influence him and the manner in which such duties are performed (Thach 1935, pp. 278–9; original emphasis).

They would be free to harm people or deprive them of rights both by judgments and by issuing regulations, and except in extreme cases where they were found to be acting outside their official duties, were free of personal legal responsibility for doing so. It was consciously anti-democratic, in the sense that implementing such a system would deprive voters of the power to remove these officials directly.

Not only the voters but the courts themselves would be limited in their power to police administrators:

> Granting that the original statute is constitutional and that the terms of the "completing" ordinances are within the four corners of the statute, the question is posed, shall the meaning of such ordinances in terms of the individual case be left to uncontrolled administrative agents? (Thach 1935, p. 276).

The answer was an unambiguous "yes." And the rationale was no longer efficiency but the pressing need to "get things done":

> No one who believes in the orderly processes of government can maintain a brief for arbitrariness. On the other hand, the insistent demand on modern government is to get things done. The plain truth is that we can no longer afford the luxury of the law's delay. Administrative action is demanded in no uncertain terms. The possibility of delay, if nothing more, is an insuperable barrier to this solution of the problem (Thach 1935, pp. 276–77).

The issue of delay was real, though ironically, it became a central tactic of the administrative state to control activities of the market by "permitting" processes that required public comment, studies conducted by or under the control of the agencies. But the "if nothing more" of this phrase was also telling. There was of course much more, as the courts granted by substituting for strict adherence to the law and legislative intent a large element of purpose which the agency was allowed to discern on its own. With this, the state of laws became the discretionary state.

## After 1946

The discussion of the role of discretionary power in democracy continued for sixty years from Wilson's initial defense of the administrative state. It was largely discontinued after the passage of the Administrative Procedures Act in 1946, which turned the issue into a legal and constitutional question. The major legal issue, which will not concern me here, involves delegation: the constitution forbids the delegation of legislative power from congress; the practice of administrative agencies in "interpreting" the law in the form of regulations is difficult to regard as anything other than legislative, even on Kelsenian grounds. My concern will be different: with the fate of discretion as a problem for liberal democracy.

The defenders of discretion reacted with undisguised hysteria to the passage of this act (Blachley and Oatman 1946). The arguments they gave are of historical interest only: none of the things they predicted came to pass, for reasons they concede in their discussion: the requirement of the act were so ambiguous that they could be interpreted by the courts in a way favorable to the discretionary power of the agencies (Blachley and Oatman 1946, p. 226). The major aim of the act was to provide for some transparency and public involvement in the rule-making process (Vermeule 2015) and to provide for judicial review of agency actions. Both were systemically evaded, in large part because the courts themselves avoided these cases, in part because the transparency of these processes was turned into an agency-governed public comment system in which the public was simply ignored. The two parts were connected. The judicial response to the act assured that the public could be ignored, by gutting judicial control of the administrative state itself. The agencies, knowing they would not be held accountable, could treat public commentary as powerless. The legislative branch was not a factor: it rarely returned to the legislation it enacted to clarify ambiguities in a way that would constrain agencies.

The key judicial doctrines that eliminated judicial control were "standing" and "deference." These require some additional explanation, for they go to the heart of one of the issues that motivated Wilson and the early reformers: what they took to be the obsolescence of the doctrine of the separation of powers. The doctrine was effectively undermined by the creation of administrative law: this amounted to an appropriation of judicial power. It represented a fundamental constitutional change. But it was affirmed legislatively in the Administrative Procedures Act, and acquiesced to by the courts, in the form of these two doctrines, as well as many supporting decisions.

The doctrine of deference was a response to the question of "who decides" in the face of ambiguity in the law. The Supreme Court ruled that

> allowing a judicial precedent to foreclose an agency from interpreting an ambiguous statute ... would allow a court's interpretation to override an agency's. Chevron's premise is that it is for agencies, not courts, to fill statutory gaps. The better rule is to hold judicial interpretations contained in precedents to the same demanding Chevron step one standard that applies if the court is reviewing the agency's construction on a blank slate: Only a judicial precedent holding that the statute unambiguously forecloses the

> agency's interpretation, and therefore contains no gap for the agency to fill, displaces a conflicting agency construction (Shriver Center 2013, 5.1.C.4.b. Deference to Agency Interpretation of Statutes, n.p.).

Ambiguity, or "gaps," in short, was to be treated as the agency's affair: the courts would not intervene unless there was a judicial precedent that the agency had gone too far.

"Ambiguity," however, is also ambiguous. So court rulings on administrative law, and the use of its larger degree of discretion, introduces the element of "purpose" as, for example, in an opinion stating that "Title IX must [be] accord[ed] … a sweep as broad as its language."[3] The language of title IX is simple and restricted to the prohibition of discrimination. The purpose was taken to justify actual discrimination in favor of previously discriminated against groups, and to include under the heading of "discrimination" numerical differences between groups that resulted from individual choices and characteristics. The court ruled that actual discrimination was permissible, because the action was related to the purpose rather than the text of the law.

The cases in which these precedents were established, however, were themselves limited to cases that were actually made subject to judicial review. The most powerful way that agencies preserve their discretion is to avoid review through the doctrine of standing. The basics of standing is contained in this test:

> In order to bring a claim in federal court, plaintiffs must demonstrate all three elements of standing: injury-in-fact, causation, and redressability. An injury-in-fact is an injury that is concrete, particularized, and actual or imminent. Proving causation requires plaintiffs to show that the injury is "fairly traceable" to the challenged action such that the challenged action has a "determinative or coercive effect" in causing the injury (Yan 2012, p. 596).

The tests exclude merely challenging agencies' abuses of discretion as a right of citizens: the plaintiff must meet the test of direct personal harm, a test that is usually understood to mean that even a hypothetical action by a third party that might be thought to intervene between the action of the agency and the harm invalidates the claim of causation. Thus a policy that actually has, according to normal notions of causation, a profound effect on the injured party, is excluded on the grounds that a third party might have done otherwise. Profoundly casual actions of the sort social scientists routinely examine, those which affect the conditions of choice and therefore have predictable behavioral results are thus excluded, and the affected persons lack standing (Yan 2012, p. 598). The arguments for this doctrine are the same as those we encountered in the democracy and efficiency debate: allowing agencies to be held judicially accountable would interfere with the agencies efficiency, and agencies are more expert than the courts (Yan 2012, 593).

Examples of agencies flouting the law, violating the principles of transparency to avoid judicial scrutiny, extending their authority, and threatening legislators are easy to find. What is more important to understand is that these are systemic issues. A footnote to one of the pre-1946 texts captures the problem for democracy that comes from discretionary power:

> The aggressiveness of administrative officials in relation to expressions of public opinion through the initiative and referendum is well brought out by Coker, "The Interworkings of State Administration and Direct Legislation," in *Annals*, vol. 64, p. 122, at pp. 128–30, illustrating also how state officials under a centralized system may be tempted to use their powers over local subordinates to promote attacks upon measures enacted by the legislature against their opposition. In the national administration, compare the alleged attempt of agents of the department of justice to intimidate members of Congress conducting inquiries into the Departments of Justice and the Interior during 1924 (White 1926, p. 419n1).

These remain problems: there was legal opposition by the federal government to referenda against affirmative action, for example (Mears 2014). And the use of threats against legislators, implied or open, is the norm.

## The Challenge to Liberalism

Why are these problems for liberalism, rather than mere problems of administration? Answering this question requires a return to fundamentals. Liberalism is inseparable from the idea of freedom from the authority of the state, and of the restriction of the authority of the state. Democracy implies that the definition of these restrictions be decided through democratic procedures. Constitutionalism implies that these procedures be both rooted in the fundamental legal norms of the regime in question, and that decisions about the application of these norms be governed by constitutional procedures as well, meaning, in practice, either judicial review or legislative or constitutional change. Discretionary power is inherently a challenge to liberalism and democracy: it represents a usurpation of state power beyond those agreed on through democratic procedures, in the name of purposes the state itself sets or discerns in the law on its own authority.

Donoso Cortes and Carl Schmitt were critics of liberalism for the failure of liberalism to come to decision, and defenders of state power against liberal restrictions. The leftist critics of liberalism in Britain in the 1930s made a parallel case, repeatedly, as did the New Deal defenders of administrative power against the courts. Schmitt's "decisionism" (2005) was a defense of discretion, and he asserted that discretionary power was more fundamental than law itself, because of the discretionary power of the executive to suspend the law and decide when the conditions for suspending the law had been met. The case for administrative discretion is a variant of this argument: the processes in which liberal discussion comes or fails to come to a conclusion are inadequate for the "needs" or "demands" of society. This means simply that within the agreed processes of decision-making based on discussion, no proposal has been sufficiently persuasive to lead to a decision. The necessity for a decision is not itself a matter of agreement within these processes. It is something higher—and often this "higher" necessity is presented as genuinely democratic, inasmuch as it reflects someone's view of what is best for society. The case for claiming that this kind of discretion is consistent with democracy is that there is some ultimate accountability, however indirect, in the form of elections of the legislature and executive, or in the acquiescence of the public to the state's claim to legitimacy.

If liberalism is, as Donoso Cortes claimed, government by discussion (Schmitt 1985, pp. 48–50), discretionary power is the antithesis of liberalism. To reclaim liberalism is to reclaim this power or limit it. And this produces a fundamental dilemma for liberalism. The expansion of discretion has occurred through the same liberal democratic means that were supposed to control discretion: the law as interpreted by the courts and the power of the elected executive and the legislature. At the root of the power of the discretionary state is the abdication of these restraining bodies. Part of the reason for this abdication is explained by the critics themselves: the inability of liberal discussion to come to decision, including the decision to restrain discretionary power.

The contemporary justification for this abdication is that the courts and the people should defer to experts, the experts in and employed by agencies—and not merely to decide through discussion to defer to experts on a case by case basis, but to accept the discretionary power of agencies as part of a general acquiescence to state power. And this means that the specific acts and rules produced by these agencies are not subject to discussion, except in an ineffective way. Nor is it helpful to refer to "experts" as a source of neutral authority: in the cases in question, matters of policy, value judgments which are controversial are mixed in not only with policy choices but in matters of acceptance of findings. The fact that agencies pay the people they take advice from, choose them, judge their advice or have their wards judge one another, and often conceal the data and methods the experts use to validate the agencies choices, means that the communities of experts are subject to epistemic capture—to the induced dominance of a given expert opinion (Turner 2001).

Schmitt argued that the conflict between liberalism and democracy would result in the democratic rejection of liberalism and the replacement of interest-based parties by totalizing parties. But he also believed as a corollary to this that liberalism would die, in effect, by its own hand, as a result of its failure to come to a decision to suppress the anti-liberal totalizing parties arrayed against it. But there are other ways for liberalism to die. The administrative state from its origins has aimed at making public opinion ineffective or undermining its independence, often in the name of leading it, educating it, or providing "justice," that is to say something beyond mere "opinion." Its theorists understood that the best means of making public opinion and liberal discussion producing public opinion effective, and to put teeth into the idea of government by discussion, was the practice of voting for officials with real power. White observed, "As late as 1918 a well-known Democratic newspaper of

Boston, opposing a constitutional amendment to extend the governor's term to two years, took up again the famous dictum of Samuel Adams, 'where annual elections end, tyranny begins'" (White 1926, p. 438n1) (in fact it is the words of Jefferson, in a letter to Sam Adams, recalling the maxim of the revolutionaries[4]). Perhaps it is no longer the case that direct electoral means are the condition of effective liberal democracy, and there are better means. But if any are devised, they too need more teeth than is provided by the very indirect and mediated effect on the state of "public opinion" on its own. We know enough about the administrative state to know that it does not limit itself. Reclaiming liberalism, however, requires reclaiming control over the administrative state. The discretionary state, the *Obrigkeitsstaat* which German liberalism sought to replace with the *Rechtstaat*, is the antithesis of liberalism as well as of democracy. An uncontrolled administrative state, limited only by the need for a general sense of legitimacy, and what Wilson sought, a population trained in docility, is nothing more than a new *Obrigkeitsstaat*. And faith in the power of the discretionary state to do better than the electorally controlled state is the wedge for bringing it about, now as in Wilson's time.

## Notes

1. The classic formulation of the narrow conception is Kelsen (1955), in the journal *Ethics*.
2. Chevron U.S.A., Inc. v. Natural Resources Defense Council, Inc. 467 U.S. 837 Chevron U.S.A., Inc. v. Natural Resources Defense Council, Inc. (No. 82-1005) Argued: February 29, 1984; Decided: June 25, 1984 [*] https://www.law.cornell.edu/supremecourt/text/467/837
3. *N. Haven, 456 U.S.* at 521 (quoting *United States v. Price*, 383 U.S. 787, 801 (1966)). https://supreme.justia.com/cases/federal/us/456/512/case.html; see also *Dickerson v. New Banner Inst. Inc.*, 460 U.S. 103, 118 (1983).
4. Thomas Jefferson to Samuel Adams, February 26, 1800. The Thomas Jefferson Papers at the Library of Congress: Series 1: General Correspondence. 1651 to 1827 (25,884). https://www.loc.gov/resource/mtj1.022_0124_0124/?st=text

## References


Blachly, F. F., and M. E. Oatman. 1946. Sabotage of the Administrative Process. *Public Administration Review* 6: 213–227.

Chevron USA, Inc. V. Natural Resources Defense Council, 467 U.S. 837 (1984). https://supreme.justia.com/cases/federal/us/467/837/

Crews, Clyde Wayne, Jr. 2017. How Many Rules and Regulations Do Federal Agencies Issue? *Forbes*, 15 August. https://www.forbes.com/sites/waynecrews/2017/08/15/how-many-rules-and-regulations-do-federal-agencies-issue/#594d24081e64 (accessed 3 December 2018).

Dicey, Albert Venn. (1914) 1962. *Lectures on the Law & Public Opinion in England: During the Nineteenth Century*, 2nd edn. London: Macmillan and Company.

Eckart, Kim. 2017. Q & A: Sarah Quinn Lifts the Curtain on the 'Hidden State'. *UWNews*, 17 August. http://www.washington.edu/news/2017/08/17/q-a-sarah-quinn-lifts-the-curtain-on-the-hidden-state/ (accessed 15 November 2018).

Hamburger, Philip. 2014. *Is Administrative Law Unlawful?* Chicago: The University of Chicago Press.

Hoxie, R. Gordon. 1955. *A History of the Faculty of Political Science, Columbia University.* New York: Columbia University Press.

Kelsen, Hans. 1955. Foundations of Democracy. *Ethics* 66(1): 1–101.

Levitan, D. M. 1943. Political Ends and Administrative Means. *Public Administrative Review* 3 (Autumn): 353–359.

Mears, Bill. 2014. Michigan's Ban on Affirmative Action Upheld by Supreme Court. *CNN*. April 23. https://www.cnn.com/2014/04/22/justice/scotus-michigan-affirmative-action/index.html

Millspaugh, A. C. 1937. Democracy and Administrative Organization. In: *Essays in Political Science*, pp. 64–73. Edited by J. M. Mathews. Baltimore: The Johns Hopkins Press.

Pfiffner, J. M. 1935. *Public Administration*. New York: Ronald Press.

Schmitt, Carl. (1928) 2008. *Constitutional Theory*. Translated and edited by Jeffrey Seitzer. Durham, NC: Duke University Press.

_____. (1932) 2004. *Legality and Legitimacy*, trans. Jeffrey Seltzer. Durham, NC: Duke University Press.

_____. 1985. *The Crisis of Parliamentary Democracy*. Translated by Ellen Kennedy. Cambridge, MA: MIT Press.

_____. 2005. *Political Theology: Four Chapters on the Concept of Sovereignty*. Translated by George Schwab. Chicago: University of Chicago Press.

Shriver Center. 2013. 5.1.C Express Causes of Action, Administrative Procedure Act. *Federal Practice Manual for Legal Aid Attorneys*. http://www.federalpracticemanual.org/chapter5/section1c

Small, Albion. 1909. *The Cameralists: The Pioneers of German Social Policy*. Chicago: The University of Chicago Press, London: T. Fisher Unwin.

Thach, C. E. 1935. The Inadequacies of the Rule of Law. In: *Essays on the Law and Practice of Governmental Administration*, pp. 269–286. Edited by C. G. Haines and M. E. Dimock. Baltimore: Johns Hopkins.

Turner, Stephen. 2001. What Is the Problem with Experts? *Social Studies of Science* 31(1): 23–49.

Vermeule, Adrian. 2015. 'No' Review of Philip Hamburger, *Is Administrative Law Unlawful? Texas Law Review* 3: 1547–1556. http://texaslawreview.org/wp-content/uploads/2015/08/Vermeule-93-6.pdf

White, L. D. 1926. *Introduction to Public Administration*. New York: Macmillan.

Wilson, Woodrow. (1886) 1941. The Study of Administration. *Political Science Quarterly* 56(4): 481–506.

_____. 1901. Democracy and Efficiency. *Atlantic Monthly* (March): 289–299. https://www.theatlantic.com/magazine/archive/1901/03/democracy-and-efficiency/520041/

Yan, Jerett. 2012. Standing as a Limitation on Judicial Review of Agency Action. *Ecology Law Quarterly* 39: 593–618.

# Ordoliberalism as the Operationalisation of Liberal Politics

Mikayla Novak

## Introduction

A view which seems to infuse through much of the contemporary discourses is that the philosophy of classical liberalism is unfriendly, if not hostile, towards notions of political management. It is widely accepted, amongst liberals and non-liberals alike, that a normative stance favouring voluntary action in market-based economic settings distinguishes liberalism from other strands of thought. What is more contentious is the proposition that liberalism has been, since its very inception, a doctrine of political conduct.

Disagreement over the status of politics in liberalism perhaps rests in the reception towards highly vocalised exponents of liberal (and especially its rather Americanised cousin, libertarian) ideas who seek to downscale governmental activities, or to put it more crudely, to "privatise all the things." Speculatively, it is held that vocalisation for a reduced profile

M. Novak (✉)
School of Sociology, The Australian National University, Canberra, Australian Capital Territory, Australia
e-mail: Mikayla.Novak@anu.edu.au



D. F. Hardwick, L. Marsh (eds.), *Reclaiming Liberalism*, Palgrave Studies in Classical Liberalism, https://doi.org/10.1007/978-3-030-28760-3_3

for politics in economic and social life might be seen, especially by liberalism's detractors, as somehow representative of the liberal view commonly held by liberals themselves. This proposition is readily contraindicated by a reading of the iconic texts of liberalism, stretching from Locke to Smith and from Hayek to Friedman, which diagnose political problems and explicate reforms to institutions and policies. Recent research endeavours also contradict the notion that investigations about the nature and consequences of political action are the intellectual preserve of non-liberal philosophers (e.g. Aligica 2015; Boettke 2018).

This chapter provides an outline of the political perspectives raised by the "ordoliberal" school of law and economics. In a similar vein to other classical liberals, ordoliberal theorists take seriously the institutional and operational qualities of public sector administration whilst remaining critical of the weaknesses and deficiencies of state-collectivism. What is distinctive about ordoliberalism is that its emphasis upon the development and maintenance of institutional rules is inspired by its commitment to develop a model of political conduct that curtails public *and* private power. Ordoliberal strictures concerning the undesirability of concentrated power by firms and governments alike reflect an understanding of the inherently *entangled* nature of economic-political relations, which was in some respects ahead of its time. For the ordoliberals, entanglement between economics and politics cannot be avoided so it needs to be managed in accordance with certain ordering principles that guarantee the maintenance of liberty, and ensure political activity is accountable, intelligible and acceptable to those being governed.

The political relevance of ordoliberalism is magnified by its history. The first generation of ordoliberal thought, devised by a loose intellectual alliance between German economists, jurists and sociologists, was a distinctly classical liberal response to the emergence of authoritarianism in Germany during the first half of the twentieth century. Given the obliteration of the German public administration system in the immediate aftermath of World War II, ordoliberal principles happened to serve as some inspiration for political actors seeking to rebuild the country's government along liberal-democratic lines. Thus, there is an element of conscious planning for, and building of, liberal institutions which would, in turn, be conducive to market-tested betterment in the longer term.

We think ordoliberalism serves as a potentially suitable framework to resuscitate liberalism into the future, should severe retrogressive drift in (and decay of) political institutions lead to bouts of populism if not authoritarianism (Wagner 2006). Far from representing an anti-democratic project, ordoliberalism is intended to overcome the workings of special interests and other insiders which thwart the application of politics as a means through which all of us deliberate and collaborate over projects in the public interest.

## Ordoliberalism: Historical Context, Key Personalities and Basic Principles

The first half of the twentieth century proved to be a traumatic period for Germany and its peoples. Vanquished militarily by allied forces during World War I, millions of German military personnel and citizens perished as a result of conflict and vast amounts of infrastructure and other forms of productive capital were destroyed. Germany was also obliged, under the Treaty of Versailles provisions, to repay the Allies reparations for war damages. The German Empire collapsed as a result of internal rebellion in late 1918, with the subsequent establishment of the Weimar Republic which lasted until 1933.

Historical accounts of Weimar are punctuated by episodes of internal political instability, hyperinflation and the deleterious effects of the Great Depression. The troubles afflicting Weimar were especially compounded by the rise of the fascistic, and deeply anti-Semitic, Nazi Party, led by Austrian-born Adolf Hitler, which assumed German political leadership in 1933. The Nazi political takeover of Germany thus instigated the demise of the Weimar Republic, sweeping away any semblance of liberal democracy in that country.

The Nazis grafted a centralised state that mercilessly engaged in the horrific persecution of German Jewish citizens and other minorities and, shortly thereafter, transmogrified into an aggressively expansionist force internationally. Germany's territorial aggression led to World War II, which commenced in 1939 and ceased in 1945. During that historically brief period, the world witnessed the tragedy of the countless deaths of more Germans, and peoples from other countries beside. For all of its murderous activity on an industrial scale the Nazi regime—just like any other political arrangement centrally planned—was characterised by its gross economic ineptitude, with ceaseless production bottlenecks and a perennial struggle to provide adequate supplies of consumer goods (Eucken 1948a, b). Naturally, the cost of Nazism on Germany, and upon the world as a whole, was immense and in some respects is still being felt to this day.

A small group of economists and jurists initially sought to conceptually describe the factors underlying Germany's worsening fortunes but, especially as post-war reconstruction became a realistic prospect, also became involved in outlining the policy framework for recovery. These figures, largely referred to today as ordoliberals (also known as the "Freiburg School"), explicitly diagnosed problems confronting Germany on a political economy foundation. Essentially, they hypothesised the transition of Germany from war to economic-political dysfunction and, again, to war as the result of a complex breakdown in esteem for classical liberal ideas economically, politically and socially.

Prior to a more complete description of the theoretical foundations of ordoliberalism, it is necessary to briefly indicate the roles and contributions of the key contributors to this unique strand of liberal philosophy. We start with Walter Eucken (1891–1950) and Franz Böhm (1895–1977), who received professorships at the University of Freiburg and were primarily, but not exclusively, concerned with intersectional studies of economics and law. Eucken and Böhm contributed to the formative texts of what came to be known as ordoliberal theory, and were founding editors of the "ORDO Yearbook" first published in 1948 (and which remains in existence).

Certain other academics and policymakers have come to be seen as fellow travellers of ordoliberalism, to some extent, even if views surrounding certain economic, social and political issues were sharply divided. Wilhelm Röpke (1899–1966) and Alexander Rüstow (1885–1963) were exiled to Turkey during the 1930s in opposition to the Nazi regime. The works of Röpke and Rüstow complemented the legal-economic doctrines of Eucken and Böhm, proffering a view of the cultural and sociological determinants of liberalism. Alfred Müller-Armack (1901–1978), who was professor of economics at the University of Cologne, coined the term "social market economy" partly in a quest to forward a politically palatable vision of a political order balancing economic and social justice considerations. The post-war German politician, and liberal reformer, Ludwig Erhard (1897–1977) is widely touted to have been inspired by ordoliberal thinking, both through his reading of key texts and the receipt of policy advice from yet another ordoliberal, Leonhard Miksch (1901–1950).

There have been significant refinements to ordoliberal theory over the past few decades, which have been propelled by some of the Yearbook's editorial board members such as Viktor Vanberg. As will be seen throughout this chapter, the evolution of ordoliberalism has entailed the incorporation of economic process and consent-oriented constitutional design theories from the likes of Austrian economics, evolutionary economics, constitutional political economy and institutional economics.

A hallmark of classical liberal philosophy is its emphasis upon the concept of the "spontaneous order" (Barry 1982; D'Amico 2015). The spontaneous order notion embodies the age-old idea that certain social phenomena are oftentimes the emergent, but not consciously designed, by-product of actions undertaken by innumerable people seeking to pursue their ambitions and objectives. The normative implication is not that individuals undertake plans, but that a wide range of economic, social and political phenomena are not commandeered or directed by a single individual, or a small group, in place of all others. Spontaneous order is largely associated with Scottish Enlightenment figures such as Adam Ferguson and Adam Smith, and more recently Hayek.

Vanberg helpfully reminds us that the likes of Eucken and Böhm "acknowledged that all empirical societies and economies are to a considerable extent the product of evolutionary forces and not the creation of a master plan" (Vanberg 2002, p. 41). Nevertheless, a defining feature of the ordoliberal school is that market institutions are not inherently self-generating, and do not possess self-correcting properties. In other words, "[s]pontaneous orders are seen to have endogenous degenerating tendencies, for example the rise of private monopoly power" (Sally 1996, p. 242). This core position both distinguishes and contrasts the more optimistic vision, most conspicuously associated with contemporary libertarian thinkers, that spontaneous orders are both desirable and inevitable (at least once the domain of governmental action is narrowed considerably).

Drawing upon their observation of economic developments in Germany, and in other locations, the first generation of ordoliberals warned that the spontaneous conduct of economic activity risks a concentration of market power at the expense of consumers. Böhm identified the onset of anti-competitive, cartel-like behaviour amongst major German firms as a key contributor towards the economic dysfunctionality of the Weimar Republic. In this context legal developments, such as the 1897 ruling by the German Supreme Court (*Reichsgericht*) upholding cartel arrangements as legally binding contracts under civil law, contributed to cartelisation becoming "a fully legitimate and accepted form of market organization in Germany" (Windolf and Beyer 1996, p. 206). As for the hyperinflation episode, the ordoliberals suggested the root cause was a political inability to guarantee monetary stability. All in all, it is posited that economic problems stem from a lack of attendance to spontaneous ordering processes. As Wilhelm Röpke vividly expressed it, "a satisfactory market economy capable of maintaining itself does not arise from our energetically doing nothing" (cited in Tatchell 2015).

Ordoliberalism stresses the desirability of *rules* to influence economic interactions in a constructive manner. The so-called "Freiburger Imperative" is to design a rule-structure so as to maintain market competition, and to uphold productiveness. This position is very much in tune with the Smithian classical political economy tradition in one sense (Hutchinson 1979), but by the same token it is seen as something of a precursor for late-twentieth century constitutional political economy (Vanberg 1988; Leipold 1990). The prominence that ordoliberals attach to rules underpinning the economic order, and the quality thereof, is aptly gleaned from their manifesto statement of 1936 which stated:

> The treatment of all practical politico-legal and politico-economic questions must be keyed to the idea of the economic constitution. … the economic constitution must be understood as a general political decision as to how the economic life of the nation is to be structured (Böhm et al. 1936 (1989), pp. 23, 24).

What are the component parts of the economic constitution, as the original ordoliberals saw it? After careful deliberations, Walter Eucken and his intellectual peers established several "constitutive principles" for a functional, liberal-oriented economic order: protection of private property; freedom of contract; complete liabilities for those causing economic harms; open markets, domestically and internationally; monetary stability centred upon anti-inflationism; and economic policy consistency (Kasper and Streit 1993).

By this point it should be apparent that the motivation of ordoliberal figures extended beyond considerations of the theoretical dimensions of economic order (*Ordnungstheorie*), and into the designation of rule-based policies which may be practically applied to sustain such an order (*Ordnungspolitik*). The emphasis upon "the rules of the game" suggests, to an extent, the ordoliberals harboured an aversion towards public policies which attempted to directly rearrange outcomes in the form of reallocation or redistribution (*Prozesspolitik*). As stated by Eucken, "the state should influence forms of economy, but not itself direct the economic process. … State planning of forms – Yes; state planning and control of the economic process – No! The essential thing is to recognize the difference between form and process, and to act accordingly" (Eucken 1951, pp. 95, 96).

Even though ordoliberalism elevates economic constitutionalism as the normative standard of economic policy, the key figures within the school provided policymakers with an outlet to redress any problems which remain after the instillation of the constitutive principles. To this end, the ordoliberals specified a range of "regulative principles" including policies to constrain market concentration, ensure fairer income and wealth distributions, correct any external effects, and address supply abnormalities (Grossekettler 1989).

The key point to be made here is that ordoliberals are prepared to tolerate some outcome-oriented policy action, insofar as it remains compatible with the broader project of upholding a liberal economic order. To establish what styles of *Prozesspolitik* are deemed appropriate, the ordoliberals made the distinction between "market conformity" and "market non-conformity" criteria. Market-conformable policy is consistent with the constitutive principles allowing the market process to remain intact, and is thus adjudged to be appropriate, whereas market non-conformity policies distort economic activity threatening to privilege some interests over others. Whereas these criteria are intended to present workable guidance for policymakers as to when governmental action is warranted, there is admittedly considerable ambiguity surrounding the use of these concepts in practice.

Whereas economic constitutionalism not only as theoretical agenda but as political practice arguably represents the core of the ordoliberal research program, there is also keen interest among ordoliberal scholars, and especially among their associates, concerning the moral and ethical underpinnings of the competitive market economy. Chiefly attributable to the works of Röpke and Rüstow, this strand of research serves as a key contribution towards the development of a "sociological liberalism."

The ordoliberals and their sympathisers sought to understand, if not promote, certain cultural and social conditions that go "beyond supply and demand," but perceived as integral to sustaining valour for liberal values within the community. As stated by Röpke, "the market economy is not everything. It must find its place within a higher order of things which is not ruled by supply and demand, free prices, and competition" (Röpke 1960, p. 6). Crucially, Röpke went on to say that, "nothing is more detrimental to a sound general order appropriate to human nature than two things: mass and concentration. Individual responsibility and independence in proper balance with the community, neighborly spirit, and true civic sense – all of these presuppose that the communities in which we live do not exceed the human scale" (ibid., pp. 6–7). Those who keenly pursued the sociological turn tended to advocate an expansive array of end-state policies which were purported to uphold a liberal life-world. However, many of these ideas appear to not only contravene the evolutionary spirit of many of the unfolding extra-economic changes, but were in some respects deeply illiberal in nature. These matters will be discussed in detail later in this chapter.

That the socio-cultural determinants of a sustained liberal order were entertained by certain ordoliberal associates points to a generic interest in the ways in which distinct domains of human action coordinate with one another. In another distinctive contribution brought forward by the ordoliberal school, an emphasis was placed upon the "interdependence of orders." Economic, social and political actions "follow different internal logics and are not to be perceived as an organic whole. However, an isolated perspective only on the economic or the legal order might be strongly misleading. Instead, these suborders are to be seen as a system of manifold links and feedback mechanisms, an image that contains the notion of mutual dependencies and patterns of (in)compatibility between them" (Kolev 2015, p. 427). When implementing a rules-based, constitutive framework for a liberal order, careful attention needs to be given to a delicate institutional balance supporting freedom of action in all relevant fields of human endeavour.

The distinctiveness of ordoliberalism within the broad-ranging cluster of ideas under the heading of classical liberalism has led some to suggest this school of thought is strictly the product of the cultural, historical and political events pertaining to the German nation. This impression may be magnified to some degree by the tendency of some key ordoliberal scholars to distinguish their brand of liberalism with the so-called "paleo-liberal," *laissez faire* offerings seen as evident within British liberalism. However, in recent years researchers have drawn links between ordoliberalism and classical liberal scholarship originating from places outside of continental Europe.

The "Old Chicago" liberal tradition of Henry Simons and, to a lesser extent, Jacob Viner and Frank Knight emphasised the desirability of constraining the exercise of capricious public power through rules (Oliver 1960; Köhler and Kolev 2013; Feld et al. 2017). The study of interdependencies between differing systems of ordering are perhaps most vividly expressed in its contemporary form under "entangled political economy" scholarship (Wagner 2014, 2016). Others have viewed ordoliberalism as presenting a precursor to the economics of rent seeking, as well as institutional economics, public choice theory and constitutional economics (White 2012; Goldschmidt and Wohlgemuth 2008). Finally, one may perceive that certain tenets of ordoliberalism—including an aversion towards power accumulation and influence-peddling within politics, and an advocacy for corporate unlimited liability—would find an element of support amongst modern-day "left libertarians."

The upshot of the statements contained in the previous paragraph is to suggest that the rule orientation that is the focus of ordoliberalism is, in fact, generically familiar to policy participants in the Anglosphere and beyond. However, the direct impact of German ordoliberalism on the economic reform programs outlined in the United Kingdom, Australia and New Zealand in recent decades had been very minimal, carrying weight only to the extent that the insights of *Ordnungspolitik* were subsumed into the recent, and more influential, scholarship on the importance of economic institutions (Centre for Policy Studies 1975; Kasper and Streit op. cit.; cf. Wohlgemuth 2001). This dim assessment of ordoliberalism's past influence is not to suggest that it is irrelevant to the political challenges presently confronting the Western world, especially given that the present-day crisis is, under no uncertain terms, the result of divisive and often chaotic departures from liberally grounded policy rules and norms.

## Containment of Power as Core Ordoliberal Strategy, and the Role of Competition

An important explanation for the "wealth of nations," to paraphrase the title of Adam Smith's famous book, resides in acts of economic competition. Economic actors (primarily, but not exclusively, individuals and firms) will rival each other in producing outputs, and incurring the costs of production in doing so, which satisfy the needs and desires of consumers. Given the unit price at which products are being sold, those actors who are able to attain an excess of (sales) revenue over costs, thereby receiving a profit in satisfying a critical mass of consumers, are able to sustain if not expand their operations. Actors which incur a loss—that is an excess of costs over revenue—are encouraged to revise their production strategies and plans should they wish to avoid future losses and potential economic unviability.

In neoclassical economics, competition is said to promote efficient resource allocations, implying that no one can be made better off in a potential reallocation without making all others worse off (referred to as the "Pareto efficiency criterion"). The alignment of competition and efficiency is posited to hold true within the perfect competition market structure, which bears several important characteristics which do not translate to economic reality. A sufficiently large number of producers are assumed to sell a homogeneous good or service, such that the market share of any given producer has no bearing upon the output prices that are offered to consumers. The assumption of complete information possessed by market participants, and unrestrained resources mobility, effectively takes opportunities for profit-seeking price manipulation or product differentiation by any particular market player out of the economic picture.

There are many criticisms levelled against the perfect competition model, notwithstanding its conceptual elegance in reconciling competition with efficiency in ways reminiscent of physics and similar natural sciences (Potts 2000). Scholars versed in the Austrian school of economics, and fellow travellers such as Joseph Schumpeter, J. M. Clark and Erich Hoppmann, emphasised that competition is an economically dynamic process conducted by fallible-yet-capable heterogeneous individuals and their agencies. In this context competition is very much conducted on a trial-and-error basis (or, using parlance adopted by Karl Popper, "conjectures and refutations") without the precisions or comforts of risklessness or certainty regarding the outcomes of competition *ex-ante*. What these heterodox scholars share is the conviction that entrepreneurship, or improvised human action undertaken with the hope of securing gains (Koppl 2006), plays an integral part within the competitive process but which is ignored by the neoclassical emphasis upon perfect competition.

The ordoliberals, especially those represented in the first generation of scholarship, are widely seen to have focussed upon the combined theoretical-historical study of deviations from perfect competition (Eucken 1950 (1992); Kolev 2015; Meijer 1987). Although the first generation ordoliberals were aware of process-oriented perspectives (e.g. Anchustegui 2015; Vatiero 2010; Sally op. cit.), and Hayek's framing of competition as a "discovery procedure" doubtlessly added impetus towards the modern ordoliberal appreciation of non-static approaches, such observations do not diminish the key perspective of ordoliberalism: competition is a means of *disempowerment*. This view is exemplified by one of the most famous statements in the ordoliberal canon, conceptualising competition as "the greatest and most ingenious instrument of disempowerment in history" (Böhm 1961, p. 22).

Whereas the perfect competition model, by its very definition, depicts an economic powerlessness arising from the passivity of part of agents to influence market outcomes (Herrmann-Pillath 2000), the ordoliberals made sufficient conceptual accommodations encapsulating freedom of action by competitors vying for support from consumers. Eucken, Böhm and others highlighted the economic desirability of competition insofar as those participating were dedicated to striving for productive outcomes that benefitted consumers in general. This style of "competition through achievement" is referred to, in German, as *Leistungswettbewerb* (Vanberg 1999), and would involve the selection and variation of goods and services, price arbitrage and process innovations promoting economic welfare. The ordoliberals indicate there is also a potential for competitive impulses to yield unproductive or even destructive outcomes (*Behindesrungswettbewerb*), which are, naturally, best avoided. In terms of the latter, forms of "competition to subdue competition" could include the outright destruction of rivals' businesses, attaining superior market share by committing fraud, establishing price- and quantity-fixing cartels and other restraints upon competition, and lobbying governments to introduce competition-suppressing regulations and taxes.

In the ordoliberal framework entrepreneurs can exercise discretion in terms of how they act economically, but surely the reason of rules is to influence the way individuals and organisations compete within the market. An economic constitution would be regarded as effective to the extent that rules facilitated productive entrepreneurship and, through it, merit-based competition directed towards serving consumers better. Conversely, rules that help minimise outbreaks of economic predation are viewed as desirable. As noted by Vanberg (Ibid.), creating the institutional environment conducive to *Leistungswettbewerb*, given the lack of guarantee that spontaneously ordered economic processes will not degenerate into market power concentration, is seen by ordoliberals as firmly within the purview of political action.

It is important to signify the importance of the relationship between the competition-promoting properties of *Ordnungspolitik* and maintenance of democratic political values, as seen by the ordoliberals. As mentioned earlier, ordoliberalism served as something of a diagnosis of the economic, political and social problems besetting Germany during the first half of the twentieth century. The development of heavily concentrated markets and the concomitant accumulation of *private* economic power reflected, in ordoliberal thought, a departure from an ability of economic agents to participate, let alone compete in a productive manner, within the market on equal terms. In no uncertain terms, the cartelisation of the economy spilled over into the political arena:

> [P]owerful market players were able to convert their economic into political power and corrupt via interest capture various political institutions. … These economic phenomena transformed the Weimarian economic and political system into a 'neo-feudal' system, undermining the independence of the state, as well as the supporting social structures of democracy. Therefore, the concentration of market power did not only jeopardize the competitive process, but also harmed the input-oriented legitimacy of the political system by curtailing the procedural guarantees of equal participation in the political game. Such development also had significant ramifications on the political rights of the citizens (Deutscher and Makris 2016, p. 187).

The ability of special economic interests to produce for themselves, *and not for others*, fiscal and regulatory privileges is reasonably considered an affront to democratic political values resting upon the fundamental equality of persons under the rule of law, and generality of political access and treatment. In this context it is not that liberal values are at risk of the improbable event of being overturned by the citizenry-at-large, but that liberal values in the broad sense are undermined by rent seeking motivated by a desire to subvert competition.

Having established the desirability of competitive acts that are innovative and supportive of economic development, the critical question is: how to best uphold competition, and ensure it is not undermined by unproductive or destructive ventures? It is in this regard that solution is more difficult to establish than the underlying sentiment, as reflected in the disagreements between ordoliberal figures themselves regarding the best strategy to maintain, if not promote, market competition.

Most of the originating ordoliberals provided support towards specific, pro-competitive public policies which they saw as market conforming. Walter Eucken and Franz Böhm suggested that government establish an anti-cartel bureau, with a sufficient degree of statutory independence from the legislature, to eliminate cartels and restrain the exercise of other forms of market power, such as boycotts and price discrimination. Wherever possible, monopolies should be disbanded and prohibited. Given their insistence upon economic policy consistency, the ordoliberals also called upon government to check that bankruptcy laws, taxes, intellectual property did not advantage larger over smaller firms, and incumbents against potential entrants (Vanberg 1988 op. cit.).

Ordoliberals did not share a common view when it came to competition policy, however. Of particular note is the contribution of Leonhard Miksch, who developed the concept of "as-if competition" (Goldschmidt and Berndt 2005; Vatiero op. cit.; Mestmäcker 2011). In the event that some monopolies (e.g. natural monopoly) could not feasibly be eliminated, Miksch suggested that government regulation could control prices and other aspects of monopoly conduct so that they behaved "as if" they existed in a highly competitive environment. The "as-if" competition notion proved controversial, even amongst ordoliberals who feared that very substantial, illiberal public-sector power would substitute for market power if attempts were made to enforce this proposal. Subsequent scholarship in relation to the epistemic merits of technocratically designed-and-implemented public policies (Hayek 1945, 1989; Koppl 2018) also cast severe doubts over the applicability of such a policy stance.

Ordoliberal scholarship towards competition has also been revised considering the advent of globalisation over recent decades (Kasper and Streit op. cit.; Kolev op. cit.). The reduction of tariffs other "trade protection" barriers, combined with cross-border supply chain integration and improved communications techniques, have, inter alia, facilitated the inflow of additional, and often cheaper, imports. This phenomenon, in turn, increased competitive pressures upon domestic industries to better meet the needs and desires of their customers. While governments in developed countries continued to maintain their formal competition policies, the policy settings themselves were reformed to take greater account of these beneficial implications of globalisation upon market concentration.

A noticeable element of populism's resurgence in advanced economies is the preparedness of governments to reimpose trade barriers, as part of a broader, yet reactionary, political project to denigrate the effects of globalisation. For example, the United States under the Trump administration has aggressively re-imposed tariffs on a wide range of manufactures in an attempt to maintain jobs as well as pursue geo-political objectives (Bryan et al. 2018; McCloskey 2019). In the face of the anti-globalisation challenge which, if anything, is likely to lead to a dampening of competition within countries as import penetration recedes, one is mindful of the pro-globalist economic orientation of the ordoliberals.

Generally speaking, the ordoliberals were not attracted to the imposition of trade barriers by government. Whilst there was some debate concerning to what extent light or modest tariffs (however defined) were market conformable or not, the general consensus was that tariffs and certain other forms of trade-suppressing policies would merely insulate domestic producers from a global impetus to compete on merit and to innovate. Wilhelm Röpke was particularly notable for his suggestion that countries engage in unilateral trade liberalisation to benefit domestic consumers, rather than wait for the conclusion of oft-drawn out multilateral trade negotiations (Sally 1997). More recently, Viktor Vanberg argued that in a choice between a competitive, privilege-free economy and a protectionist, privileged economy, "we would have good reasons to prefer the first environment because it promises to make for a much richer society" (Vanberg 1999, p. 146). In common with other classical liberals, the ordoliberals thus continue to warn of the deleterious effects of anti-globalisation.

## The Socio-Cultural Element Associated with Ordoliberalism: A Critical Assessment

Much of twentieth-century political economy tended to consider the richly varied domains of human action as largely separated phenomena. To the extent that different ordering principles were held to impact each other, the "strong separability" thesis of political economy saw impacts as largely occurring in an exogenous fashion. Taking the example of the interaction between people in economic and political realms, "polity and economy [are seen] as distinct analytical objects, each of which can be usefully analyzed without taking the other into account, and with polity acting on economy to modify economy in some fashion" (Wagner 2016, p. x). The analytically mutual estrangement of kinds of human action would appear to be grounded in certain historical, scientific and other developments—for example, the emergence of specialisation within the social sciences, but nevertheless represents what could be described as a conceptual "flight from reality" (Boettke 1997).

One of the distinctive intellectual contributions of the ordoliberal school is its insistence that the economy, polity and society are deeply embedded phenomena which cannot be entirely considered in isolation from each other. This perspective lends itself to a genuinely integrative view of human conduct along ethical-normative lines. Consider the following statement by Wilhelm Röpke as a representative account of the ordoliberal emphasis upon the interdependence of orders:

> We move in a world of prices, markets, competition, wage rates, rates of interest, exchange rates, and other economic magnitudes. All of this is perfectly legitimate and fruitful as long as we keep in mind that we have narrowed our angle of vision and do not forget that the market economy is the economic order proper to a definite social structure and to a definite spiritual and moral setting. … Extra-economic, moral, and social integration is always a prerequisite of economic integration (Röpke 1960, pp. 93, 124).

Acceptance of an existent of interdependent economic, political and social action led the ordoliberals to consider the extent to which profit-seeking economic activity is consistent with associational forms of cooperation, undertaken for altruistic, solidaristic and other socially meaningful purposes, often referred to in shorthand as "civil society." In many ways this line of investigation has animated classical liberal scholarship, such as the work of Adam Smith who contemplated how self-regarding economic transactions could be reconciled with observations of broad-scale social harmony. The ordoliberals harboured some doubts about the applicability of spontaneous order within the economy, as mentioned previously, and those who formally indulged in socio-cultural investigations also proffered a view that alignment of economic prosperity and social harmony is a contingency.

The cohort of scholars specialising in sociological thought, and who are seen in some quarters as sympathetic to ordoliberalism, namely Röpke, Alexander Rüstow and Alfred Müller-Armack, supported in principle the maintenance of a competitive economic order. This kind of arrangement would serve to undermine cartelised and monopolistic power structures within the marketplace, and the ensuing economic growth would redress social disaffection by providing secure employment and reasonable wages. It is arguably with respect to the extra-economic underpinnings of liberalism, however, that the ordoliberals most consciously explicated a catalogue of high specific, end-state conditions to be satisfied. Writing in the 1950s, Röpke insisted that a society conducive to productive entrepreneurship, and performance competition, would consist of peoples possessing virtues such as: public spiritedness; civic mindedness; a sense of social responsibility; honesty; fairness; reciprocal altruism; moderation and self-discipline; respect of human dignity; solidarity; benevolence; and Christian love respectively love of neighbour (cited in Wörsdörfer 2013).

Walter Eucken warned that certain social forces may contribute towards widespread "de-souling" and "de-individualisation," implying that "the individual becomes increasingly incapable of expressing his or her right to self-determination" (Wörsdörfer 2010, p. 25). Along with the rise of private economic centralism and industrial gigantism, the sociological ordoliberals expressed reservations about what the processes of urbanism, secularisation, political party development, unionism and other forms of so-called "massification" would do to the maintenance of a liberal order. For Rüstow (1942) part of the discontent felt by union-organised manufacturing workers, which threatened to undermine liberal political institutions, resulted from their residential detachment from nature and economic divorce from entrepreneurial self-employment.

The ordoliberals feared the trend towards ethical and moral conformity amongst the citizenry would instigate the degradation of the political order. The creation of a proletarianised "mass man" risked creating a political climate less conducive to the toleration of entrepreneurial novelties within the market sphere, and more supportive of collective forms of economic organisation which could translate into political authoritarianism (Hayek 1944 (2001)). This fear of economic illiberalism spilling over into political illiberalism helps to explain why ordoliberals such as Röpke maintained strident opposition towards the welfare state (beyond old-age pensions, unemployment payments and insurance for those unable to participate in the economy).

The aforementioned statements indicate that ordoliberals, and those in their broad intellectual circles, did identify circumstances under which they saw economic action posing as a threat to the specific, yet fragile, ethical and moral qualities deemed necessary to preserve a liberal order. The socio-cultural element presaged the scholarship undertaken by communitarians, such as Amitai Etzioni, Robert Putnam and Michael Sandel, whose work came to prominence during the "Great Moderation" period of the 1990s. What was the ordoliberal solution, or set of solutions, to ensure a bourgeois social order complementing the competitive, market-based economic order and liberal-democratic order? The social policy platforms espoused by ordoliberals came in varied nomenclatures—for example Rüstow's *Vitalpolitik*, Müller-Armack's "social irenics" and Ludwig Erhard's "social market economy"—but each of these platforms shared a commitment to holistically consider human activity in an effort to reconcile divergent ordering principles.

Inspired by the Catholic social principle of subsidiarity, an enduring position of the ordoliberals is that actions and tasks should be delegated to decentralised, local forms of association best equipped to undertake them. The virtue of decentralisation in an economic context is that society as a whole can benefit from the distillation of personalised, tacit knowledge about how to entrepreneurially cater to the wishes of idiosyncratic and heterogeneous consumers. To this end, the ordoliberals expressed support for the continuation of small, family-owned businesses as part of a broader effort to retain economic diversity and, through it, a variation in styles of economic entrepreneurship within society.

Decentralisation is also seen as advantageous politically. In one sense the "democratic deficit," borne of a variation between the interests of political and non-political actors, can be abridged by the existence of smaller electorates and the greater ease of political communication this provides. To the extent that decentralisation corresponds with a sizeable number of sub-national jurisdictions, individuals and groups can constrain political excess and enhance politician-citizen accountabilities by threatening to move to another locality. The ordoliberals say one of the keys to a revitalised society is to avoid the strictures of socio-political centralism to the greatest extent possible.

Other features of the ordoliberal decentralisation agenda are more contentious, even to classical liberals. Röpke and Rüstow upheld the virtues of geographic decentralisation, seeking the introduction of planning and other policies to halt the seemingly rapid flow of people from rural to urban areas. Given his valorisation of the economic self-sufficiency of farmers, and the purported social values that go with such occupations (including a strong work ethic and adherence to religious values), Röpke unsurprisingly sought to advance agricultural policies to assist the preservation of smaller scale, non-industrialised agricultural activity (Gregg 2010).

As mentioned previously it was within the realm of social policy that certain ordoliberals were inclined to exhibit an obsession with form rather than function. To no small extent this notion is exemplified by ordoliberal policies aimed at tilting social structures in favour of small business, geographic decentralism and subsistence agriculture and crafts. Proponents of the sociological strand were also dedicated to policies supporting the status of the heterosexual nuclear family structure as a bulwark against the perceived atomisation being threatened by large-scale corporates and bureaucracies. There seems an element of tension between this view and the somewhat quixotic concerns of Röpke and Rüstow in relation to overpopulation (Hartwich 2009; Lantink 2018). As illustrated by Julian Simon and other analysts of long-term progress, calls to restrain population growth had proven to be unfounded as productivity growth both supported urban agglomeration and labour-saving increases in agricultural output.

Even if the maintenance of the liberal social order necessitates the specification of definitive proposals, it would be difficult to mount a reasonable case for some of the more extreme agendas pursued by some figures bracketed with the first-generation ordoliberals. We challenge the legitimacy of Röpke's support for South Africa's apartheid regime (Goldschmidt and Dörr 2018; Röpke 1964; Slobodian 2014, 2018), which is grossly at odds with the venerable classical liberal principles of equality and justice for all peoples. Formalised restrictions against pathways to opportunity, including the "freedom to compete," are also likely to reduce the scope of productive economic coordination (Novak 2016; Boettke and Candela 2017). Röpke also expressed antiseptic views towards the rights of women during his career—including in relation to the merits of women participating in the labour force (Röpke 1942)—which clearly runs counter to the enunciated ordoliberal respect for individual autonomy and freedom.

All in all, the cultural-sociological element often attached to first-wave ordoliberalism has not aged particularly well. The likes of religious affiliation and unionisation are on the wane in many developed countries, causing some consternation amongst conservatives and social-democrats nostalgically yearning for the cultural and social certainties exemplified by these mass structures of yesteryear. These and certain other forms of mass association (e.g. political party membership) have experienced decline, but it is far from clear that such developments have necessarily coincided with the atrophy of economic activity let alone degradation of civil society (Novak 2018). In the place of certain popular mass structures of the past have come other mass structures albeit of smaller scale (e.g. groups centred about environmental amenity), as well as more dynamic sub-groups and counter-cultures providing a more "individuated" experience of human association. The evolution of civil society combined with the significant advance of economic development on a global scale and spread of democracy, certainly in the decades prior to the onset of the 2007–2008 "global financial crisis," places a great shadow over the usefulness, or even reasonableness, of the end-state socio-cultural turn in thinking.

Whilst ordoliberals should disavow the racist, sexist and other anti-humanistic indulgences carried by certain figures of the past, the suggestion posited here is that proponents for ordoliberalism today can still uncover intellectually fertile ground in the studies of cultural and social concerns and their relations with other features of human life. As highlighted by the now-extensive scholarship in institutional economics, ethical and moral concerns such as fairness, reputation and trustworthiness are at the heart of a functioning competitive, market-based economy (Schmidtchen 1984; Wörsdörfer 2013 op. cit.). One might also add that the aforementioned attributes have, once again in recent years, been revealed as indispensable components of consensus-building democratic political conduct which appears to be in short supply over recent years.

One potential avenue for fruitful investigation along socio-cultural lines is to advance an ordoliberal interpretation of recent work, by Choi and Storr (2018), over the "culture of rent seeking." In essence, the cultural precepts operating within a given political jurisdiction are said to resemble a rent seeking culture to the extent that citizens perceive expending resources to secure governmental favours as an acceptable path to economic success. The degeneration of economic, social and political relations identified by the ordoliberals during the Weimar and Nazi eras could be interpreted as the emergent result of the legitimation of a culture of rent seeking in Germany, only to be nullified by that country's defeat at the end of World War II. The post-war deregulatory moments enshrined by Erhard in (West) Germany is said to have facilitated the rapid recovery of the German economy, and these policy events could be interpreted as having facilitated cultural development adverse to rent seeking—but not on a permanent basis (Giersch et al. 1992; Lenel 1971 (1989); Watrin 1978 (1982); Witt 2002).

## Conclusion

The theory of ordoliberalism not only sought to present economic thought in a more realistic frame, contrasting the theoretical drift towards the institution-less conceptualisation of the economy in mainstream thinking during the early to mid-twentieth century. Proponents of ordoliberal thought, such as Walter Eucken, Franz Böhm and Wilhelm Röpke, aimed to politically reposition classical liberalism in an age exemplified by extreme political polarisation which descended into tyranny, mass murder and chaos throughout Europe.

Ordoliberalism poses as *politically aware liberal theory* in ways not seen in classical liberal scholarship, not least until the advent of public choice theory during the 1940s and 1950s. Acknowledging the existence of power structures, and the need to constrain discretionary political action within a framework of agreed and well-known rules, are among the most noteworthy of ordoliberal innovations. Being especially animated by a fear that interest groups could accumulate power and privilege by successfully petitioning for fiscal and regulatory advantages from the state, the ordoliberals attempted to elevate political action to a rule-based position of imperviousness to rent seeking conduct. In putting forward such solutions, the ordoliberals challenged power concentrations, acute inequality and a lack of distributed opportunities that, incidentally, are major subjects of contemporary discourses.

Both ordoliberalism's intellectual proponents and critics have conceded the immense practical difficulties surrounding the high-threshold objective of immunising politics from rent seeking. Claims by aspirants to political office that knowledge, if not success, in business deal-making is direct transposable to the political arena, or that "what is good for business is good for the country," does more than blur what are already fuzzy boundaries between economic and political orders of human activity. The expression of such sentiments, and the efforts to act upon them, threaten to normalise a culture of rent seeking throughout society.

The composition of "Big Players" (Koppl 2002) threatening a thriving liberal economy and robust democracy might have changed in the wake of globalisation and low-cost communication, but the threat of power accretion remains all too real. It is in this context that enunciating better rules, as illustrated by ordoliberalism since its inception, is properly seen as a pro-democratic project insofar as the Big Players, and other carriers of privilege, do not enjoy inside-running in terms of political access and participation. In other areas there remains the need to remodel ordoliberalism, including with respect to more dynamic, pluralistic theories of culture and society, but the key working elements of the theory are in place and, most importantly, are adaptable and subject to improvement. On this basis, we suggest ordoliberal precepts could more than capably serve as intellectual inspiration for a reformist *and* anti-authoritarian liberal political agenda of the future.

**Acknowledgements** The author wishes to thank two anonymous referees for feedback on a draft version of this chapter.

## References

Aligica, P. D. 2015. Public Administration and the Classical Liberal Perspective: Criticism, Clarifications, and Reconstruction. *Administration & Society* 49 (4): 530–551.

Anchustegui, Ignacio Herrera. 2015. Competition Law through an Ordoliberal Lens. *Oslo Law Review* 2: 139–174.

Barry, Norman. 1982. The tradition of spontaneous order. *Literature of Liberty* 5 (2): 7–58.

Boettke, Peter J. 1997. Where did economics go wrong? Modern economics as a flight from reality. *Critical Review* 11 (1): 11–64.

______. 2018. Economics and Public Administration. *Southern Economic Journal* 84 (4): 938–959.

Boettke, Peter J. and Rosolino A. Candela. 2017. The Liberty of Progress: Increasing Returns, Institutions, and Entrepreneurship. *Social Philosophy and Policy* 34 (2): 136–163.

Böhm, Franz. 1961. Demokratie und ökonomische Macht. In *Kartelle und Monopole im modernen Recht*, ed. Institut für ausländisches und internationals Wirtschaftsrecht, Volume I, 3–24. Karlsruhe: C. F. Müller.

Böhm, Franz, Walter Eucken and Hans Grossman-Doerth. 1936 (1989). The Ordo Manifesto of 1936. In *Germany's Social Market Economy: Origins and Evolution*, ed. Alan Peacock and Hans Willgerodt, pp. 15–26. London: Macmillan.

Bryan, Bob, Shayanne Gal and Jenny Cheng. 2018. Trump's trade war is getting serious. *Business Insider*, July 23. Accessed 21 August 2018. https://www.businessinsider.com.au/trump-trade-war-tariffs-effect-on-economy-prices-consumer-stocks-2018-7?r=US&IR=T

Centre for Policy Studies. 1975. Why Britain needs a social market economy. Accessed 16 August 2018. https://www.cps.org.uk/files/reports/original/111028103106-WhyBritainneedsaSocialMarketEconomy.pdf

Choi, Seung Ginny and Virgil Henry Storr. 2018. A culture of rent seeking. *Public Choice*. Accessed 21 August 2018. https://doi.org/10.1007/s11127-018-0557-x

D'Amico, Daniel J. 2015. Spontaneous Order. In: *The Oxford Handbook of Austrian Economics*, ed. Peter J. Boettke and Christopher J. Coyne, pp. 115–142. New York: Oxford University Press.

Deutscher, Elias and Stavros Makris. 2016. Exploring the ordoliberal paradigm: The competition-democracy nexus. *Competition Law Review* 11 (2): 181–214.

Eucken, Walter. 1948a. On the Theory of the Centrally Administered Economy: An Analysis of the German Experiment, Part I. Translated by T. W. Hutchinson. *Economica* 15 (58): 79–100.

_____. 1948b. On the Theory of the Centrally Administered Economy: An analysis of the German Experiment, Part II. Translated by T. W. Hutchinson. *Economica* 15 (59): 173–193.

_____. 1951. *This Unsuccessful Age, or The Pains of Economic Progress*. London: William Hodge & Company.

_____. 1950 (1992). *The Foundations of Economics: History and Theory in the Analysis of Economic Reality*. Translated by T. W. Hutchinson. Berlin: Springer Verlag.

Feld, Lars P., Ekkehard A. Köhler and Daniel Nientiedt. 2017. The "Dark Ages of German macroeconomics" and other alleged shortfalls in German economic thought. In: *Ordoliberalism: A German Oddity?* Ed. Thorsten Beck and Hans-Helmut Kotz, pp. 41–51. London: CEPR Press.

Giersch, Herbert, Karl-Heinz Paqué and Holger Schmieding. 1992. *The Fading Miracle: Four Decades of Market Economy in Germany*. Cambridge: Cambridge University Press.

Goldschmidt, Nils and Arnold Berndt. 2005. Leonhard Miksch (1901–1950). A Forgotten Member of the Freiburg School. *American Journal of Economics and Sociology* 64 (4): 973–998.

Goldschmidt, Nils and Julian Dörr. 2018. Wilhelm Röpke on Liberalism, Culture, and Economic Development. In: *Wilhelm Röpke (1899–1966): A Liberal Political Economist and Conservative Social Philosopher*. Eds. Patricia Commun and Stefan Kolev, pp. 203–217. Berlin: Springer.

Goldschmidt, Nils and Michael Wohlgemuth. 2008. Social Market Economy: origins, meanings and interpretations. *Constitutional Political Economy* 19: 261–276.

Gregg, Samuel. 2010. *Wilhelm Röpke's Political Economy*. Cheltenham: Edward Elgar.

Grossekettler, Heinz G. 1989. On designing an economic order. The contributions of the Freiburg School. In: *Twentieth-Century Economic Thought*, Volume 2, ed. D. A. Walker, pp. 38–84. Aldershot: Edward Elgar.

Hartwich, Oliver Marc. 2009. Neoliberalism: The genesis of a political swearword. The Centre for Independent Studies (CIS) Occasional Paper No. 114. St. Leonards: CIS.

Hayek, Friedrich A. 1944 (2001). *The Road to Serfdom*. London: Routledge.

_____. 1945. The Use of Knowledge in Society. *American Economic Review* 35 (4): 519–530.

_____. 1989. The Pretence of Knowledge. *American Economic Review* 79 (6): 3–7.

Herrmann-Pillath, Carsten. 2000. How to Research Complex Systems: A Methodological Comparison of Ordoliberalism and Regulation Theory. In: *Institutional Economics in France and Germany: German Ordoliberalism versus the French Regulation School*, eds. Agnès Labrousse and Jean-Daniel Weisz, pp. 272–301. Berlin: Springer.

Hutchinson, T. W. 1979. Notes on the Effects of Economic Ideas of the German Social Market Economy. *Zeitschrift für die gesamte Staatswissenschaft/Journal of Institutional and Theoretical Economics* 135: 424–441.

Kasper, Wolfgang and Manfred Streit. 1993. Lessons from the Freiburg School: The Institutional Foundations of Freedom and Prosperity. The Centre for Independent Studies (CIS) Occasional Paper No. 44. St. Leonards: CIS.

Köhler, Ekkehard A. and Stefan Kolev. 2013. The Conjoint Quest for a Liberal Positive Program: "Old Chicago," Freiburg, and Hayek. In: *F. A. Hayek and the Modern Economy: Economic Organization and Activity*, eds. Sandra J. Peart and David Levy, pp. 211–228. New York: Palgrave Macmillan.

Kolev, Stefan. 2015. Ordoliberalism and the Austrian School. In: *The Oxford Handbook of Austrian Economics*, ed. Peter J. Boettke and Christopher J. Coyne, pp. 115–142, New York: Oxford University Press.

Koppl, Roger. 2002. *Big Players and the Economic Theory of Expectations*. New York: Palgrave Macmillan.

_____. 2006. Entrepreneurial Behavior as a Human Universal. In *Entrepreneurship: The Engine of Growth—Volume 1: People*, ed. Maria Minniti, pp. 1–20. Westport: Greenwood Publishing.

_____. 2018. *Expert Failure*. New York: Cambridge University Press.

Lantink, Frans Willem. 2018. Cultural Pessimism and Liberal Regeneration? Wilhelm Röpke as an Ideological In-Between in German Social Philosophy. In: *Wilhelm Röpke (1899–1966): A Liberal Political Economist and Conservative Social Philosopher*, eds. Patricia Commun and Stefan Kolev, pp. 187–200. Berlin: Springer.

Leipold, Helmut. 1990. Neoliberal ordnungstheorie and constitutional economics: A comparison between Eucken and Buchanan. *Constitutional Political Economy* 1 (1): 47–65.

Lenel, Hans Otto. 1971 (1989). Does Germany Still Have a Social Market Economy? In: *Germany's Social Market Economy: Origins and Evolution*, eds. Alan Peacock and Hans Willgerodt, pp. 261–272. London: Macmillan.

McCloskey, Deirdre Nansen. 2019. Quit Worrying and Learn to Love Trade with China. *Reason Magazine*, March 17. Accessed 21 March 2019. https://reason.com/archives/2019/03/17/quit-worrying-and-learn-to-lov

Meijer, Gerrit. 1987. The History of Neo-Liberalism: Affinity to Some Developments in Economics in Germany. *International Journal of Social Economics* 14 (7/8/9): 142–155.

Mestmäcker, Ernst-Joachim. 2011. The development of German and European competition law with special reference to the EU Commission's Article 82 Guidance of 2008. In: *European Competition Law: The Impact of the Commission's Guidance on Article 102*, ed. Lorenzo Federico Pace, pp. 25–64. Cheltenham: Edward Elgar.

Novak, Mikayla. 2016. Deirdre McCloskey, Kirznerian Growth and the Role of Social Networks: Comment. *Economic Affairs* 36 (2): 217–220.

_____. 2018. Civil Society as a Complex Adaptive Phenomenon. *Cosmos + Taxis* 5 (3+4): 3–13.

Oliver, Henry M. Jr. 1960. German Neoliberalism. *The Quarterly Journal of Economics* 74 (1): 117–149.

Potts, Jason. 2000. *The New Evolutionary Microeconomics: Complexity, Competence, and Adaptive Behaviour*. Cheltenham: Edward Elgar.

Röpke, Wilhelm. 1942. *The Social Crisis of Our Time*. Chicago: University of Chicago Press.

_____. 1960. *A Humane Economy: The Social Framework of the Free Market*. Chicago: Henry Regnery.

_____. 1964. Südafrika: Versuch einer Würdigung *Schweizer Monatsheft* 44 (2): 97–112.

Rüstow, Alexander. 1942. General Sociological Causes of the Economic Disintegration and Possibilities of Reconstruction. In: *International Economic Disintegration*, Wilhelm Röpke, pp. 267–283. London: William Hodge & Company.

Sally, Razeen. 1996. Ordoliberalism and the Social Market: Classical Political Economy from Germany. *New Political Economy* 1 (2): 233–257.

_____. 1997. The International Political Economy of Wilhelm Röpke: Liberalism 'From Below.' *Millennium: Journal of International Studies* 26 (2): 321–348.

Schmidtchen, Dieter. 1984. German "Ordnungspolitik" as Institutional Choice. *Zeitschrift für die gesamte Staatswissenschaft/Journal of Institutional and Theoretical Economics* 140 (1): 54–70.

Slobodian, Quinn. 2014. The World Economy and the Color Line: Wilhelm Röpke, Apartheid and the White Atlantic. *German Historical Institute Bulletin* 10: 61–87.

_____. 2018. *Globalists: The End of Empire and the Birth of Neoliberalism.* Cambridge: Harvard University Press.

Tatchell, Jessica. 2015. Understanding the main tenets of ordoliberalism and its links to biopolitics. *Warwick Sociology Journal* 1 (4): 16–24.

Vanberg, Viktor. 1988. "Ordnungstheorie" as constitutional economics – the German conception of a "social market economy." *Ordo* 39: 17–31.

_____. 1999. Constitutionally constrained and safeguarded competition in markets and politics: with reference to a European constitution. In: *The Politics and Economics of Power*, eds. Samuel Bowles, Maurizio Franzini and Ugo Pagano, pp. 141–166. New York: Routledge.

_____. 2002. The Freiburg School of Law and Economics: Predecessor of constitutional economics. In: *The Constitution of Markets: Essays in political economy*, ed. Viktor J. Vanberg, pp. 37–52. London: Routledge.

Vatiero, Massimiliano. 2010. Ordoliberal Competition. *Concorrenza e Mercato: Rivista annuale di concorrenza* (July 29, 2010): 371–381.

Wagner, Richard E. 2006. Retrogressive regime drift within a theory of emergent order. *Review of Austrian Economics* 19: 113–123.

_____. 2014. Entangled political economy: a keynote address. *Advances in Austrian Economics* 18: 15–36.

_____. 2016. *Politics as a Peculiar Business: Insights from a Theory of Entangled Political Economy.* Cheltenham: Edward Elgar.

Watrin, Christian. 1978 (1982). Does Germany still have a social market economy? In: *Standard Texts on the Social Market Economy: Two Centuries of Discussion*, ed. Wolfgang Stützel and Horst Friedrich Wünsche. Translated by Derek Rutter, pp. 91–100. Stuttgart: Gustav Fischer.

White, Lawrence. 2012. *The Clash of Economic Ideas: The Great Policy Debates and Experiments of the Last Hundred Years.* New York: Cambridge University Press.

Windolf, Paul and Jürgen Beyer. 1996. Co-Operative Capitalism: Corporate Networks in Germany and Britain. *The British Journal of Sociology* 47 (2): 205–231.

Witt, Ulrich. 2002. Germany's "Social Market Economy": Between Social Ethos and Rent-Seeking. *The Independent Review* 6 (3): 365–375.

Wohlgemuth, Michael. 2001. The Present Relevance of Ordnungstheorie for the Politics and the Economics of the Social Order. In: *Institutional Economics in France and Germany: German Ordoliberalism versus the French Regulation School*, eds. Agnès Labrousse and Jean-Daniel Weisz, pp. 200–243. Berlin: Springer.

Wörsdörfer, Manuel. 2010. On the Economic Ethics of Walter Eucken. In: *60 Years of Social Market Economy: Formation, Development and Perspectives of a Peacemaking Formula*, eds. Christian L. Glossner and David Gregosz, pp. 20–41. Berlin: Konrad Adenauer Stiftung.

_____. 2013. Individual versus Regulatory Ethics: An Economic-Ethical and Theoretical-Historical Analysis of German Neoliberalism. *Œconomia* 3 (4): 523–557.

# Liberalism, Through a Glass Darkly

David F. Hardwick and Leslie Marsh

Philosophical liberalism leads a double life. On the one hand (analytically discursively), it is a closely studied tradition of political thinking, extending from Locke to Hayek, of appreciable internal diversity and recognisable stages of development. On the other hand (rhetorically responsively), it is the hegemonic, all-purpose negative frame of reference. As the dominant First World ideology, or (if one prefers) political theory, it is the viewpoint in terms of which other ideologies define themselves. It is an important counterpoint to Marxism, to socialism, to conservatism, to libertarianism, and even to anarchism, despite the fact that each of these doctrines contains liberal elements to a greater or lesser degree.

Of late, there has been a spate of books either touting the demise of liberalism (most notably Patrick Deneen's *Why Liberalism Failed*, 2018) or expressing a hyper-ebullience concerning liberalism's achieve-

D. F. Hardwick • L. Marsh (✉)
Department of Pathology and Laboratory Medicine, The University of British Columbia, Vancouver, BC, Canada
e-mail: david.f.hardwick@ubc.ca; leslie.marsh@ubc.ca



D. F. Hardwick, L. Marsh (eds.), *Reclaiming Liberalism*, Palgrave Studies in Classical Liberalism, https://doi.org/10.1007/978-3-030-28760-3_4

ments and prospects (most notably, Steven Pinker's *Enlightenment Now*, 2018). These perspectives were foreshadowed two to four decades earlier. Judith Shklar wrote that "it may be a revolting paradox that the very success of liberalism in some countries has atrophied the political empathies of their citizens" (Shklar 1998, p. 17). Edward Shils, even earlier, wrote, "The cause of liberalism is not a lost cause, but much reflection and many repairs are needed if it is not to become one" (Shils 1978, p. 123). In contrast to the quiet circumspection of Shklar and Shils' work, Francis Fukuyama's bullish and best-selling grand narrative *The End of History and the Last Man* has had the shelf-life of a loaf of bread, despite his protestations that he was misread (Fukuyama 2018). Though Deneen and Pinker (as does John Gray contra Pinker)[1] each present and represent helpful perspectives, in the ever-shifting sands of political life, it is not immediately obvious which one of these perspectives has a more accurate correspondence with reality—hence the "glass darkly" of our title. It is our contention that these perspectives converge around the political sociology of liberalism, whereby liberalism is being *leached* by its opponents and is *gamed* by its ostensible advocates, paradoxes that may well be inherent to the logical structure of liberalism.

While the thought might be implicit in Deenan, Pinker, and others, a deeper diagnostic was articulated by Michael Oakeshott some seventy years ago (1991; 1996). That is, we have long since been within the throes of a crisis of modernity, and all the twentieth-century *isms* (the politics of *faith* as opposed to the politics of *scepticism*) are merely various responses to this crisis. Modernity announced the individual's independence of arbitrary external authorities and urged that everyone draw upon the rational faculties with which we are endowed. Whatever else separates the several variants of liberalism, anything worthy of the name must turn upon the idea of individual autonomy. Identitarianism is merely the most recent instantiation of a long-germinating manifestation of those unable or unwilling to embrace individual autonomy. This sublimation of individuality is an inversion of the central liberal tenet not to treat others as a means to an end.

In the discussion that follows, we examine the conceptual relationship between two key liberal values—justice and rights—especially in light of the rise of "social" justice and its now prominent driver, identitarianism. This is especially challenging to standard conceptions of liberalism and its identity-neutral vocabulary of justice, that is, *cives*, persons, and agents (Appiah 2005, pp. 99–105). We do not deny that there are instances whereby *relevant* collecting features can be picked out, but the problem, as we see it, is that identitarianism and its ever more obscure permutations have been made to do duty for the whole of liberal political theory, thereby creating an ontological slum of rights-claims, an abstract and axiomatic foundationalist conception *demanding a corresponding morality not deduced from morally relevant considerations*. Through this gold-rush to secure ever more obscure rights, the politics of relevant similarity (liberalism) has morphed into a politics of divisiveness (*ressentiment* and *mauvaise foi*), significantly reducing the prospects for practicable remediation.

This has resulted in ideological viewpoints being deployed "like switchblades against the enemy of the moment" (Percy 1991, pp. 58; 416), or as David Corey following Eric Voegelin has termed it, "dogmatomachy" (Corey 2014), each side guilty of an over-sacralisation of one value. In the case of the Left, the over-sacralisation of equality of *outcomes* necessarily stirs an authoritarian impulse in its implementation. We concede, however, that liberalism has been tarnished by an over-sacralisation from within the tradition itself—that is, the marketocrats (Hardwick and Marsh 2012a, b; Abel and Marsh 2014). Liberalism's fortunes have waned, tarnished by zero-hours contracts, wildly fluctuating business cycles, widespread crony capitalism/corporate welfare (Munger and Villarreal-Diaz 2019), and rent-seeking (Taleb 2018).

## Liberalism: Three Theses

It is seldom worthwhile to treat particular ideologies as closed concepts that one can define in terms of necessary and sufficient conditions. Liberalism, like other ideologies, displays a great deal of diversity among different theorists, past and present (Marsh 2018, pp. 169–172). So we are not going to find a unique set of values, ideals, and general theoretical beliefs common and distinctive to liberals. However, at the level of values and ideals, we think that we can pick out three *typical* liberal beliefs. These are as follows:

- the personal autonomy thesis,
- the state forbearance thesis, and
- the rule of law thesis.

The personal autonomy thesis assumes (1) that people have ideas about living rightly or living well, (2) that these ideas can inform their practical reasoning and explain their actions, and (3) that when such ideas do fulfil this practical role, there is at least one good element in any situation in which it occurs. Where a person is autonomous be it intrinsically or instrumentally, he or she would have a personal conception of the good, and this conception is part and parcel of the causal aetiology of their choices.

The state forbearance thesis holds that the state should not exclusively or predominantly promote any particular conception of the good. According to the state neutrality thesis, the state should be equally indifferent to all conceptions of the good. As we've already indicated, a cynical exploitation from within liberal democracy has corroded this notion.

To effect the first two theses, liberalism requires that there should be a just political order. Under liberalism the main purpose of law as a just system of rules is to ensure that no agent, pursuing a conception of the good, is set arbitrarily at a disadvantage by the force, fraud, or deception of *other agents or by the state itself* as lawmaker, law-enforcer, or law-evader.

The personal autonomy thesis, in the form in which it is stated above, is "thin" or minimalist in two respects. In the first place, it does not assume a particular view of the self or person in respect of egoism or (in Pettit's sense) individualism. That is, on the one hand, it does not assume that agents are exclusively or predominantly egoistic, doing what (and only or mainly what) they take to be in their overall self-interest. Nor, on the other hand, does it assume that there is a fixed, context-independent human nature of the kind that informs, say, Hobbes' political theory (Pettit 1985–86, pp. 174–75).

Secondly, the thesis does not involve, in Richard Double's terminology, a content-specific notion of autonomy (Double 1992, p. 68). Such notions are normative and significantly contentious; they tell us what autonomy properly, authentically, or most deeply, consists in. Kantian autonomy is a matter of the noumenally free agent prescribing consistently universalisable maxims to him or herself as a requirement of pure practical reason. Sartrean existentialist ideas of self-creation, with radical freedom in respect of values and ideals, is in much the same line of business. Other notions of autonomy invoke the Cartesian idea of complete personal responsibility for one's beliefs. And so on. In a more direct account we can say that conceptions of the good, or substantive theories of the good,[2] are views (more or less systematic) about living rightly or living well. Theories of living rightly are theories of conduct, telling us how we should behave; theories of living well spell out the personal, social, or even ecological conditions for a rewarding, satisfying, fulfilling life. Kant's normative ethics is a theory of living rightly which says virtually nothing about living well. Religious theories of living well often specify some purpose in life that gives point or "meaning" to one's existence. But there are broader, non-religious possibilities. Living well might be a matter of the maximum gratification of desire, or of living up to one's major expectations, or (with a nod to Aristotle) of actualising one's potential for full human functioning. Brian Barry's categorisation of anthropocentric, zoocentric, and ecocentric theories of the good can comfortably overlay this account (Barry 1995, p. 20).

For the state exclusively or predominantly to promote a particular conception of the good, X, is approximately for the following probability to hold. Given the state's policies, to the extent to which the successful pursuit of a conception of the good is affected by those policies, the probability of X's being successfully pursued is higher than that of any other conception's being so.

If this is what the state forbearance thesis rules out, and if conceptions of the good are roughly as just explained, the question of a rationale arises. On what grounds should the claim be made that the state should not exclusively or predominantly promote any particular conception of the good? In detail there are, we think, a variety of (not wholly consistent) epistemological and metaphysical grounds for this claim within liberalism.

As nearly as we can tell, three such bases are discoverable historically:

1. One view (hardly widespread among liberals nowadays) is that there is an objective human good, which is known to be valid—or in which, at any rate, we have reasonable grounds for belief. But, the point is, this good must be freely acknowledged and voluntarily acted on. Locke takes this view of Christianity. He is totally convinced of "the reasonableness of Christianity" (that very phrase is, of course, the title of one of his books). A Christian way of life cannot, however, be enforced at the level of deepest spiritual value. *This is why the state should practice forbearance, on pain of attempting the impossible.* (There is, so far as we can see, no inconsistency between this view and Locke's refusal to tolerate atheists, on the ground that they could not recognise the sanctions of the divine law. This is not an imposition of Christianity but *a defence of the community against harm.*) Rephrasing Locke in terms of the above formula, we can say that by virtue of the kind of resources available to the state, it cannot through its policies increase the probability of a certain kind of spiritual life's being successfully pursued. The means, as Bosanquet would later say, are not in *pari materia* with the end.
2. Another view is that there is an objective human good, but we do not yet possess anything amounting to knowledge or rational belief about its specific nature. This is J. S. Mill's position; the recommendation in *On Liberty* (1858) to encourage "experiments of living" is designed to create the conditions (rather like laboratory conditions in experimental science) in which people acting innovatively may bring the true human good to light. This is the kind of view normally tagged as "perfectionist liberalism", though the precise aptness of the term "perfectionist" is elusive. There is no specific notion of perfection, only of indefinite improvability towards substantive standards of excellence not yet fully known.
3. The final view, which has enjoyed most support in the twentieth and current century, is that there is no such thing as a unique, objective human good to be known. A person's interests are properly defined by his or her own choices. In other words, interests have no objective status over and above what each person prefers; preferences reflect values, and values are ultimately subjective. This is the pluralist stance.

If we abstract from their differences, the second and third views both assume that conceptions of the good are matters of reasonable disagreement. In the case of the second view, we do not know the good (though such is knowable) and therefore there is scope for reasonable disagreement about it. In the case of the third view, we do not know the good (because there is nothing to be known) and hence our divergent preferences are not unreasonable. The first view is prima facie resistant to the assumption of reasonable disagreement, but it is now historically rather isolated within liberalism, and it does recognise the fact of conscientious disagreement and hence (we hope the inference is not too precarious) of reasonable disagreement at one remove. This is so if we accept that it is reasonable for people to argue from their conscientiously held beliefs, including their conscientiously held conceptions of the good. (Cf. Aquinas 1981 on the "rights" of erroneous conscience: *Summa*, i. 2, sq. 19, aa. 5, 6.) Incidentally, one of our dissatisfactions with *A Theory of Justice* is that, operating barely on the level of reasonable disagreement about conceptions of the good, Rawls has no need on his own terms to probe the bases of such disagreement or to explore the varied possibilities represented by views 1–3. But no adequate political theory can avoid confronting these views or choosing between them.

Socialist (or more accurately, Marxist) political theories are typically marked by a particular stance towards the plurality of conceptions of the good that gives liberalism its point. In a socialist (especially Marxist) perspective, when a specific source of conflict and alienation has been removed, that is, when the economic system is no longer exploitative, then the kind of lifestyle pluralism that liberalism so jealously guards will be sidelined. Lifestyles implicated with exploitation (notoriously, religious lifestyles à la Marx's 1843 *Critique of Hegel's Philosophy of Right*) will fall away, and the remaining variety will cease to matter politically.

We distinguish the state forbearance thesis from two other positions. The state forbearance thesis holds that the state should not exclusively or predominantly promote any particular conception of the good. According to the state neutrality thesis, by contrast, the state should be equally indifferent to all conceptions of the good. This means, in the terms used above, that given the state's policies, to the extent to which the successful pursuit of conceptions of the good is affected by those policies, the probability of successful pursuit is equal for all (relevant) conceptions of the good. The state impartiality thesis yields the same result but works from the more positive basis that the state, so far from being equally indifferent to all conceptions of the good, should equally promote them.

The state neutrality and state impartiality theses entail the state forbearance thesis; to affirm the two former and deny the latter would be a contradiction.[3] But the state forbearance thesis does not presuppose either of the two other theses. This is just as well, for there are familiar reasons for thinking that the neutrality and impartiality theses are nugatory. On realistic assumptions *any* policy or set of policies is likely to promote or hinder the pursuit of different conceptions of the good to different degrees (Appiah 2005).

## Liberal Justice

For classical liberalism, justice involves the maintenance of a general body of formal rules and procedures (Vincent 1992, p. 41). We agree, but liberal views on justice are not limited to classical liberalism and there are ambiguities in the idea of procedural justice.

All ideologies run on dominant descriptions—fundamental descriptions under which persons are identified or recognised. For Marxism, for example, the fundamental descriptions are "exploited" and "exploiter". Liberalism has a single dominant description, that of the autonomous agent—the agent pursuing a conception of the good, which is part of the causal aetiology of his or her choices. "Citizen" or *cive* is secondary to this; citizenship arises from the needs of autonomous agents for a political system. Justice is a matter of treating like cases equally. Under liberalism, the main purpose of law as a just system of rules is to ensure that no agent, pursuing a conception of the good, is set arbitrarily at a disadvantage by the force, fraud, or deception by other agents, or by the state itself. This is the classic doctrine of the rule of law, whatever its variations of formulation by Dicey, Hayek, and other liberal theorists of law.

But liberal theory has not stopped at purely legal justice. One way of reading the "New Liberalism" of T. H. Green, J. A. Hobson, and L. T. Hobhouse, in the late nineteenth and early twentieth centuries, is as an application of justice to the social distribution of goods, services, and opportunities. From the perspective of New Liberalism it is arbitrary, an irrelevant difference, that one agent should be able to pursue a conception of the good, or should have access to a plurality of such conceptions and the means of pursuing them, by accident of birth or circumstances.

This is a slight over-statement of what we find explicitly in Green, but it is the logical direction of his thought and the perspective is clearly present in the work of Hobson and Hobhouse. No commitment to markets or any other form of capitalism need block this perspective. Conceptually, there is no necessary connection between liberalism and capitalism. It is impossible to derive the moral or practical desirability of capitalism of any variety from the three theses set out above. Even a rights-based liberalism, running on the right to acquire and transfer private property, will not work the conceptual trick: it is logically possible to possess and exercise this right in pre-market, pre-capitalist conditions.

Empirically, the salient point in capitalism's favour is that, inasmuch as it separates political from economic power (and decentralises economic power, dispersing it in a multiplicity of points), *it reduces the state's power to act arbitrarily against the individual agent*. And precisely inasmuch as separation and dispersal fail in the real world of capitalism, the empirical argument is less convincing. The historical-sociological correlation of liberalism as a "living" ideology—a set of institutionalised ways of thinking, talking, perceiving, acting, and so on—with capitalism as a separate matter, is not considered here.

Liberalism is thus not committed to a purely procedural view of justice. The distribution of goods, services, and opportunities is not to be justified solely in terms of the rules by which the relevant holdings have been acquired or transferred. It is answerable to a more substantive criterion, independent of the rules themselves, in terms of the social equality of persons' *ability* to pursue conceptions of the good. Moreover, given this view of the relevance of social inequality, it is not really accurate to characterise liberalism, in the familiar way, as representing "the politics of citizenship" rather than "the politics of difference". Liberal political theory *does not* ignore the specific descriptions—of nationality, ethnicity, skin colour, gender, sexuality, age, and so on and so forth (cf. Alcoff 2003, p. 6). If there are systematic connections with social inequality in respect of the ability to pursue conceptions of the good, then liberal justice is the "politics of difference".

The charge might rather run that autonomy is conceptually an identity notion. Two ideas are involved here. One is that the liberal autonomous agent is a life-planner with (in self-image and on ideal conditions) a heroic trajectory of achievement across the stages of a lifespan. This executive, managerial view may well be identitarian, but liberalism is uncommitted to it. The causal aetiology of which we have spoken, connecting ideas about living rightly or living well with actual choices and actions, is consistent with having no such "executive, managerial" view. The autonomous agent, who may rely on an "art of improvisation", does not even have to take Nagelian prudential cognisance of the future on the grounds that all stages of a lifespan are of equal importance. Liberal political theory, as such, takes no stand on these matters.

It is true that rule-governed accounts of rationality abound; one thinks immediately of Kant's attempt to derive exceptionless, abstract laws from the principle of the categorical imperative. But we can offset Kant with Aristotle; the *phronimos* has perception into the mean in any situation for action (1893, NE, ll, 6. 1106b36-1107a2, and cp. ll, 9. 1109b20-23). There is no reliance on abstract rule-following; Aristotle is here as contextual and "judgmental" as one could wish.

The social contract is only an evocative metaphor. The point is really the one that Locke made against Filmer—that there is no such thing as natural political authority, with one person or group having the inherent right to make decisions with which some other person or group is obliged to comply. It is not that conditions of contractual liability hold between state and citizen such that there is a distinct statement or understanding of the terms of the agreement, fully informed consent, and the rest. It is simply (a) that the imagery of a contract, as something "artificial", makes the right point against claimants to inherent authority; and (b) that political obligation is voidable just as a civil contract is.

Liberalism in any case is not a theory of contractual consent—entered into by autonomous agents—as the basis of political authority and legitimacy. The justification of a liberal political order is *not* that citizens consent to it. The liberal state is legitimate in its own right as an appropriate, historically specific response to pluralism—to the *fact* (Walzer 1997) of there being divergent lifestyles, rival conceptions of the good, which are matters of reasonable disagreement and none of which are known to be the correct account of human flourishing. Liberalism is consistent with autocracy, provided the autocrat is a liberal.

We just referred to divergent lifestyles, rival conceptions of the good, which are matters of reasonable disagreement and none of which are known to be the correct account of human flourishing. But "known" by the criterion of what epistemology? This project branches in two directions. The first follows the path of sociology of knowledge and seeks for beliefs, experiences, forms of consciousness, to which x identity has sole or predominant access by virtue of their social situation. This is the content of the knowledge angle. Along the other direction, the concern is with the logical form of knowledge. Traditional epistemology is charged by identitarian critics with androcentricity[4] in respect of seeking to close the concept of knowledge under necessary and sufficient conditions: "S knows that p if and only if …".

*It is not clear how the sociological approach, relying on forms of consciousness to which x identity has sole or special access, will reduce society-wide disagreements about the good. There is no coherence in the idea that there is an epistemic community that corresponds to say black, female, Jew, &c.* Neither, on the other hand, is there much plausibility in the idea that the "reasonable" disagreements that are central to liberalism arise *only* on androcentric "closure" of the concept of knowledge. Suppose, with Locke and Mill, that the human good is knowable. Still, with the underdetermination of theory by data, more than one theory of the good will be tenable. Disagreements will be reasonable. Suppose, with twentieth-century non-cognitivism, that there is nothing to be known about the human good: then divergent preferences will not be unreasonable. Disagreements will be reasonable. *None of this rests, so far as we can see, on an androcentric epistemology: standards of good evidence and justified belief cannot and should not be merely political.* As Susan Haack pointedly writes, the mistake is in "confusing the perspectival character of judgements of evidential quality for relativity of standards of evidence" (Haack 1998, p. 144).

There is an issue within identitarianism concerning the moral status of justice. We can be fairly brief on this because, though the issue goes deep in theoretical ethics (Appiah 2005), it is not one on which liberal political theory need take a stand. A moral theory to which justice is central is taken to be rule-governed. A morality of justice "excludes the care-orientation to the extent that it subordinates relationships to rules and context to abstraction" (Austen 1995, p. 35). The critical perspective is one which we have already encountered in considering rationality. Clearly there are two sets of questions. The first, if we consider rules to be products of reason, concerns the role of reason versus the emotions in the moral life, and the second relates to the adequacy of abstract, context-free rules (whatever their origin) versus the situational particularity of the moral life.

Liberalism, in its commitment to a just political order, is not signing up for a total morality of justice in these questions. Considering citizens as agents pursuing conceptions of the good, the liberal state is concerned to ensure that, like cases are treated equally.

And so we return to the points about the rule of law and social inequality noted earlier. Justice fulfils an essential role in the political morality of liberalism; liberalism is not committed to a morality of justice. This distinction enables liberal political theory to sidestep the otherwise extremely important issue about justice with which feminist ethics, for example, is properly concerned. Our suggestion is that so-called second-wave feminism is assimilable to liberalism; and that radical third-wave feminism of the essentialist kind must either embrace liberalism or must sideline itself as non-political.

Against this there is an argument, quite without merit, that liberalism cannot, by virtue of its commitment to the private/public distinction, fully address the systematic social injustice to which women are exposed. The criticism runs that liberal political theory assumes the patriarchal family, with its power and property relationships, as "prior" to politics and hence (as part of the private sphere) beyond the scope of public debate and political action. There is a keen irony in this charge against liberalism when one recalls that the central liberal theorist of the private/public distinction, J. S. Mill, was concerned to intervene in family matters to revise legally the property and other rights of women. History aside, the position is clear. Any non-totalitarian political theory accepts a private/public distinction of some kind; and liberal theory is under no constraint to assign family matters to the private sphere if this results in or prolongs systematic social injustice to women. Feminism of the essentialist kind, for example, does face a dilemma. If, from an adequate essentialist theory, we can deduce a distinct conception (or set of conceptions) of the female good, these conceptions are grist to the liberal mill. We can now feed into liberal politics a fresh set of conceptions for liberal pluralism to recognise. On the other hand, if the female essence is a separating factor such that we no longer all share the single dominant description, "agents pursuing personal conceptions of the good", then it is hard to see what coherent politics is possible. That is, if we now have two irreducible dominant descriptions, "women" and "men", then *there is no commonality for a shared politics to run on and this state of affairs can be extrapolated for any other dominant identitarian descriptors.* There is a tension in the positing of identitarian descriptors. On the one hand, these identities are ostensibly socially constructed, yet on the other hand, they point to an ontology that relies on some objective designation.[5]

## Liberal Equality

It is our purpose now to (a) conceptualise the notion of equality, and (b) show its inextricable and intimate link with the concept of justice.

One is not sure exactly when equality surfaced as a major political value. Certainly it is present in the 1789 French Declaration of the Rights of Man and even earlier there is the famous statement in the American Declaration of Independence. A useful port-of-call is John Dunn (1984, pp. 7–9). Dunn stresses that

- equality is socialism's major value, just as freedom is liberalism's;
- equality can quite easily be made to look an absurd notion if it is taken descriptively;
- even prescriptively the claim of equality has important limitations—it is not the case that all are entitled to equal respect; and
- the politically important role of the idea of equality is "in the systematic criticism of arbitrariness in the distribution of social, economic or political advantages".

We have two reactions:

1. On Dunn's first point, if we are talking about the requirement for like cases to be treated equally, that is, for treatment not to depend on arbitrary or otherwise irrelevant differences, isn't this the basic idea of justice? Isn't justice rather than equality at stake here? And aren't we caught up in the traditional problem of justice, that of specifying a valid ground of differential treatment?
2. Dunn says that to espouse equality is not to see equality "as the overall goal of social organization" (Dunn 1984, p. 8). But we think Dunn neglects one strand of the socialist tradition. At the very least, socialists have traditionally assumed that if arbitrary grounds of differential treatment were cut out, variations in the distribution of social, economic and political advantages would be sharply reduced.

We think that what is missing from Dunn's characterisation is this. Individuals can be "scored" or "rated" for equality along many dimensions, and if you eliminate unfair differences (so far as possible) you will give people overall equality in their life-chances. Everyone will command the conditions for a satisfying life. We think that's the positive content to the idea of equality as a political ideal, however briefly and naively we've expressed it, and it's missing from Dunn's remarks.

In "The Idea of Equality" Bernard Williams (1969, pp. 153–180) gives a more elaborate conceptualisation of equality than Dunn; and he is more closely argumentative in trying to vindicate a political use for the idea of equality. What Williams is trying to do is to derive a substantive rule of distribution from a specification of the logical object or internal goal of an activity:

1. Activities have logical objects (internal goals).
2. Activities provide services.
3. There are criteria or rules for the distribution of services.
4. Those rules should be defined by the logical object (internal goal) of the corresponding activity.
5. The logical object of medical activity is the promotion of health and the cure of illness.

6. Health services should be distributed so as to promote health and cure illness (from 1–5).
7. This instantiates the rule: "To each according to their health needs".
8. No other rule of distribution is valid.
9. In particular, the following rule is invalid: "To each according to their ability to pay for health services".

Robert Nozick questions item 4. In fact he rejects it altogether in favour of the suggestion that rules for the distribution of a service may be defined by the particular purpose of the person who performs the activity (Nozick 1974, pp. 233–235). Nozick says of Williams' item 7 that this is simply a specific version of a wider and quite familiar claim ("stated many times before"—Nozick 1974, p. 234) for the distribution of social benefits; to each according to their important need: Nozick's critical claim is that this rule or principle has to be argued for in its own right. His suggestion is that this kind of distributive principle "ignores the question of where the things or activities to be allocated or distributed come from" (Nozick 1974, p. 235). Nozick argues elsewhere in his book that the rights of those who create the relevant things or do the relevant actions set limits to (re-)distribution on the basis of important needs.

We're not entirely happy with Nozick's procedure here. In the first place, Williams has not argued for the general rule, "To each according to their important needs", even if the particular rule he does try to vindicate, "To each according to their health needs", is a special case of it. And secondly, he does produce an argument (good, bad, or indifferent: but certainly original and not banal) for his particular rule—precisely the argument we have set out in points 1–9.

One comment we'd offer on Williams' argument is that he appears to us to be arguing for a principle of justice. We think that all criteria for the distribution of benefits and burdens are rules of justice. However, if you take Dunn's line on equality, Williams is arguing for equality. He is criticising the distribution of health services on the basis of ability to pay as arbitrary relative to the logical object or internal goal of medical activity. We repeat, however, that we don't think this involves the idea of equality, but of justice.

Plato's *Republic* is an attempt to define the nature of justice in the individual and the state. But the first really systematic and refined conceptualisation of justice comes from Aristotle. In his *Nicomachean Ethics*, Book V, Aristotle makes a string of distinctions. But let's first play around with the language of "just" and "justice" to see what distinctions we can establish for ourselves.

One point to note is the usage in which "justice" is simply a name for legality. Some countries have ministries of justice, which are concerned with the operation of the legal system. This sense of justice is not particularly relevant to political philosophy; we have the concept of law itself to cover this sense of "justice". Another point is that "just" is often merely a synonym for "exact". "Just so", we say. Not much philosophical interest there. Sometimes in ethics we refer to someone as "just" or (more likely) "fair" when we may not find them very lovable but do want to stress, with a sort of grudging admiration, that they are not arbitrary in their treatment of others or apt to make exceptions in their own favour. In ethics again there is, vestigially, a usage in which somebody is said to be "just" if their moral conduct is upright. For a pre-war generation this usage lingers in the title of Edgar Wallace's story, *The Four Just Men* (1905).

Aristotle recognises this last sense of "just" when he speaks of general justice. However, he has much more to say about particular justice. Particular justice is about the rules for distribution of benefits and burdens; for punishment or the correction of harm by one person to another; and for exchange. Aristotle's name for these types of justice have stuck. They are as follows:

- Distributive justice
- Remedial justice
- Reciprocal or commutative justice

The relationship between these types of justice is a matter of controversy. It has been interestingly suggested that the need for distributive justice arises only, or at least mainly, because reciprocal or commutative justice has not been secured. To fix on distributive justice is to do only the ambulance work, and leave the causes of the trouble (the failure to get reciprocal or commutative justice) untouched.

Let's take a look at distributive justice, on which political philosophy has mainly concentrated. Distributive justice is about the distribution or allocation of benefits and burdens. An elementary requirement of justice is that like cases be treated equally, which gives us an immediate connection back to the concept of equality. But what descriptions do we use to secure the proper basis for comparison? In respect of what quality or characteristic are like cases to be treated alike and unlike cases differently? In other words, how are we to give specific content to the purely formal idea of treating like cases equally? Chaim Perelman (1963, pp. 5–10) offers six formulas for justice:

- To each the same thing
- To each according to their merits
- To each according to their works
- To each according to their needs (cf. Nozick and Williams)
- To each according to their rank
- To each according to their legal entitlement

At first glance these formulas are not all compatible. They could not all be applied simultaneously to the allocation of the same benefits and burdens. If you wish to apply different formulas at different times and to different areas of social life, you need a principle on which to do so.

At second glance it is not entirely clear what the different formulas mean exactly. One basis for adopting a particular formula might be that it matches people's rights. If, for example, there is a natural or human right to be paid according to one's work or to have one's needs met (so far as the social system allows), that would be a ground on which the formulas would rest. Market theory appears to rely on a principle of justice, something like "To each according to their returns in a competitive situation of exchange". Perhaps the most controversial applications of distributive justice is in connection with so-called social justice.

*The hallmark of social justice is that the relevant characteristic belongs, not to an individual but to a class or group.* According to the class's or the group's characteristics, the whole class or group is to be treated in a similar fashion. Social justice operates at the level of some characteristic(s) of a group of people. One thing that it typically inspires is a policy of reverse discrimination and compensatory justice. Such policies involve logical problems of apparent contradiction. Policies of reverse discrimination also attract criticisms of unfairness to individuals. Social justice produces individual injustice. There's no way of avoiding it. If I am a member of group X, an unfavoured or disfavoured group relative to Taylor's (1973) group G under a policy of reverse discrimination, I am discriminated against purely by virtue of my membership of group X even if I have no responsibility for the historical discrimination against group G (see also Bayles 1973).[6]

Roger Scruton (1980, pp. 86–89) suggests two further points against policies of social justice:

- the false presuppositions of distributive justice in respect of the redistribution of wealth, and
- the gross relationship of group characteristics to individual circumstances (see his example of the house-owning widow, Scruton 1980, p. 88).

Hayek has a rather different argument against social justice, namely, the emptiness of the concept of social justice relative to the market. Hayek denies that "the concept of 'social justice' has any meaning or content whatever within an economic order based on the market" (Hayek 1982, pp. 62–70; 1976). Hayek's criticism of the concept of social justice is plainly conditional on the case for the market, a case which he has probably argued with greater clarity, sophistication, and comprehensiveness than any other social or political theorist (Miller 1999).

This is not to say that there aren't instances whereby *relevant* collecting features cannot be picked out: the Married Women's Property Act, female suffrage, 15th Amendment ratified in 1870, and gay rights—are notable examples of the remedying of social incoherencies with wide (liberal) applicability. The *concept* of justice is the formal idea of treating like cases equally, while the various formulas for justice ("to each according to their merits", etc.) are *conceptions* of justice (Flew 1986, p. 203).

Though we fully accept that personal identity is deeply entangled with social identity, identitarianism as a quasi-organising role, has deeply distorted the real-life complexity of the phenomena in question crisply articulated by Amin Maalouf (1998, pp. 16–17).

## Liberal Rights

Insofar as corresponding rights are concerned, there are two central questions we need to ask:

- What is the structure of rights-statements (of statements like 'X has a right to X')?
- What is the fundamental basis of rights?

The most celebrated modern analysis of rights, and of the logically distinct structures which rights-statements involve, is that of Hohfeld (1964). Hohfeld analyses "P has a right to X" in four ways, as:

- A privilege
- A claim-right
- A power
- An immunity

The immediate context of Hohfeld's classification is legal; but the classification is clearly capable of application to moral rights.[7]

We now move on to consider some issues connected with certain kinds of rights which human beings may possess, namely human rights and natural rights (Ignatieff 2001). Like Mayo (1965), we shall take these notions as interchangeable. There are, though, possibilities for distinguishing between human and natural rights. Human rights might be a sub-set of the wider class of natural rights, rights possessed by creatures other than human beings. For most purposes in political philosophy, however, unless we're discussing the politics and ethics of animal welfare, talk of human rights is just an updated version of talk of natural rights.

Any theory claiming that there are human or natural rights has a number of tasks on its hands:

1. It must observe the discriminations we picked up from Hohfeld and tell us whether the rights in question are privileges, claim-rights, powers, or immunities.

2. It must provide an ordered list. It would be very strange for a theory to succeed in showing that there are such things as natural or human rights without being able to give the slightest indication—even a specimen list if not a complete enumeration—of what they are and of the relations between them.
3. It must supply a basis for natural or human rights. Unless the claim that there are such rights is to be mere rhetoric, we'd quite like some argument to support the idea that there are such things.

This final argument will carry a particular burden. Human or natural rights have been generally taken to have two special characteristics or features. Aside from their logical form—that is, how they fit into Hohfeld's classification—there is the point that these rights are widely regarded by espousers of them as being both inalienable and non-social. The idea of inalienable rights is the idea is that human rights, possessed in virtue of our characteristics as human beings can never be forfeited or lost as long as we remain human beings. To talk of the "imprescriptibility" or "absoluteness" of human or natural rights, is another way of making this point (See Hart in Waldron 1984, p. 78, Mayo 1965, p. 220). Talk of rights as "absolute", a term of appalling slipperiness, can also be a way of saying that "rights are trumps". For an explanation of this phrase, see below.

Human or natural rights are commonly regarded by the relevant theorists as "individualistic". People do not have them by virtue of their social milieu. There is a social context–independent character or property that a human being has, namely, his or her possession of these rights; and no matter how a human being's social context may vary, the right remains intact.

Now this idea is plainly problematic in one way. Rights-talk is inherently interpersonal. Rights are, for example, privileges that a person has in relation to other people. But we don't think a human rights theorist need be completely embarrassed by this elementary point. It depends on the kind of property a natural right is. Consider a parallel: solubility in water is an inherent property of salt. It still has that property even if no salt is ever put in water. The human rights theorist need only say that people have an inherent property, which is the basis of their human or natural rights, but that in the absence of other people, the right remains latent and the property relevantly inoperative.

More worrying, perhaps, is the slack ambiguity involved in talking of social-context independence. Is the idea that of independence of (a) any social context or of (b) any particular social context?

Hart's "Are there any natural rights?" (1984) is a classic expression of this view. The basic shape of his argument is this: assume that one person can have moral rights against another. For example, you have a moral right against me if I promise to pay you $100. Hart calls this a "special" right because it is specific to our relationship. I haven't promised to pay anybody else $100 and so they don't have a corresponding right against me. A right is, from one point of view, a restriction of freedom. In the example, if you have a right of payment against me then I am not morally free to do what I want with my money. Ethically $100 of it is reserved for you. Hart argues that if my freedom is now restricted in this way, then prior to the promise and before the creation of the special right, I had a general moral freedom which has now been subtracted from. No-one conferred that freedom; it is in that sense a natural right.

Hart's argument is conditional on there being special moral rights. It's hypothetical, that is to say, on the assumption that one person can have special rights against another. Deny that assumption, and the argument is blocked. There are ethical theories which make do without the notion of special rights. The issues here are complex and the problem belongs really to ethics. Hart is careful to deny that he is setting out to prove the existence of, natural rights as traditionally understood. So he doesn't claim that the natural right of which he has proved the existence, conditional on there being special rights, is inalienable (Hart 1984, p. 78).

Mayo (1965) is not a proponent of human or natural rights, but he has a good discussion (much better than Raphael's flaccid contribution to which he's replying). One of the matters in which Mayo is interested is that of the logical basis of natural or human rights. There are two possibilities, assuming that we have human rights simply by virtue of our characteristics as human beings:

1. That possession of these rights is a genuine "metaphysical" property, one belonging to the general character of reality. If one did a metaphysical count of fundamental properties in the world, human beings' possession of human or natural rights would be among them.

2. John Locke regarded natural rights in this way in the seventeenth century. But he had Christian theology to fall back on. More likely, the possession of natural or human rights is regarded (by those who believe in them) as supervenient on other characteristics that we have, not a primary characteristic of reality on its own account.

What are these characteristics? This question, of course, takes us into the tricky territory of identitarianism. If we are to produce a list of human characteristics not dependent on particular social milieus, what will it contain? (see note 5).

If we can agree on a social-context independent list, there is a clear problem of seeing how the possession of human or natural rights is to supervene on the relevant characteristics. It is hard to see the logical basis of supervenience:

A. Does having one or more of the relevant characteristics entail the possession of a human or natural right? so that if we said, for example, "We both have imperfect information but you do not have a natural right to X", our remark would be contradictory (a standard test of entailment.)
B. Or is it just that possession of natural rights presupposes the possession of one or more of the relevant characteristics? So that, for example, if one possesses none of the above characteristics, the question of ones having natural rights does not arise. That would tell us something about the concept of a natural right, but without entailment between possession of characteristics and possession of rights, we don't think the natural rights theorist could be said to have accomplished very much.

However, we do not dispose of the place of rights in politics by exercising our logical acumen at the expense of natural and human rights theorists. If one goes back to Hohfeld's classification then we'd say it's just obvious that *any social system will make provision for privileges, claims, powers, and immunities*. The questions are: (a) which ones, (b) for whom, and (c) with what rationale? Whatever we think of human or natural rights, they set a political "problem of rights" which remains.

To handle that problem one needs an ideology (see Williams quoted in Nielson 1983, pp. 11–12), characterised by

1. a set of beliefs about human beings, society, and the state
2. that embody values or ideals, together with
3. associated principles of action.

(a), (b), and (c) will derive from 1 and 2; then 3 will involve the political implementation of rights, the making of practical provision for them.

Though one wouldn't guess as much from common-place politico prattle, there has been a tradition of hostility to rights-talk from the Left (Campbell 2010, pp. 1–12). Pressing ourselves just a bit, we should say that this antipathy (supposing it exists) rests on three interpretations of rights:

α. Rights are confined to individuals.
β. Rights are wholly or mainly privileges.
γ. Rights are "trumps".

If one interprets rights in these ways, one is bound to encounter drastic stops on collective action, unwelcome to the Left. But, in the first place, there is no conceptual reason to confine rights to individuals. For example, what of rights of self-government or national self-determination, which logically cannot be individual rights? (See Ginsberg 1947, p. 278).

Secondly, there is conceptually no reason to restrict rights to privileges, to exemptions from interference, with the associated idea of negative freedom.

Thirdly, there is no conceptual reason to treat rights as "trumps" (Dworkin 1977, XI). Rights can set prima facie obligations, obligations *ceteris paribus*, which may be properly overridden in particular circumstances.

## Liberalism and Human Nature

Academic clerisies are the current instantiation of the "engineers of the soul". Nicholas Taleb (2016, p. 100) writes that "[t]he rationalist imagines an imbecile-free society; the empiricist an imbecile-proof one".

Leftist Peter Singer (2000, pp. 60–63) is that rare bird who writes that any Leftism worthy of its name cannot (a) deny the existence of human nature, or insist that human nature is inherently good, or that it is infinitely malleable; (b) expect to end all conflict and strife whether by political revolution, social change, or better education; (c) assume that all inequalities are due to discrimination, prejudice, oppression, or social conditioning. Some will be, but this cannot be assumed in every case; and (d) expect that, under different social and economic systems, many people will not act competitively in order to enhance their own status, gain a position of power, and/or advance their interests and those of their kin.

J. R. Lucas (1966, p. 2) argues that political systems presuppose five characteristics of human nature:[8]

1. Some interaction
2. Some shared values
3. Incomplete unselfishness
4. Fallible judgment
5. Imperfect information

Our claim is this: not only do political systems presuppose human characteristics; more than that, behind all political discourse (empirical or evaluative) is a conception of human nature. In some political theorists, the conception is fully explicit. For Hobbes there is a fixed, essential human nature which politics cannot alter but can only "contain". His recommendation of absolute autocracy is his remedy for the social chaos that otherwise results from the three central human characteristics of competitiveness, diffidence (fear), and glory (pride). Other theorists see different permanent characteristics or (on a crude reading of Marxism), only variable characteristics which are social products open to alteration through political action.

From another angle, when in *Politics*, I.2 Aristotle says that man is a political animal (*zoon politikon*), he is not uttering some dreary and indefinite generality about the tendency or capacity of human beings to enter political systems. He is telling us that well-being (*eudaimonia*) can only be achieved by taking part in the specific institutions of the Greek city or polis. This Aristotelian claim pulls a tight connection between human nature, as regards the conditions of well-being, and a specific type of political system. To not need the polis, says Aristotle, you must be a beast or a god. From Hobbes in the seventeenth century back to the ancient Greeks and down to present-day sociobiologists, you can't talk politics without making significant, challengeable assumptions about the nature (fixed or alterable) of human beings.

Two comments are in order. We do not think that any explanatory theory of human nature currently on offer has progressed beyond Hume's theory (*Treatise* II.l.ll; III.2.l; Marsh 2018, pp. 168, 171, 173–174). Hume rejects the "selfish theory" of Hobbes. He offers a descriptive moral psychology and makes no attempt to determine rational choice. Indeed, the very idea of rational choice is nonsense in Hume's theory of mind. Hume is equally critical of the agent who doesn't experience benevolence and rides the social system (cf. Oakeshott 1991).

One doesn't require a theory or an ideology to run on "strong" epistemological assumptions of human nature; a more subtle "thin" theory of human nature is more able to accommodate differing conceptions of the human good and flourishing.

## Liberalism: Religion and State

As we indicated earlier in the discussion, liberalism is being leached from within: there are apologists[9] for political Islam who fail miserably to critically address certain key questions:

- What, if any, are the connections between religion and politics?
- Is the only acceptable political order a secular one?
- Is the conflation of religion and politics a category mistake?

These questions come into sharp relief when one considers the tendency of those who seek a tight and formal logical correspondence between religion and politics, a tendency known as "fundamentalism". There is a significant logical difference between Judaism's, Christianity's, and Islam's relationship to politics. Though the *Old Testament* provides paradigmatic expression for the oppression and freedom of a people, politically speaking, it has informed the rhetoric of the Civil Rights Movement. Those who argue for the notion of the Jubilee (Leviticus 25: 8–24) typically do so through a tenuously imposed (Marxist) liberation theology. The central text of Christianity, the *New Testament*, and the time-hallowed creeds and confessions (the Nicene Creed, the Athanasian Creed, the Augsburg Confession, and so forth) contain hardly any political reference. Nothing like a definite and comprehensive view of political life can be extracted straightforwardly from the prime traditional sources. So, for example, the inference

1. love your neighbour as yourself (religious premise) therefore, or
2. support democracy (political prescription)

is not a valid inference in any known system of logic, yet many blithely gloss over such derivations, giving political Islam/Islamism a free pass (Marsh 2019). Any vestige of liberal thought that these apologists might have laid claim to has been completely and utterly undermined by (a) the uncritical acceptance of an ideology that sees no separation of religion and state, and (b) the derivative acceptance of Sharia Law and its rejection of the core values that liberalism has secured. This sorry state of affairs must, in no uncertain terms, be laid at the door of identitarianism/intersectionality's self-consuming logic. In effect, those who have permitted the profoundly illiberal concept of blasphemy back on the table have wielded as the bluntest of cudgels to *stifle* critical analyses within liberal society.

## Some Concluding Observations

Recall the prime liberal thread we specified at the outset, that is, the personal autonomy thesis? What Oakeshott termed the politics of the "felt need" standardly demands remedies that necessitate some form of economic and social coercion and the politicisation of the law. Autonomy and individuality become the undifferentiated "individual manqué"[10] or "anti-individual" forestalling the inextricable link between choice, the contingency afforded by that choice and correlate responsibility (Oakeshott 1991, p. 370; Capaldi 2018).

We think it would be far more helpful to substitute talk of "rights" with talk of "moral obligations". Rights-talk encourages unfocused discourse, whereas the term "moral obligation" is explicitly a two-term relationship—that is, the individual as part of a society. It should be recognised that *politics at the best of times is a defective experience*: no country has the resources to satisfy everything claimed as a human right by its *cives*. While "democracy" is still a powerful term, so is "human rights" and it could well be that everything that was once seen as good about liberalism is now subsumed under these two terms.[11] But in the rush to secure ever more obscure rights permutations, the politics of *relevant* similarity (liberalism) has morphed into a politics of divisiveness (*unbridgeable* difference), thereby reducing the prospects for practicable remedies.

While there is no conceptual link between liberalism and democracy, there is a practical one, a marriage of convenience (Mill and Tocqueville had already noted this). We don't see any *privileged* connection between liberalism and capitalism or the market—which in *no way* is meant to imply that we do not support the epistemic benefits and associated freedoms accrued by markets.

The liberalism that best matches that which we are recommending, a situated liberalism, has been termed by Judith Shklar as the "liberalism of fear" best expressed by Bernard Williams (2009, p. 61):

> The approach of the liberalism of fear is bottom-up, not top-down. Just as it takes the condition of life without terror as its first requirement and considers what other goods can be furthered in more favourable circumstances, it treats each proposal for the extension of the notions of fear and freedom in the light of what locally has been secured. It does not try to determine in general what anyone has a right to under any circumstances and then apply it. It regards the discovery of what rights people have as a political and historical one, not a philosophical one.

To reiterate. Liberal political theory *does not* ignore the specific descriptions of nationality, ethnicity, gender, sexuality, age, or whatever. Where identitarianism has gone dreadfully awry is in its apriori specification of socio-societal anomalies, *short-circuiting the very tradition best equipped to make meaningful remedies.* This goes some way towards explaining our now deeply dysfunctional socio-political culture. *The liberal state is legitimate in its own right as an appropriate, historically specific response to pluralism—to the fact of there being divergent lifestyles, rival conceptions of the good, which are matters of reasonable disagreement and none of which are known to be the correct account of human flourishing.*

When we think of liberalism in political theory, we think of the rule of law, constitutionalism, and political pluralism, under which the state does not promote a substantial conception of the good. The sinking enthusiasm for these concepts manifest as identitarianism has let in (again) the most historically and conceptually illiterate fanaticism (Hoffer 1951), with the embodied public policy "remedies" requiring various degrees of authoritarian implementation. Moreover, with the ostensible advocates of liberalism gaming the system, aided and abetted by bloated bureaucracies, surveillance capitalism,[12] and the rise of non-liberal states challenging the West's economic hegemony, liberalism, as we've presented it, has been corroded.

## Notes

1. John Gray, *The Guardian* https://www.theguardian.com/books/2015/mar/13/john-gray-steven-pinker-wrong-violence-war-declining. See also Botting et al. (2006).
2. The phrase "conception of the good", implicit in the first and second theses, equates with John Rawls' locution "substantive theory of the good" (Rawls 1971). Rawls never provides a close characterisation of what such a theory involves; he says much more about the "thin theory of the good", the idea (we suppose) that we are to supply the characterisation by contrast.
3. A prominent multicultural theorist writes: "Minorities should not be subjected to coercive assimilation and should be free within the limits of the law to maintain their identity" (Parekh 2019, p. 161) and that cultural diversity should be guided by three core values—liberty, equality, and national unity. This is perfectly consistent with the liberalism we

have outlined, and as such, it is redundant. *But* Parekh (p. 162) does acknowledge that though conceived within the liberal framework, multiculturalism now has assimilated non-liberal strands, the upshot being a revitalised corresponding identitarianism on the far Right. Alert to this, one of the major advocates for multiculturalism along with Canadian Prime Ministers Trudeau Sr., Jr., and German Chancellor Merkel was former British Prime Minister Tony Blair who now concedes that "multiculturalism has been misinterpreted as meaning a justified refusal to integrate, when it should never have meant that". Moreover, "there is a duty to integrate, to accept the rules, laws and norms of our society that all British people hold in common and share, while at the same time preserving the right to practise diversity, which is fully consistent with such a duty." "Our tolerance is part of what makes Britain, Britain", he said in 2006. "Conform to it; or don't come here." *The Guardian* 20th April, 2019: https://www.theguardian.com/politics/2019/apr/20/tony-blair-says-migrants-must-integrate-to-combat-far-right

4. The idea that white heterosexual men have undeserved epistemic authority.
5. In just the same way as racial supremacists appeal to some notion of biological essentialism, constructivists also engage in biological "woo": that is, transracialism and the smorgasbord of genders with a proliferation of ever-more obscure permutations.
6. Consider the fashionable virtue-signalling and "processional justice" incoherency posited by those actually born in some area but still calling themselves "settlers".
7. Questions one might ask of Hopfield include:

   1. Are the four specifications (as made by Hohfeld 1964, pp. 6–7) clear?
   2. Are the four types of right distinct? Or is one type a special case of, or otherwise reducible to, another?
   3. Is the list complete?
   4. Is any one of the four fundamental in the sense that, without it, the other types would be empty or useless?

8. Cf. Hart's (1961, pp. 189–95) list in *The Concept of Law*:

   (a) Human vulnerability
   (b) Approximate equality
   (c) Limited altruism

(d) Limited resources
(e) Limited understanding

9. This "progressivist" identitarianian stance has been mocked by Maajid Nawaz as being, in effect, *regressive* (Nawaz 2016). Those of an ostensible liberal orientation have shamefully failed to support reformists: for an unflinching assessment of political Islam/Islamism from *within* the tradition, see Tawhidi (2018) and Husain (2018) (see note 3). In their *wilful* mendaciousness, the aforementioned apologists' typically, by sidestepping people such as Tawhidi, resort to the circular "no *true* Scotsman" fallacy, satirised by evolutionary behavioural scientist Gad Saad as "Ostrich Parasitic Syndrome".
10. Mass man is not necessarily coextensive with the poor: there is the anti-individual "intellectual" correlate who, much to their chagrin, are as Trotsky and Gramsci put it, handmaidens to some amorphous grouping or other, their activism a disease of the rich (Stove 2003).
11. This said, even "inconvenient" democratic enthusiasms have been stymied by the technocratic-managerial classes and the intelligentsia.
12. Peter Viereck (2004, p. xiv) wrote "Today is not so much politics as meta-tech that crushes the private life."

## References

Abel, C. and Marsh, L. 2014. A Danse Macabre of wants and satisfactions: Hayek, Oakeshott, Liberty and Cognition. In: G. L. Nell (ed.), *Austrian economic perspectives on individualism and society: Moving beyond methodological individualism*. New York: Palgrave.

Alcoff, L. M. 2003. Introduction: Identities: Modern and Postmodern. In: Alcoff, L. M. and Mendieta, E. (Eds.). *Identities: Race, Class, Gender, and Nationality*. Oxford and Malden: Blackwell.

Appiah, K. A. 2005. *The Ethics of Identity*. Princeton: Princeton University Press.

Aquinas, T. 1981. *Summa Theologica*. Westminster, MD: Christian Classics.

Aristotle. 1893. *The Nicomachean Ethics*. https://oll.libertyfund.org/titles/aristotle-the-nicomachean-ethics

Austen, A. 1995. Bradley and Feminist Ethics. *Bradley Studies* 1(1): 30–44.

Barry, B. 1995. *Justice as Impartiality*. Oxford: Oxford University Press.

Bayles, M. D. 1973. Reparations To Wronged Groups. *Analysis* 33(6): 182–184.

Botting, E. H. et al. 2006. The End of Enlightenment? *American Behavioral Scientist* Vol. 49 Number 5: 643–749.
Campbell, T. 2010. *The Left and Rights: A Conceptual Analysis of the Idea of Socialist Rights. Radical Philosophy*. Abingdon: Routledge.
Capaldi, N. 2018. The Pathology of Identity Politics. *Academic Questions* 31:281–288.
Corey, D. D. 2014. Dogmatomachy: Ideological Warfare. *Cosmos + Taxis* 1(3): 60–71.
Deneen, P. 2018. *Why Liberalism Failed*. New Haven: Yale University Press.
Double, R. 1992. Two Types of Autonomy Accounts. *Canadian Journal of Philosophy*, 22 (1): 65–80.
Dunn, J. 1984. *The Politics of Socialism*. Cambridge: Cambridge University Press. 1984.
Dworkin, R. 1977. *Taking Rights Seriously*. Cambridge, MA: Harvard University Press.
Flew, A. 1986. Equality, yes surely; but Justice? *Philosophical Papers* VOL XV, No. 2+3:197–204.
Fukuyama, F. 2018. *Identity: The Demand for Dignity and the Politics of Resentment*. New York: Farrar, Straus and Giroux.
Ginsberg M. 1947. *Reason and Unreason in Society*. New York: Longmans, Green.
Gray, J. 2015. John Gray: Steven Pinker is wrong about violence and war. *The Guardian*, Friday 13, March.
Haack, S. 1998. *Manifesto of a Passionate Moderate*. Chicago: University of Chicago Press.
Hardwick, D. and Marsh, L. 2012a. Clash of the Titans: When the market and science collide. In: R. Koppl, S. Horwitz, & L. Dobuzinskis (Eds.), *Experts and epistemic monopolies* (*Advances in Austrian economics*, Volume 17). Bingley: Emerald.
______. 2012b. Science, the market and iterative knowledge. *Cosmos + Taxis* (SIEO), 5: 26–44.
Hart, H. L. A. 1961. *The Concept of Law*. Oxford: Oxford University Press.
______. 1984. Are There Any Natural Rights? In: Waldron 1984.
Hayek, F. A. 1976. *Law, Legislation and Liberty, vol. II: The Mirage of Social Justice*, London: Routledge and Kegan Paul.
______. 1982. *Law, Legislation and Liberty*. London: Routledge and Kegan Paul.
Hoffer, E. 1951. *The True Believer: Thoughts on the Nature of Mass Movements*. New York: Harper & Row.

Hohfeld, W. N. 1964. *Fundamental Legal Conceptions As Applied in Judicial Reasoning*. New Haven: Yale University Press.
Husain, E. 2018. *The House of Islam: A Global History*. New York: Bloomsbury.
Ignatieff, M. 2001. *Human Rights as Politics and Idolatry*. Princeton: Princeton University Press.
Lucas, J. R. 1966. *The Principles of Politics*. Oxford: Oxford University Press.
Marsh, L. 2018. Pathologizing Ideology, Epistemic Modesty and Instrumental Rationality. In: *The Mystery of Rationality: Mind, Beliefs and the Social Sciences*. G. Bronner and F. Di Iorio (eds.). Cham: Springer.
_____. 2019. Diachronic Identity: Intimations, Perturbations, Antifragility and Toleration. *Cosmos + Taxis* 6:3+4: 78–83.
Maalouf, A. 1998. *Les identites meurtrieres*. Paris: B. Grasset.
Marx, K. (1843) 1970. Marx's Critique of Hegel's *Philosophy of Right*. Oxford: Oxford University Press.
Mayo, B. 1965. Human Rights. *Proceedings of the Aristotelian Society*, Supplementary Volume XXXIX: 219–236.
Mill, J. S. (1858) 2016. *On Liberty*. Ballingslöv: Wisehouse.
Miller, D. 1999. *Principles of Social Justice*. Cambridge, MA: Harvard University Press.
Munger, M. and Villarreal-Diaz, M. 2019. The Road to Crony Capitalism. *The Independent Review*, v. 23, n. 3: 331–344.
Nawaz, M. 2016. *Radical: My Journey out of Islamist Extremism*. Guilford: Lyons Press.
Nielson, K. 1983. A Marxist Conception of Ideology. In: ed. A. Parel, *Ideology, Philosophy and Politics*. Waterloo, ON: Wilfrid Laurier University Press.
Nozick, R. 1974. *Anarchy, State and Utopia*. New York: Basic Books.
Oakeshott, M. 1991. The Masses in Representative Democracy. In: *Rationalism in Politics and other essays*. Indianapolis: Liberty Fund.
_____. 1996. *The Politics of Faith and the Politics of Scepticism*. New Haven: Yale University Press.
Parekh, B. 2019. *Ethnocentric Political: Theory The Pursuit of Flawed Universals*. Cham: Palgrave.
Percy, W. 1991. *Signposts in a Strange Land: Essays*. Patrick Samway (ed.). New York: Farrar, Straus and Giroux.
Perelman, C. 1963. *The Idea of Justice and the Problem of Argument*. London: Routledge.
Pettit, P. 1985–86. Social Holism and Moral Theory. *Proceedings of the Aristotelian Society*, 86: 173–197.

Pinker, S. 2018. *Enlightenment Now: The Case for Reason, Science, Humanism, and Progress*. New York: Viking.
Rawls, J. 1971. *A Theory of Justice*. Cambridge, MA: Harvard University Press.
Scruton, R. 1980. *The Meaning of Conservatism*. Harmonsworth: Penguin.
Shils, E. 1978. The Antinomies of Liberalism. Reprinted in *The Virtue of Civility: Selected Essays on Liberalism, Tradition, and Civil Society* (1997), ed. Steven Grosby. Indianapolis: Liberty Fund.
Shklar, J. 1998. The Liberalism of Fear. In: Stanley Hoffmann ed. *Political Thought and Political Thinkers*. Chicago: University of Chicago Press.
Singer, P. 2000. *A Darwinian left: Politics, evolution and cooperation*. New Haven: Yale University Press.
Stove, D. 2003. *On Enlightenment*. New Brunswick: Transaction.
Taylor, P. W. 1973. Reverse Discrimination And Compensatory Justice. *Analysis* 33 (6): 177–182.
Taleb, N. N. 2016. *The bed of procrustes: Philosophical and practical ap*horisms. New York: Random House.
_____. 2018. *Skin in the Game: Hidden Asymmetries in Daily Life*. New York: Random House.
Tawhidi, M. 2018. *The Tragedy of Islam: Admissions of a Muslim Imam*. Adelaide: Reason Books.
Viereck, P. 2004. *Unadjusted Man in the Age of Overadjustment*. New Brunswick: Transaction
Vincent, A. 1992. *Modern Political Ideologies*. Oxford: Oxford University Press.
Waldron, J. ed. 1984. *Theories of Rights*. Oxford: Oxford University Press.
Wallace, E. 1905. *The Four Just Men*. London: The Tallis Press.
Walzer, M. 1997. *On Toleration*. New Haven and London: Yale University Press
Williams, B. 1969. The Idea of Equality. In: *Moral Concepts*, ed. Joel Feinberg. Oxford: Oxford University Press.
_____. 2009. *In the Beginning Was the Deed: Realism and Moralism in Political Argument*. Ed. Geoffrey Hawthorn. Princeton: Princeton University Press.

# Liberalism and the Modern Quest for Freedom

David D. Corey

The effort to reclaim liberalism will require some understanding of what *kind* of liberalism to reclaim. What is liberalism? What has happened historically such that it needs to be reclaimed? These turn out to be difficult questions. In this essay I propose a theoretical account of liberalism, a way of understanding what it is and why it has undergone such dramatic changes over the course of its history. At the heart of my account is the claim that liberalism did not come into being as an independent historical phenomenon but was rather a contingent aspect of a much broader, more powerfully sweeping historical movement, the "modern quest for freedom," which predates liberalism, gives rise to it, and eventually overtakes it—at which point the quest for freedom itself (notoriously) retains the name "liberalism" in the United States for reasons partly principled, partly expedient.[1] The theory of liberalism on offer here occupies the bulk of this essay, but it is not the only contribution I hope to make. My account of liberalism facilitates a unique assessment of some of

D. D. Corey (✉)
Honors Program, Baylor University, Waco, TX, USA
e-mail: David_D_Corey@baylor.edu



D. F. Hardwick, L. Marsh (eds.), *Reclaiming Liberalism*, Palgrave Studies in Classical Liberalism, https://doi.org/10.1007/978-3-030-28760-3_5

its current weaknesses. And this in turn makes possible a concrete analysis of what an effort to reclaim liberalism might look like. In the end, I argue that the politics of warring freedoms (what contemporary liberalism has in part become) should give way to a markedly different conception of politics, which I call the politics of liberal truce.

## Puzzles

A common way of understanding liberalism and its history is to distinguish between "classical" and "new"—classical liberalism emphasizing freedom from the state, especially in economics (*laissez faire*); "new" liberalism (sometimes called social liberalism) emphasizing social solidarity and individual welfare, using the state to regulate and distribute goods.[2] This is no doubt a helpful distinction, capturing a monumental shift in the focus of liberalism at or around the beginning of the twentieth century. But as a way of understanding liberalism's history in general, it leaves much to be desired. What gave rise to classical liberalism in the first place? Why does classical liberalism emphasize economic freedom instead of other "classic" freedoms such as religious liberty, freedom from foreign domination, and freedom from tyrannical rule?[3] Under what pressures did classical liberalism give way to the more collectivist and statist "new liberalism"? Why has this so-called new liberalism not remained dominant but instead given way (as it has to some extent) to even newer liberal trends, from sexual revolution to civil rights to identity politics and "LGBTQIA+" issues?

These questions cannot be answered by pointing to the distinction between classical liberalism and new. In fact, the history of liberalism is more complex than any binary distinction can capture, including that equally popular distinction made famous by Isaiah Berlin between "negative" and "positive" liberty (Berlin 1969). Perhaps one reason why such distinctions fail to capture liberalism's complexity is that they were never meant to do so. They were rather forged at moments of conflict within liberalism and were intended rhetorically to carry normative weight. Those who promoted the term "new liberalism" were *recommending* it, not engaging in disinterested analysis.[4] So too with the defenders of "classical liberalism." And Isaiah Berlin was not making a merely academic distinction when he separated liberty into negative and positive varieties; he was making a moral argument.

It follows that those of us who wish to "reclaim" liberalism will need a better, less tendentious way of understanding its history. We should begin by frankly admitting that terms like classical and new, positive and negative, are not the same as true and false or good and bad. Liberalism, as Michael Freeden has persuasively argued, is an "essentially contested concept" (Freeden 1996, ch. 2, 2005, pp. 131–143; cf. Gallie 1955–56). There is no uncontroversial *essence* of liberalism to reclaim (Gottfried 1999, p. 28).

## An Account of Liberalism

But important insights into liberalism emerge when it is considered in the context of the broader, constantly evolving quest for freedom that has been and continues to be a prominent feature of modernity in the West. Over the course of modern history individuals and groups in the West have agitated for various kinds of freedom and endeavored to secure these both theoretically and practically. Below is a list of nine distinct kinds of freedom arranged in rough chronological order, accompanied by a characteristic thinker or set of thinkers commonly associated with each:

1. Freedom from religious domination (Luther)
2. Freedom from foreign domination (Machiavelli, enshrined at Westphalia)
3. Freedom from religious civil war (Bodin, Hobbes)
4. Freedom from arbitrary rule, tyranny (Locke)
5. Freedom from government interference in the economy (Smith, Say, Cobden)
6. Freedom from rule by another, that is, by some person or group that does not include oneself or one's representative (Rousseau, Publius, Kant)

7. Freedom from economic exploitation by privileged social groups (Marx, Green, Hobhouse)
8. Freedom from discrimination based on the moral prejudices of privileged social groups (Mill)
9. Freedom from biological inequality and constraint (Nick Bostrom and the transhumanists)

What is the relationship between this historical stream of freedoms and liberalism? The answer is complex but not unfathomable. Liberalism as a self-conscious movement, a set of ideas and practices bearing the name "liberal," appeared on the scene in the early nineteenth century (more about its debut below).[5] Its aim was the advancement of the political and economic freedoms (numbers 4 and 5) whose philosophical articulation had already begun up to a century before liberalism itself became self-conscious. From its inception, moreover, liberalism quickly latched onto all the movements of freedom that preceded it in the West (freedoms 1–3) and made these a part of its platform. Nascent liberalism, in other words, embraced religious freedom, freedom from foreign domination, and freedom from civil war. But here one must be careful not to suppose that the original advocates of these pre-liberal freedoms—thinkers such as Martin Luther, Niccolò Machiavelli, and Thomas Hobbes—were *themselves* liberal.[6] In fact, they neither knew of "liberalism" nor would have approved of much of its political content. Nevertheless, during the nineteenth century, self-styled "liberals" latched onto these prior freedoms and managed to blend them into a doctrinal and practical amalgam along with political and economic freedoms.

What happened next to liberalism accounts for much of the confusion surrounding the term. To some extent, the liberals of the nineteenth century attempted to arrest the flow of the modern quest for freedom. They tried to freeze it at the exact point of freedoms 1–5. But they were not successful. For reasons I explore below, partly practical, partly psychological, citizens of liberal regimes in the West refused to suspend the quest for freedom at the point of freedoms 4 and 5. Instead, they pressed for "democratic" freedoms, "social" freedoms, and more. The fact that this development occurred in every liberal state in the West is one indication—perhaps even a proof—of my claim that liberalism did not arise as an independent historical phenomenon, but was rather from the start a contingent aspect of a broader historical movement.

One may wonder: if the modern quest for freedom passed beyond liberalism, why does the word "liberalism" continue to be used today? What do contemporary authors mean when they write about liberalism's "future" (Wolfe 2010) or its "end" (Lowi 1969) or its "failure" (Deneen 2018), as if liberalism were still an extant political category? The answer is that when the modern quest for freedom began to overtake liberalism in the early twentieth century, the advocates of the newer freedoms, especially in the United States, retained the word "liberalism" (some would say *usurped* it) to describe their new socio-political ideals. This in effect means that liberalism today has three distinct significations. It may refer (1) to the theory and practice of social organization that prioritizes the first five liberties on the list above. Or (2) it may refer to the effort in theory and practice to advance newer freedoms either singly or in combination. (In this case, defense of the first five freedoms appears "conservative.") Or it may refer (3) to the overarching character of regimes that have been and still are living on this historical trajectory. The second and third senses of "liberalism" will be of particular interest in the final, more evaluative sections of this essay.

Two more features of my account need to be mentioned. The first is the phenomenon of *liberal accretion*. This refers to the fact that as new freedoms are pursued over the course of liberalism's history, older freedoms do not cease to be politically relevant but rather continue to attract adherents and are typically even *enlarged* beyond their initial scope. For example, religious freedom (freedom 1), which aimed initially at securing a place for Lutheran worship in a hegemonically Catholic world, over time came to include a place for numerous other Protestant sects, and eventually expanded into a blanket doctrine of "toleration." I shall comment on the development over time of particular kinds of freedom below, but for now let me suggest that "liberal accretion" presents a serious problem, one which liberal writers have historically tended to ignore. Liberal writers and activists alike have tended to adopt what I call the "harmony assumption," the belief that all freedoms are inherently compatible. But all freedoms are *not* compatible. Thus the more freedoms liberalism takes on, the more do problematic clashes of freedom arise within liberalism itself—sites of conflict where the practical incompatibility of certain freedoms must somehow be resolved. I shall return to the problem of warring freedoms near the end of this essay.

The final feature of liberalism I want to mention is the engine or engines that drive its change. What animates the choices made by those who endeavor to alter the character of liberalism? Even more broadly, what motivates the constantly changing character of the modern quest for freedom? Certainly, one way to answer this question is to notice that large-scale revolutions such as the Reformation, the French Revolution, and the Industrial Revolution, bring unintended, negative or problematic consequences in their wake. On this account, the pursuit of new kinds of freedom may sometimes be motivated by the fact that the pursuit of earlier freedoms resulted in unexpected forms of servitude or dependence. For instance, the Industrial Revolution certainly produced unintended levels of social upheaval, geographical dislocation, and poverty among the working class. It makes sense, then, to suppose that the desire for the seventh kind of freedom (freedom from economic exploitation) arose partially in response to the unintended consequences associated with the fifth form of freedom (freedom from government interference in the economy). I try to show below (section "Illustrations of the Nine Freedoms: The Rise and Development of Liberalism") that this kind of account does shed considerable light on some developments in the history of the modern quest for freedom. But it is not exhaustive, and I am inclined to look elsewhere for other factors.

Beyond unintended consequences there appears to be something psychological at work, a kind of "eudaimonic expectation" that develops as the quest for freedom proceeds. At the outset of modern history this expectation is notably absent. The freedoms being agitated for were perceived as rather *existentially* needful, not a recipe for happiness. The quest for religious freedom, for instance, was a quest for salvation, eternal life, not a quest for worldly happiness per se. Freedom from foreign domination was similarly a matter of national *existence*; so too with freedom from civil war. But after these initial freedoms became relatively secure, the character of the quest for freedom seems gradually to have changed. It seems to have become increasingly bound up with the hope and expectation that new forms of freedom would somehow bring happiness and fulfillment in their wake. And yet they never do. Rather, each newly secured freedom gives way eventually to a vague sense of disappointment: Freedom achieved, where is the expected result? It is not hard to imagine how liberals who felt such disappointment might search for, and then discover, certain new, previously undetected forms of constraint that now appear to stand intolerably in the way of genuine freedom and fulfillment. On this account, some of the later changes that occur in the modern quest for freedom seem to be driven by the alluring dream of human perfection. More on this below in section "Assessing Contemporary Liberalism."

## Cautions

If this account of liberalism has any degree of illuminative power, as I hope it does, it certainly does not illuminate everything; and I want to be clear about the limits of what I am offering.

First, my inventory of modern freedoms is not meant to be exhaustive but merely indicative. I have tried to include enough freedoms to illustrate the existence of this distinct thread of modernity and to show the point at which liberalism arises within it. Moreover, I have *not* tried to include in my account other important liberal goods besides freedom (for instance, equality and justice), though these would have to be factored into a fuller account. I have, however, noticed an interesting phenomenon on this score, which is that when goods such as equality and justice become the focus of liberal debate, they tend to be defended not for their intrinsic worth but for the contribution they make to a fuller, more humane kind of freedom.[7] Freedom, in other words, in all its variety, seems to be the basal good of liberalism.

Another cautionary remark about the freedoms on my list is that they are more like families of freedoms than individual freedoms. For instance, "religious freedom" includes within it such particulars as freedom of worship; freedom of belief; and freedom to live out one's belief in society by evangelizing, for instance, or engaging in conscientious objection. All the freedoms listed above prove similarly multiform. This will be important when it comes to considering the potential conflicts within and among liberal freedoms.

Next, extreme caution must be taken with respect to chronology. Though I present the freedoms above in a "rough chronological order," this in fact requires a *significant* degree of abstraction from historical particulars. I am confident that this act of abstraction is useful for purposes of analysis, but I do not wish to mislead. In England, the United States, France, Spain, and Germany (the countries I have studied) the exact ordering of modern freedoms varies for reasons peculiar to each country.[8] The actual history is much more contingent than any uniform list can convey. And yet to present the evolving quest for freedom in a rough chronological order remains useful if only to dispel the tendency to view liberalism *a-historically* as a free-floating set of "basic liberties" (Rawls 1971; 1993) or, worse, as a univocal "theory" of some kind (Deneen 2018). Liberalism is not *a theory*, though it certainly has theoretical content. It is rather a messy admixture of thoughts and practices that develop over time, simultaneously affecting and being affected by competing thoughts and practices.

With respect to these competing thoughts and practices still more cautions are in order. In the account of liberalism above, I have deliberately kept my gaze fixed firmly on the movement for freedom. But this quest for freedom is by no means the only feature of modernity; and significant developments within liberalism would not be fully intelligible without broadening the analysis. For instance, I have not factored in the power of such restraining forces as conservatism, reaction, skepticism, and religious revival, even though these have had a considerable impact on the character of Western liberalism. Similarly, liberalism's shift from "classical" freedoms to "new" could scarcely be intelligible without considering the exogenous influence of socialist thought in the West and various practices of collectivism taking shape in non-liberal countries such as Soviet Russia and Fascist Italy.[9] To attain a fuller understanding of the history of liberalism one would certainly have to consider the numerous competing forces in opposition or apposition to which it partly defines itself.

With all these cautions in mind, is the account of liberalism on offer here still worth anything? Obviously, I think it is. But perhaps I can make its worth seem less dubious if I say a word about "understandings." The achievement of an understanding (such as this account of liberalism) does not exclude the possibility of other understandings. Nor need these alternatives be incompatible rivals. It is possible to understand a phenomenon in multiple ways, each furnishing its own kind of illumination. The test of an understanding is thus not whether it removes controversy, explains *everything*, or commands consensus, but rather whether it throws fresh light on a subject that would otherwise remain obscure. The task I have set for myself in offering this account of liberalism is thus to achieve some degree of illumination and, simultaneously, to facilitate the substantive philosophical criticism of liberalism to which I turn in section "Assessing Contemporary Liberalism."

## Illustrations of the Nine Freedoms: The Rise and Development of Liberalism

In this section I try to fill out my account of liberalism by viewing its relationship to the modern quest for freedom in slightly more specific terms. What I offer here is *not a history*, though I adduce historical examples. Rather, I intend (1) to *illustrate* the nine kinds of freedom, (2) to show that each freedom, once introduced, does not vanish but rather continues to develop over time, and (3) to show how "liberalism" appears and develops within this broader movement of freedoms. Along the way, I comment on some of the reasons why a strictly linear presentation of modern freedoms (such as the overly simplistic list above) distorts historical reality.

### Freedom 1: "Freedom from Religious Domination"

Religious freedom is frequently described as a "first freedom" for good reason. Not only was it the first to receive mention in the U.S. Bill of Rights, it was also the freedom that arguably gave birth to the modern quest for freedom in the West. This is a grand claim, and I do not mean to imply that the Protestant reformers intended to ignite what now seems a perpetual movement of freedom. Far from it. Yet their fateful act of renouncing the religious and political authority of the Roman Catholic Church produced unintended consequences that likely necessitated or at least encouraged the pursuit of further freedoms (freedoms 2–4).[10]

Religious freedom at the time of the Reformation was not the sort of thing one typically thinks of today. As Lord Acton famously pointed out, the most influential of the magisterial reformers, Luther and Calvin, were themselves supporters of religious persecution—not of their own sects, of course, but of others (Acton 1907). One may thus say that early on, religious freedom "meant the right to dissent from Rome and to agree with Wittenberg." This "was for the times a new degree of religious freedom, and it brought about real and lasting change in contemporary religious life." And yet, "it was also a new bondage to a new dogmatic creed" (Ozment 2003, p. 77).

A more thoroughgoing religious freedom came only gradually and with much bloodshed. The principle, "cuius regio, eius religio" (princes have the right to determine the religion of their own state) did not emerge until the Peace of Augsburg in 1555, and even then was not consistently respected. The legal right of different Christian sects to practice their faith in private did not emerge until the Peace of Westphalia in 1648, and yet that treaty only recognized the legitimacy of Lutheranism, Catholicism, and Calvinism. Smaller sects such as the Anabaptists had no legal rights. In fact, full religious toleration in Europe was still a desideratum during most of the seventeenth century, as evinced by the persecution of the Huguenots in France and the Waldensians in the Piedmont in 1688. Thus, the movement for religious freedom that began at the time of the Reformation continued to develop over time and has, indeed, remained an active force in liberal politics today.

## Freedom 2: "Freedom from Foreign Domination"

What I call "freedom 2" followed at least in part from the unintended consequences of freedom 1, because when the Protestant reformers attacked the authority of the Catholic Church, they attacked an indispensable part of the network of powers that had held European civilization together during the Middle Ages. For this reason, the Reformation sparked a massive political crisis. As it happens, the Reformation coincided with a crisis of authority within the Holy Roman Empire, a conflict between Charles V's Spanish and German inheritances, and it exacerbated that crisis by enticing local dukes to challenge Charles' hegemony. In the wake of the Reformation the empire rapidly divided along religious lines, with southern and western regions remaining Catholic while the north, east, and many large cities became Protestant. For the next century and a half, Europe would be enveloped in wars to increase either the Catholic or the Protestant territories and to unify religion within state borders.

During this initial Reformation period, the problem of securing the state against foreign invasion (freedom 2) occupied the minds of Europe's most gifted statesmen and theorists. Machiavelli's best-known political texts, *The Prince* and *The Discourses on Livy* date precisely to this period and present the problem literally as a matter of freedom. Indeed, the final chapter of *The Prince* is a direct call "to liberate Italy" from foreign invaders (Machiavelli 1985, p. 101). Of course, the term "freedom" in Machiavelli's texts often refers to "republican freedom," the form of self-rule that, for instance, Florence managed to achieve for a period during Machiavelli's lifetime. But for Machiavelli such freedom was always a contingent and, ultimately, instrumental good. The overriding concern of his texts is with the freedom of the state itself as an entity continuing through time with the power to acquire. And Machiavelli makes clear that this demands that the constitution of the state (what he calls its "orders") be adaptable (a) to the moral conditions of its citizens and (b) to the geopolitical situation in which the state finds itself. Machiavelli wanted nothing more than a unified and freed Italy. He studied Livy because that Roman historian narrated the development of ancient Italy from a congeries of regional powers into a republic with the power to acquire and, finally, into an ever-expanding empire. Not since Livy's time had Italy been so united and free.

Another example of freedom 2 (this one practical rather than theoretical, and much further down the historical stream) was the Peace of Westphalia, negotiated in 1648, which legalized the concept of territorial sovereignty and forbade states from intervening in the affairs of other states. It is estimated that approximately eight million people perished during the European wars of religion including the Thirty Years' War (Clodfelter 2017, p. 40). The treaties of Westphalia aimed at putting a stop to such bloodshed. This partly attests to the claim I made above, that originally the modern quest for freedom involved freedoms that were *existentially* needful.

## Freedom 3: "Freedom from Religious Civil War"

Well prior to the Peace of Westphalia the quest for the third kind of freedom, release from religio-political conflict *within* states, had already begun. What this problem seemed to demand was a new understanding of the grounds of political authority for an age in which neither Pope nor Emperor commanded universal respect. And the problem was so keenly felt in the kingdom of France in the final quarter of the sixteenth century that it attracted the attention not only of the Politiques, but also of one of France's most talented political theorists, Jean Bodin. In his *Six Livres de la République* published in Paris in 1576 (four years after the St. Bartholomew's Day massacre), Bodin distinguished between a happily homogeneous political association in which law, custom, language, and religion are uniform, and a more complicated kind of political association where sharp differences along these lines are reconciled within a self-sufficient whole called a state or commonwealth (*république*). Bodin went on to describe in great detail the appropriate form of political authority in a state, which he called *souveraineté*. And though he ascribed a virtually unlimited power to the sovereign, he did so in the belief that this would foster the possibility of different religions' living side by side under an authority that makes a place for them all.[11] Thomas Hobbes's (no doubt more familiar) theory of sovereignty contained in *De Cive* (1642) and *Leviathan* (1651) was animated by a similar concern for civil peace in an age of civil war, though his approach was to strive for religious settlement rather than toleration.

In the realm of political practice, the Edict of Nantes (1598) signed by Henry IV was not far from Bodin's vision and was aimed at lessening the threat of religious civil war. Later, the Peace of Westphalia (1648) also tried to address the problem by simultaneously bolstering the principle of *cuius regio, eius religio* while guaranteeing (in section 28) rights of worship to Christians living in states where their sect was not the established church.

It is interesting to observe the dovetailing that occurs over time in the quests for freedom 1 (religious freedom) and freedom 3 (freedom from religious civil war). For it was not the doctrine of absolute sovereignty developed by Bodin and Hobbes that ultimately brought religious civil war under control in Europe (to the extent that it did come under control) but rather the development of a doctrine and practice of *toleration*. Certainly by the 1680s, toleration was being urged in Europe (especially in England and the Netherlands) not simply as a matter of religious principle, but as a carefully worked out *political* principle. John Locke in particular (though he was far from alone) had come to see that the use of absolute sovereignty in matters of religion was failing to produce either religious unity or relief from civil war. As a result, he studiously wagered that if religious differences were rather tolerated than repressed, they might eventually cease to erupt into violence (Kraynak 1980). This idea of toleration took time to catch on; and as recent historians have reminded us, the results were uneven well into the eighteenth century (Kaplan 2007, p. 352). But the main point I am making here is simply that the rise of toleration belongs as much to the third as it does to the first family of freedoms.

I have not yet commented on the endurance of the quest for freedom 3 over time. In one sense this freedom seems unique insofar as it was eventually *achieved*, even if it took time: religiously inspired civil wars came to an end. But this appearance recedes quickly upon reflection. The problem of religiously inspired civil unrest and even outright war continued to menace Western states well after Westphalia, and every effort to tamp it down constitutes an episode in the history of freedom 3. Moreover, if one takes a rather broader view of what is "religious" and includes the conflict between "secularism" and "religion" as an instance of religious civil war or at least "culture war," then it becomes clear that the effort to free ourselves from this socio-political problem is far from over. On the contrary, it sometimes seems as if contemporary politics is little more than a civil war by other means, a colossal struggle on the part of rival religious or quasi-religious factions for control of the state. Below I develop this thought into a more systematic critique of contemporary liberalism.

## Freedom 4: "Freedom from Tyranny"

As the quest for freedom 3 ensued across Europe the desire was soon felt for another kind of freedom, namely, freedom from absolute, arbitrary rule. The desire for this freedom arose in part because the theory and practice of absolute sovereignty (including the theory of the divine right of kings) that accompanied the quest for freedom 3 was beginning to seem like something ominously familiar from ancient accounts of politics, namely "tyranny," that classical nemesis of freedom. What I call freedom 4—"freedom from arbitrary, tyrannical rule"—was thus directed at removing or at least constraining this source of oppression.

The instrument that was used, first in England, then in the United States, France, and Spain, was "constitutionalism." But here I must make an important distinction. When constitutionalism was used as a check on *monarchical* rule, it was indeed an instance of freedom 4. But constitutionalism could also be used as an instrument for new experiments in non-monarchical rule, such as the "commonwealth" in England, an extended republic in the United States, and a democracy in France. These ventures in republican and democratic politics are actually instances of the sixth kind of freedom, and I shall discuss them below under that head.

European history does not display a linear movement through freedoms 4–6, but rather a halting one with significant reversals under the general heading of "restoration." To make matters worse, the emergence of freedom 5, economic freedom, occurred roughly at the same time as freedoms 4 and 6. Thus, if one tries to present the history of these freedoms as sequential, one distorts their complex reality. I remind the reader, therefore, that I present them sequentially only for purposes of exposition and analysis.

The English Bill of Rights (1689) that was drawn up after the Glorious Revolution of 1688 constitutes a prime example of the constitutionalism associated with freedom 4. Of course, England had enjoyed a long history of medieval constitutionalism stretching back to the Magna Carta (1215). But under the pressure of Stuart absolutism in the seventeenth century, significant constitutional advances were made that were captured in the Bill of Rights: That document proscribes royal interference with the law, bans the monarch from establishing new courts or acting as judge, disallows taxation without parliamentary approval, prohibits standing armies or interference with the people's right to bear arms, and guarantees freedom of speech, especially but not exclusively in parliamentary debate. The rise of these guarantees was in part the product of fierce political conflict between the crown and the parliament during the seventeenth century, but it was also influenced by theoretical writings in pamphlet and treatise form. Composed between 1679 and 1681, John Locke's *Second Treatise of Government* dates to this exact period.

In the United States, the Declaration of Independence (1776) can also be interpreted as an example of freedom 4. Although its primary purpose was to dissolve the political relationship between the colonies and England, it was not a repudiation of monarchy per se. Rather its charge was that "The history of the present King of Great Britain is a history of repeated injuries and usurpations, all having in direct object the establishment of an *absolute Tyranny* over these States." Significantly, the document endeavored to prove this in its lengthy "bill of particulars" by referring to specific constitutional and common-law limits on monarchical power that the king was said to have violated.

France's various adventures in constitution-making after the Revolution are too tortuous to describe here. They all owe a great debt to Montesquieu, whose *Spirit of the Laws* (1748) had already served to popularize the ideas of English constitutionalism in absolutist France.[12] But at least one example of the kind of constitutionalism associated with freedom 4 can be found in the "Charter of 1815," written by Benjamin Constant upon the return of Napoleon from exile on Elba. This constitution, short-lived though it was, bore some similarities to the Charter of 1814 promulgated by the Restoration King Louis XVIII, which was also quite liberal in some ways. On the one hand, the Charter of 1815 unambiguously named Napoleon "Emperor of the French," but, on the other hand, it advanced a number of unprecedented freedoms. A "chamber of representatives" was to be composed of more than 600 members elected for five-year terms, and a lengthy list of substantive rights was guaranteed to French citizens, including for example, equality before the law, freedom of worship, the right of private property, freedom of the press without censorship, and the right of petition.

The Charter of 1815 was not Benjamin Constant's only achievement in the quest for freedom 4. During the Restoration, he had been a strong advocate for placing fixed limits on monarchical power, what the French call "guarantism." Specific guarantees discussed at the time included division of powers, non-dismissible magistrates, and the independence of provincial and communal bodies.[13] Again, the effort here was not to establish a democracy or a republic, but rather to prevent monarchy from becoming tyrannical. In fact, Constant famously propounded the distinction between what he called "modern liberty" (e.g., of person, family, religion, property, and industry) and "ancient liberty," which meant freedom to participate in government (Constant [1819] 1988). Constant's view was that widespread democratic participation in government was incompatible with modern life because citizens had other, more important enterprises to pursue than political rule.

## Freedom 5: "Freedom from Government Interference in the Economy"

Freedom 5 initially consists in the movement across Western Europe away from Mercantilism toward a system of economic free trade and free enterprise. In France, for example, "physiocrats" such as François Quesnay (1694–1774) and Anne-Robert-Jacques Turgot (1727–1781) argued that the wealth of nations was best gauged not (*pace* Mercantilism) by the amount of a monarch's gold or the relative balance of trade with other nations, but rather by the amount of productive work, especially in agriculture, occurring within the nation's economy. Moreover, the physiocrats' emphasis on individual self-interest as the best guide to what ought to be produced and consumed, and at what price, was a direct attack on state intervention in the economy and certainly anticipated Adam Smith's famous account of the "invisible hand" in his monumental treatise, *The Wealth of Nations* (1776).

Another, later example of freedom 5 occurs in the middle of the nineteenth century in Manchester, the seat of the world's textile industry, where factory workers and owners alike were severely disadvantaged by the British government's "Corn Laws" (1815–1846)—protectionist tariffs on imported grain that effectively raised the price of food in England. Opposing the Corn Laws, men such as Richard Cobden and John Bright fought passionately for a system of free trade. Both men were founders of the Anti-Corn Law League and members of Parliament in a party that was already calling itself (though not yet officially) the "Liberals." (The formal creation of the Liberal Party in Britain occurred in 1859, the year Lord Palmerston formed his second government.) The success of the liberal opponents to the Corn Laws—and one should include Sir Robert Peel and William Gladstone in this group as well—marked a major victory for economic "liberalism" in Great Britain.

It is now possible to inquire into the rise of liberalism and to better understand the controversy surrounding its character. If one focuses only on England, the rise of a formal group calling themselves "liberal" appears to be associated primarily with freedom 5 (freedom from government interference in the economy, or the "doctrine of free trade"). But in fact, one of the earliest uses of the term "liberal" in the modern, political sense occurred not in England but in Spain, in 1812.[14] That was the year that a party of the Cortes (Spain's first legislature) drafted and enacted the "Constitution of Cádiz" in an effort to avoid the restoration of the absolutist Ferdinand VII and to create a constitutional monarchy instead.[15] The advocates of this constitution called themselves the *Liberales*, and their effort was clearly more bound up with freedom 4 (freedom from absolute rule, constitutionalism) than freedom 5, even though one of the provisions of their constitution also addressed free trade.[16]

This suggests (and this is the view I hold) that the rise of a self-conscious movement called "liberalism" was so bound up with freedoms 4 and 5 that to associate it exclusively with either would be a mistake. And this makes sense if we consider the extent to which the classic texts of freedom 4—texts such as Locke's *Second Treatise* and Montesquieu's *Spirit of the Laws*—already evince a deep concern for economic freedom and economic growth. The entire fifth chapter of Locke's work, we recall, concerns private property and the tremendous *economic* gain that awaits a country whose government secures it. As for Montesquieu, it was no exaggeration when Lord Keynes referred to him as "the real French equivalent of Adam Smith, . . . head and shoulders above the physiocrats in penetration, clear-headedness, and good sense" (Devletoglou 1963, p. 1).

A second point to observe about the rise of liberalism in the nineteenth century is the extent to which it immediately brought under its banner all the modern freedoms that preceded it in time. For instance, the Liberal Party in England was from the start supportive of religious Nonconformists; and both Lord Palmerston and John Bright were noted supporters of religious freedom (freedom 1) (Wolffe 2005; Holton 2002). Likewise, the Spanish Constitution of Cádiz began by asserting Spain's territorial sovereignty (freedom 2), as well as her domestic sovereign power (freedom 3), which was to be constitutionally limited rather than absolute (freedom 4). From the start, then, liberalism incorporates earlier, classic freedoms. What results is an ever-growing body of freedoms expanding over time. This much on the rise of liberalism. What remains now is to illustrate its historical development.

## Freedom 6: "Freedom from Rule by Another"

Freedom 6, "freedom from rule by another," is arguably the first of the freedoms considered here that did not owe something substantial to the unintended consequences of the Reformation.[17] Instead, it was inspired by certain Renaissance writers in Italy who had taken a renewed interest in Roman legal and political writings on "republicanism," and also by a group of writers during the Commonwealth Period in England from 1649 to 1660.[18] (Marchamont Nedham, James Harrington, and John Milton were among the principal advocates of republican theory during this period.)[19] Freedom 6 could certainly be placed earlier on the list of nine freedoms if one wanted to emphasize the importance of these influential writers. My reason for placing it later is simply that, as Quentin Skinner has pointed out, "the cause of the English republic was not to prevail" (Skinner 1998, p. 16). With the restoration of Charles II, England returned to the path of constitutional monarchy (freedom 4). Nevertheless, as Skinner continues: "The period of the Interregnum left behind it the richest legacy of neo-Roman and republican writings of the seventeenth century, in addition to nurturing the political sensibilities of such writers as Henry Neville and Algernon Sidney."[20]

I interpret freedom 6 as containing two distinct emphases: the first, republican; the second, democratic. The "Dedicatory Letter" to Rousseau's *Discourse on the Origin of Inequality* (1754), gives voice to the first emphasis, as does his *Social Contract* (1762). The basic contention of these texts is that a people cannot be truly free under a monarch, whether "constitutional" or not. The only meaningful guarantee of freedom is to live as an active citizen under a scheme of government that employs magistrates of the people for day-to-day governance.[21] Other instances of freedom-6 republicanism include the system of "representative government" created by the U.S. Constitutional Convention (1787) and defended by Publius in the *Federalist Papers* (1788); and the political system articulated by Immanuel Kant in the *Metaphysics of Morals* (1797).

The more *democratic* emphasis in freedom 6 was in evidence, but only briefly, in the immediate aftermath of the French Revolution. By "democratic," I do not mean direct popular rule, but rather the extension of individual rights (especially the franchise) to all members of the political community, and the tearing down of social hierarchies in the name of equality. After drawing up the "Declaration of the Rights of Man and of the Citizen" in 1789, for instance, the French elected their first National Convention by an almost universal male suffrage. Other examples: In the United States, the extension of the male franchise in the early nineteenth century was part of the movement for freedom 6. So too were the democratic reforms of the Jacksonian Era, and the "woman's suffrage movement" that occurred in the United States as well as in England.

## Freedom 7: "Freedom from Economic Exploitation"

The quest for freedom 7 is often referred to by scholars of European thought as a "social revolution." It involves a deliberate refashioning of liberalism in order to use the state to address the problem of economic inequality and poverty. Freedom 7 was not the first modern freedom to contemplate a fuller use of the state—this was already characteristic of Rousseau's political thought, for instance, in the *Social Contract* (freedom 6). But it was the first attempt to enlist the state in a systematic effort to redress what now seemed an unintended consequence of freedom 5 (*lais-*

*sez faire* and the dramatic dislocations and degradations of the working class associated with industrialism in the West).

The quest for freedom 7 appears at first closely bound up with socialism—for instance in the writings of Henri de Saint-Simon (1760–1825), the French economist and political theorist whose maxim was, "from each according to his capacity, to each according to his needs" (De Ruggiero 1959, p. 197ff). Indeed, many socialists, including Karl Marx and his followers, took their inspiration from Saint-Simon. But Saint-Simonism also influenced liberalism itself—not immediately in France, where the revolution of 1848 brought the dictator Louis Bonaparte to power, crushing the ambitions of liberal democrats and socialists alike, but in England and the United States.

In England, one finds, for instance in the writings of T. H. Green (1836–1882) and L. T. Hobhouse (1864–1929), many of the central ideas of Saint-Simonism—that the quest for individual freedom demands more than freedom from coercion, but requires also a positive concern for citizens' welfare; that welfare is a "right," not a matter of charity; that workers are not free merely by virtue of their freedom to sign a labor contract on terms deleterious to their well-being, but must also have an equal position in the negotiation of such contracts through trade associations and state regulation of wages; and, finally, hovering above all this, that "the state" must be more than a merely negative guarantor of individual freedom from harm, but also a "positive" guarantor of the conditions of well-being for every one of its members, as if these members combined to form a single, harmonious organism (the "organic" conception of the state). The difference between the liberal defenders of these ideas and the proto-socialist Saint-Simon is that for the latter they represented an *alternative* to liberalism while for the former they were rather a *modification*. The advocates of freedom 7 believed it was time for liberalism to transition from its early "negative phase" to a contemporary "positive phase."

The ideas associated with freedom 7 appeared in the United States in connection with the Progressive Movement and the New Deal. Herbert Croly's *Promise of American Life* (1909), for example, makes the classic case for a strong national government in order to free the economically disadvantaged from the greed and corruption of the economically privileged classes. John Dewey's political philosophy does so too, though it goes even further: "Organized social planning," he writes in *Liberalism and Social Action* (1935), "put into effect for the creation of an order in which industry and finance are socially directed in behalf of institutions that provide the material basis for the cultural liberation and growth of individuals is now the sole method of social action" (Dewey [1935] 2000, p. 60). This was as close to socialism as one could get while still calling oneself a liberal. And this movement was in no way limited to abstract speculation. Rather, it found a powerful voice in Franklin D. Roosevelt, whose "Second Bill of Rights" (1944), for instance, translated the goals of freedom 7 into the fixed language of rights—the right to work, to ample remuneration, to a home, to medical care, to security in old age and ill health, and to education. All these new rights represented Roosevelt's (freedom 7) effort to secure individuals from economic oppression and to protect the weak from the power of the strong. From the Roosevelt years on, freedom 7 in its economic aspect would become synonymous with the politics of the "welfare state," and it remains to this day a powerful force in Western liberal politics.

For many students of liberalism, freedom 7 seems to constitute something so foreign to liberalism's original character expressed in freedoms 1–5 that it seems a repudiation of liberalism itself. But that is a much-contested interpretation, and by setting liberalism in the context of the broader modern quest for freedom, one can see why. While it is true that the "new liberalism" associated with freedom 7 reverses the earlier attitude that liberals took toward the state, it does not reverse, but rather advances, the underlying thrust of the modern quest for freedom. In that quest, the state was not always the enemy of individual freedom; often it was its chief guarantor, as in the movements for freedoms 1–3. There is, thus, arguably nothing inconsistent about individuals and groups *returning* to the state when a source of oppression seems once again of the sort that the state might credibly resist. And one reason that the supporters of freedom 7 could credibly refer to themselves as "liberal" is that liberalism had from its inception become bound up with the modern quest for freedom in general.[22]

## Freedom 8: "Freedom from Discrimination Based on Moral Prejudice"

Freedom 8 takes aim not at economic privilege but at overly restrictive social norms created and maintained by society's privileged classes. John Stuart Mill's influential book, *On Liberty* (1859) offered a paradigmatic account of this concern in what scholars call Mill's "harm principle." "The only purpose for which power can be rightfully exercised over any member of a civilized community, against his will, is to prevent harm to others" (Mill [1859] 2002, p. 13). Part of what made Mill's exploration of this principle so original was that he did not limit his analysis to the power of government over individuals but extended it to the relationship between and among individuals and groups in the social sphere. The principle requires, according to Mill, "liberty of tastes and pursuits; of framing the plan of our life to suit our own character; of doing as we like, subject to such consequences as may follow: without impediment from our fellow-creatures, so long as what we do does not harm them, even though they should think our conduct foolish, perverse, or wrong" (ibid., p. 15). Mill went so far as to say that no society can be free where this liberty is not respected, no matter the form of government or institutional structures; and he insisted that this liberty be "absolute and unqualified" (ibid., p. 16).[23]

Freedom 8 has been and continues to be a powerful force at work in contemporary liberalism. Some further examples include the Bohemian movements of the nineteenth century in Europe and the United States, the hipsters of the 1940s, the Beat generation of the 1950s, and the counterculture of the 1960s and 1970s: All were engaged in the effort to free themselves from what they believed to be the overly constraining norms and prejudices of bourgeois-liberal culture. I would add that for most of its history, the quest for freedom 7 has had the status of so many "alternative" ways of life and has tended to be more social than political. That is to say, its advocates were not inclined to take the fight to political institutions. However, the last fifty years has witnessed a more aggressive form of freedom 7, one that actively seeks liberation *by the state* from what are believed to be oppressive norms, practices, institutions, and unfair inequalities within society. "Identity politics," for instance, bears *something* of the character of freedom 7. It is an attempt to eliminate cultural intolerance and inequality for myriad "intersecting" minority groups on the assumption that these groups have been and continue to be oppressed by traditional attitudes and structures. On the other hand, identity politics would scarcely be conceivable if freedom 7 were the only factor animating it. Rather, it arises primarily from the loose application of Marxist class analysis to non-economic factors combined with psychological and other theories of oppression, and proceeds in imitation of the American Civil Rights Movement even when the nature of the freedoms being sought are not equivalent.

## Freedom 9: "Freedom from Biological Inequality and Constraint"

I come at last to freedom 9. By "biological constraint" I mean to refer (rather loosely) to any "given" of our biological nature—for example, our genetic makeup, intelligence, physical appearance, reproductive powers, and gender. The advocates of freedom 9 feel unjustly hindered by these givens, not only because they are "given" and not the product of free choice, but also because their "givenness" does not accord with rational principles of equality or desert.[24] Some people are given biological advantages, others disadvantages, for no discernible reason. Instances of this freedom can be traced back to the eugenics movements of the nineteenth century in England and the United States, but the quest for it becomes more prominent in the twentieth and twenty-first centuries.[25] One reason for this is the degree of technological sophistication that is required to alter our biological nature, but another reason is perhaps the prior successes of the modern quest for freedom itself over time. To regard oneself as unfairly constrained not by another person or group but by nature herself presupposes a very high degree of security from other, more menacing forms of oppression. It would not have occurred to earlier generations of liberals that one's biological constitution could be a chief obstacle to freedom and a matter of political concern.

I include a wide range of diverse phenomena within freedom 9, and in some instances the intention of the agent matters more than the technique being used. For instance, birth control is not a freedom-9 phenomenon in itself (the use of birth control goes back to remote antiquity), but when the "right" to birth control becomes a political movement aimed at removing the inequality between women and men in their sexual status, it becomes an instance of freedom 9. Medicine too is as old as civilization, but the assertion of a right to free and equal healthcare at public expense is, again, an instance of freedom 9. The right to physician-assisted suicide, to abortion, to gender reassignment surgery: these are other well-known examples. I also group the "transhumanist" movement with freedom 9 insofar as its goal is to transcend the human species, "not just sporadically, an individual here in one way, an individual there in another way, but in its entirety, as humanity" (Huxley 1957, p. 17; see also Bostrom and Salvulescu 2009; for a critique see Lawler 2005). This is a program that will undoubtedly require the active participation of the state, not only for financial support but also to ensure the fair distribution of biological enhancements.

## Assessing Contemporary Liberalism

Again, I do not offer the foregoing as a *history*. It is rather a series of lightly sketched examples of nine kinds of freedom and the place of liberalism within it. Liberalism is, on the one hand, a nineteenth-century phase of an underlying movement for freedom stretching back to the Reformation, but it is also a continuation of that movement. Liberalism changes because the movement does not stop with the achievement of this or that particular freedom (economic, political, etc.) but continues in the pursuit of ever more freedom. In the remainder of this essay I want to hint at the power of this account to facilitate philosophical criticism of contemporary liberalism. I shall limit my analysis at this point to American liberalism; and while there is so much that could be said, I shall limit myself to three points. These three points will in turn issue in a brief reflection on how we might begin to "reclaim" some kind of liberalism worthy of reclaiming.

## Liberalism's Eudaimonic Expectation

In section "An Account of Liberalism," I teased out three potential meanings of "liberalism." In this more evaluative part of the essay, I want to focus on the second and third meanings: namely, the effort in theory and practice to advance newer freedoms either singly or in combination; and the overarching character of regimes that have been and still are living out this "modern quest for freedom." For purposes of exposition and analysis I shall refer to these as "liberal advancement" and "liberal character."

Liberal advancement is a fascinating phenomenon to isolate and study. It can be pursued in different ways. One way (presented here in the manner of an ideal type) is *incremental and organic*. Inconveniences within the practice of liberal social arrangements are detected by those experiencing them; thought is given to how these inconveniences might be remedied; costs and benefits are assessed, not just for the individuals in question, but also for the entire social organization, which is understood always to involve a delicate balance of political goods: for example, freedom, stability, predictability, justice, peace, improvability. Ultimately, a *question is posed* (rather than an answer assumed) whether the attempt to remedy the present inconvenience is worth the cost of upsetting the current balance of goods. If this question is answered affirmatively, change is cautiously pursued, and the effects are monitored for unintended consequences.

Another, virtually opposite approach to liberal advancement (also an ideal type) is *sudden and autonomous*. Inconveniences are detected. These may arise from the practice of liberal social arrangements but just as often they hail from theory: "poverty ought not to exist," "Ozone emissions should be decreased by 50% in five years." Typically, these inconveniences are understood and presented as *injustices*. Thought is given to how they might be remedied, but due to the heavy normative weight ascribed to them, they seem too urgent to permit cost-benefit analysis; indeed such calculations seem crass when it comes to such weighty moral matters; the attitude here is deontological. Accordingly, the question *whether* these inconveniences ought to be remedied is never asked. Immediate change is demanded. Its advocates act autonomously, disregarding the effects of change on the broader social organization and the delicate balance of political goods.

Glancing back at the illustrations of liberal freedoms above, I am struck by the extent to which their continual advancement has been pursued more in the sudden and autonomous manner than in an incremental and organic one. Moreover, in recent decades the very pace of sudden and autonomous change has increased, not from one family of freedoms to another, which has remained relatively consistent, as *within* each family of freedoms, especially within freedoms 7–9. In other words, American liberalism seems to be racing with unprecedented speed toward ever-new forms of economic, social, and biological freedom, all of them now cast in terms of social *justice.*

It is worth asking why this is happening and what effect it has had on "liberal character," the overarching character of a regime that lives at this breakneck speed. No doubt the intended effect was an ostensibly moral one: to improve the moral quality of liberal life by removing as many injustices as possible. Of course, the removal of so many purported injustices requires the coercive force of the state; and it would be surprising if elite liberal actors were not also motivated by power itself, perhaps instrumentalizing the cause of "justice" in order to exercise and maintain power. But be that as it may, the effects of sudden and autonomous liberal advancement are not limited to the intended ones. The side-effects are everywhere to see: political conflict, exhaustion, disorientation, and perhaps most seriously, a resulting ordering of freedoms and other political goods that is irrational and difficult to accommodate.

Why have liberal citizens not noticed this problem and taken the proper precautions? Why do we continue to celebrate "activists" and "activism" as if these were unalloyed goods? Looking beyond the love of power, which I assume to be operative but not at such levels that it accounts for the massive *number* of liberal citizens who pursue sudden and autonomous change, I can only imagine a deep (but flawed) *psychological* motivation. Contemporary liberals are motivated at least in part by a sincere belief that this constant pressing for change will eventually bring about a state of moral perfection (or at least unending moral improvement). They desire mankind's gradual release from every form of injustice and from every obstacle to complete freedom.

This motivating hope for the attainment of perfect peace, justice, and freedom, is rarely if ever articulated by the liberals who entertain it. Rather it has something of the character of a mystical belief for which no fully rational defense can be given but which, once assumed, animates an entire way of life among a community of believers. But the difficulty is that such a final state of perfection cannot in principle be attained through political activism or through any other human means. It cannot be attained because (1) the problem of evil is constitutional for man, not the result of unjust conditions and poor social planning, and (2) the problem of citizens' forming attachments to rival goods and creating factions around those goods is constitutional for society, not the result of insufficient liberal enlightenment.

## Liberal Accretion and the Warlike Quality of Contemporary Liberalism

A fundamental problem with the continual accumulation of freedoms over time (liberal accretion) is that not all freedoms are compatible; indeed, all freedoms are incompatible if pressed too far. An absolutized religious freedom—to take one example—can threaten state borders (freedom 2), undermine domestic political order (freedom 3); turn governments into instruments of religious tyranny (freedom 4); and place weighty constraints on economic activity (freedom 5). We know, moreover, that religious freedom can clash with freedom from social discrimination (freedom 8), as the recent lawsuits over same-sex weddings attest. I shall not belabor this point by showing how each of the nine freedoms exists in tension with the others, but it is a fact that can be easily demonstrated. As political philosopher John Gray has pointed out, "vitally important liberties do not dovetail into a single, harmonious pattern. They are sites of conflicts of value" (Gray 2000, p. 76).

The mere fact that freedoms exist in tension is not in itself the cause of the warlike quality of contemporary liberalism. But there are several causes related to how citizens negotiate (or fail to negotiate) the tensions in question. One cause is our contemporary "rights talk," and the underlying way we think about rights. Most rights, as I understand them, are little more than particular freedoms we desire to insulate from the vicissitudes of everyday politics. We do so by putting a rhetorical, protective shell around them, saying in effect that *these* freedoms are different; they are more fundamental and should be privileged when confronted by rival freedoms and other rival goods. A further and even more problematic step is taken when we refer to these privileged "rights" as "absolute rights." Absolute means "set loose from all contingency," and rights that acquire this status can never (in principle) be negated or diminished. Yet, if all or most of our freedoms are regarded as "rights," and *absolute* rights at that, and if these absolute rights are in fact incompatible in significant ways, then how can liberal citizens possibly negotiate the conflicts that arise among liberal freedoms? "Absolute rights" cannot be the subject of negotiation; they are by definition unconditional. This is one reason for the warlike quality of contemporary liberalism (see further Glendon 1991).

A second and related reason is the phenomenon I call "inverted liberalism." This occurs when a society enthusiastically grants recognition in law and public policy to the newest liberal freedoms without considering the potential conflicts between the new and the old. Sometimes societies deliberately sacrifice the old on the altar of the new. But because the history of liberal freedoms begins with those that are more existentially needful than later ones—indeed, a matter of life and death—the continual preference for new over old amounts to a severe curtailing, if not outright overturning, of the foundations of freedom itself. This curtailing is visible today in the areas of religious liberty, secure national borders, sovereign political authority, constitutionalism, and economic liberty (to mention only the first five freedoms). The problem is actually quite understandable: the enthusiasm for novelty and the degree to which the old and established may be taken for granted results in a discernable bias, what we might call "presentism" or simply the "progressive bias." But the problem is serious. A liberal society that eats away at its own foundations is not sustainable. Or to put this more concretely, political communities that lack religious freedom, secure borders, sovereignty (both external and internal), constitutional limits, and economic freedom, will not remain stable and productive communities for long. The "warlike" quality of liberalism results from this problem every bit as much as it results from "rights talk." The clash between the old and the new becomes a clash between the forces of revolution and preservation, between an unbounded zeal for change and the sober recognition that survival demands constraint.

A third cause of warlike liberalism builds upon and deepens the notion of competing freedoms. It is that nine freedoms are not merely freedoms; they are also so many competing conceptions of the good and, indeed, ways of life (cf. Gray 2000, pp. 69–104). For example, in the liberal West today we find citizens for whom religion (freedom 1) is the most important part of their identity. For others, a patriotic nationalism (freedom 2) fills that place, while for others still it is economic activity (freedom 5). Today, there are also many liberals for whom race, class, gender, ethnicity, and sexual orientation are by far the most important features of their identity, and they live lives devoted to the battle against discrimination in these areas (freedom 8). But if freedoms are in some respects incompatible, then the lives that are built around those freedoms will also house incompatibilities. And this too explains the warlike quality of liberalism. Liberalism leads to (or perhaps reflects) a deep-seated pluralism among possible ways of life, not just a benign pluralism of "difference," but a pluralism of conflict. Thus, all the various liberal identities, ways of life, fight for the right to thrive without constraint.

Finally, and working in concert with the causes just identified, liberalism develops warlike qualities because of the increased size and scope of government. Modern governments in the West have become increasingly "telic," by which I mean that they are devoted to the achievement of substantive sociopolitical ends. For example, a government engaged in a "total war" against another country would be a "highly telic" government. It would have a substantive purpose (victory) and would likely devote every available resource to that end. But there are many ways for governments to be highly telic without engaging in external wars. Some examples are the "war on poverty" of the New Deal, the "war on drugs" of the Great Society, the wars on crime, disease, and inequality. These are all substantive political ends that liberal societies have endeavored to pursue. The problem is that when governments attempt to pursue highly telic agendas in the context of a deeply pluralistic society, the number of citizens *opposed* to the ends that are ultimately chosen is likely to be very high. As a matter of principle, it is impossible to take a radically diverse set of people down a single political path without violating freedom and formal (political) equality, the bedrock principles of liberalism itself. Thus, as pluralism increases, the telic scope of government should *decrease*, but the opposite has been the norm for some time. The result is angry citizens who sense that their most fundamental rights to freedom and formal equality have been illegitimately taken away; and in order to defend these rights they become warlike political activists against the government and its supporters. This occurs both on the Right and the Left, depending on which side is pursuing the telic policies in question.

## The Problem of Liberal Meaninglessness

My second criticism of contemporary liberalism is that as it becomes warlike, and as more and more social institutions such as universities, churches, and businesses are pressed into service for "the cause," citizens gradually lose contact with the humane practices that bring deep meaning to human life. I shall return to some of these practices briefly, but for now let me suggest that liberalism itself, insofar as it amounts to a quest for human freedom, is to a surprising degree "meaningless."

I do not want to be misunderstood. I acknowledge that people who feel oppressed find meaning (understandably) in liberation. They often find meaning, too, in the camaraderie that the fight for freedom affords. I am not claiming therefore that the history of the struggle for freedom is entirely void of meaning. However, freedom is a paradoxical thing. Seek it as we may, its achievement never seems to bring with it the fulfillment we imagined. We remain restless and anxious about who we are and what we should be doing with our lives. Nor is this accidental. Mere freedom can never assuage the human longing for meaning because freedom is an essentially negative thing, while its meaning is positive. Freedom—even when it goes by the name "positive liberty"—is not *something*, but the removal of some felt constraint. Freedom therefore does not offer its possessor something to *do* with life, but only supplies one *condition* for doing something. Of course, it is true that the revolutionary pursuit of freedom can itself become something to do with one's life (i.e., political activism). But in the end, this too cannot satisfy, because it is scarcely more than a pursuit of preconditions for a life one never actually lives. The activist, on this analysis, sacrifices the present for a future he never lives.

## Concluding Reflections on Reclaiming Liberalism

How might it be possible to reclaim some form of liberalism that avoids the eudaimonic expectations, the warring freedoms, and the problem of meaninglessness which plague contemporary liberalism in the West today? I think our best hope lies in the uniquely human ability to understand and *re-understand* our situation in ways that are most conducive to human flourishing. Let me suggest that how we understand *what politics is* has consequences for how we practice it. If we understand politics to be a fierce battle over public resources and the ends to which these are put, then we shall likely continue to practice liberal politics in a warlike mode. Yet, the problem with political wars (as opposed to actual wars) is that no victory is ever secure. The potential is always high that "the enemy" will try to erode or reverse our latest gains. Moreover, if politics can become warlike, it can also become something like a "total war," a commitment of more and more resources (time, talent, and treasure) to the cause. But a society in the throes of total war is a society that risks sacrificing the very things that make life in general, and political life in particular, worth living. Intense and protracted political warfare represents the *failure* of politics, not its basic character.

If in a different vein we understand politics to be the creation and implementation of some great national vision, a "coming together" over what our future should be and how we might best get there, we would be entertaining a view as old as Greek antiquity, but one that is, significantly, at odds with the foundations of liberalism (*pace* Lilla 2017, ch. 3, who calls on the Democratic Party to articulate such a vision). Liberalism in its religious aspect, in its economic aspect, and in its social aspect entails a conscious rejection of the belief that politics can or should present citizens with a single vision of the good. Rather liberalism is a form of political life that tries to secure for individuals and groups the freedom to make their *own* decisions about the good. And this freedom becomes ever more important as liberal societies become more pluralistic. For, as I said above, the more pluralistic we become, the less possible is it for us to pursue a common *telos* without violating the freedom and political equality of our fellow citizens. In a society as pluralist as ours, the "politics of telic vision" leads inevitably to coercion.

I propose therefore that the first step in "reclaiming liberalism" should be a deliberate rejection of these unworkable ways of understanding politics. The "politics of war" and the "politics of vision" need to be replaced by an understanding of politics as the means by which free and formally equal citizens in a deeply pluralist society cooperate in "the art of living together." The fundamental political question that should be constantly asked by citizens is not "how can we defeat the other side?" or "how can we get 'them' to do what we want?" but rather, how can "*we*" (all of us) manage to live peacefully together, given our differences, in a way that respects the freedom and formal equality of us all? Politics on this conception resembles neither a war, nor a ship about to chart a course for an exciting destination (whether the destination be conservative or progressive), but rather the ongoing negotiation of a truce between potentially rival factions who, despite their differences, do not wish to fight and have better things to do.

Such a "negotiation of truce" will call on several virtues. It will require political restraint, by which I mean a willingness to stand down when the political goods we are pursuing lack widespread popular support. It will also require a high degree of toleration, because the failure to secure a much-desired policy at the national level does not mean citizens should not try to secure it at a more local level, where pluralism is not as severe and where displeased citizens can exercise their right of "exit" (Hirschman 1970). Toleration of different political cultures and subcultures *within* liberalism will be key to the future of liberalism. Finally, liberalism as the ongoing negotiation of truce will require dispassionate political deliberation, inside and outside the institutions of power, about the best way to balance rival freedoms. Fanaticism and the unwillingness to compromise, the entire language of "absolute rights," and the practice of moral exceptionalism, will need to be recognized as unhelpful. These are characteristics of the politics of vision and the politics of war, but they have no place in a liberalism aimed at peace, freedom, and political equality.

Lastly, a good remedy for the warlike quality of contemporary liberalism and especially for the eudaimonic expectations and subsequent feelings of meaninglessness that attends it is for citizens to place less value on politics itself. To some extent this should happen as a matter of course, when citizens drop their belief that politics is akin to "total war" or that it promises to fulfill some exciting vision of the good. When politics becomes less telic it will simultaneously become less enthralling. Yet the problem of meaningless will remain if something does not come forward to fill the void. In my view, what can fill (and *more* than fill) that void is engagement in social activities where the goods involved are deemed valuable to the participants who freely choose to engage in them. I have in mind such activities as scientific discovery, friendship, artistic creation, religion, sports, technological invention, and, especially, participation in voluntary organizations (even highly telic ones) that aim at fixing or improving some imperfect dimension of our social world. By re-conceiving the very meaning of politics in terms of truce, we create time and space for activities that stand a much better chance of delivering meaning than liberal politics ever could.

## Notes

1. The insight that liberalism is not an independent phenomenon I owe to Voegelin (1974).
2. For an exposition and defense of classical liberalism, see Mises (1927) 2002. For new liberalism, see Hobhouse (1911) 1994.
3. In Mises (1927) 2002, for example, all liberties are subordinate to and instrumentally related to the goal of greater economic productivity.
4. Thinkers such as T. H. Green, L. T. Hobhouse and J. A. Hobson. For a detailed analysis of these thinkers' contribution to the New Liberalism, see Freeden (1986).
5. For a helpful account of some of the earliest uses of "liberal" as a *political* term, see Rosenblatt (2018).
6. Cf. Laski (1936, p. 3): "To the evolution of liberalism have gone contributions of the first importance from men unacquainted with, often hostile to, its aims; from Machiavelli and Calvin, from Luther and Copernicus, from Henry VIII and Thomas More, in one century; from Richelieu and Louis XIV, from Hobbes and Jurieu, from Pascal and Bacon in another."
7. Evidence from Rousseau's *2nd Discourse* and Hobhouse's *Liberalism.*

8. I have learned the most about the history of liberalism from a very fine, if largely forgotten, comparative study—*The History of European Liberalism*—by the Italian Liberal, Guido de Ruggiero, translated into English by the late British Idealist, R. G. Collingwood. Even though De Ruggiero's text carries the history only as far as 1925 (and even though he was notoriously wrong about the future of German liberalism between the wars), it remains an invaluable resource when coupled with other studies that round out the history and bring it up to date.
9. For helpful comments on the pressures that European collectivism put on American liberalism, see Katznelson (2013, p. 5ff).
10. Brad Gregory's well-known book (Gregory 2012) about the unintended consequences of the Reformation focuses for the most part on consequences different from the ones I consider here. We both, however, see a problem with plural conceptions of the good.
11. Bodin's thoughts on toleration come out more fully in his *Colloquium of the Seven about the Secrets of the Sublime*, written in 1588; on which, see Remer (1994).
12. It is frequently remarked that Montesquieu misunderstood and misrepresented English constitutionalism.
13. De Ruggiero (1959, pp. 82–90, and pp. 158–176).
14. For other early uses of the term, see Rosenblatt (2018).
15. This liberal constitution, though short-lived (because Ferdinand reestablished an absolute monarchy in 1814), became a model for several other countries around the world: for the Norwegian Constitution of 1814, the Portuguese Constitution of 1822, and the Mexican Constitution of 1824. On the historical circumstances surrounding the constitution, see Westler (2015).
16. The constitution granted a relative increase in free trade to the Spanish colonies on the American continent.
17. Perhaps one could say this about freedom 5, but scholars have long been divided on the extent to which the Reformation played a role in unleashing economic activity. The classic text is, of course, Weber (1904–05) 2011.
18. On this movement, see Pocock (1975), esp. Part II, "The Republic and Its Fortune: Florentine Political Thought from 1494–1530," pp. 83–330. On English republicanism during the Commonwealth period, see Skinner (1998).

19. Marchamont Nedham, *The Excellencie of a Free-State* (1656), James Harrington, *The Commonwealth of Oceana* (1656), John Milton, *The Readie & Easie Way to Establish a Free Commonwealth, and the Excellence Therof Compar'd with the Inconveniences and Dangers of Readmitting Kingship in this Nation* (2nd ed., 1660).
20. Ibid. Skinner's locution, "neo-roman *and* republican writings," is crucial for understanding the difference between my freedoms 4 and 6. In his earlier writings, Skinner used the term "republican" to refer to writers who defended the classical idea of the *civitas libera* or free state. However, some of these writers, it turns out, were perfectly content to live under a constitutional monarchy. It was not "republicanism" they wanted, but strong limits upon monarchical power. In light of this, Skinner has switched his term to "neo-roman," rather than "republican" writers. However, the difference between the two groups is quite significant for my argument concerning the nine freedoms.
21. See especially Rousseau (1762) 1978, chapter 4, "On Slavery." Rousseau stands in sharp contrast to Voltaire in this respect. The latter was a constitutional monarchist. See Laski (1936, p. 238 ff)., for an argument that Voltaire, Diderot, and Helvétius all fall short of what I call freedom 6.
22. Earlier in this essay I remarked that the use of the term "liberal" to describe later phases of the modern quest for freedom occurred "for reasons partly principled, partly expedient." I have tried to emphasize the principled case here. The case for expedience is expertly laid out by Gottfried (1999, pp. 3–29).
23. An overstatement to be sure. Compare the more qualified position of Galston (2003), who refers to this kind of freedom as "expressive liberty."
24. This is an important aspect of John Rawls's political theory. See, for example, Rawls (2001, pp. 74–75): "Do people really think that they (morally) deserved to be born more gifted than others? Do they think they (morally) deserved to be born a man rather than a woman, or vice versa? Do they think that they deserved to be born into a wealthier rather than into a poorer family?" Rawls tried to address this problem of desert through his "difference principle."
25. On the eugenics movement and its connection to liberal progressivism, see Freeden (2005, pp. 144–172). Freeden's analysis shows that some, but not all, eugenicists understood themselves more in terms of my freedom 7 than freedom 9. They wanted to use eugenics as a tool for social reform.

## References

Acton, John Emerich Edward Dalberg. 1907. The Protestant Theory of Persecution. In: *The History of Freedom and Other Essays*, pp. 150–187. London: Macmillan.

Berlin, Isaiah. 1969. Two Concepts of Liberty. In: *Four Essays on Liberty*, pp. 118–172. Oxford: Oxford University Press.

Bostrom, Nick and Julian Savulescu. 2009. *Human Enhancement*. Oxford: Oxford University Press.

Clodfelter, Michael. 2017. *Warfare and Armed Conflicts: A Statistical Encyclopedia of Casualty and Other Figures, 1492–2015*. Jefferson, NC: McFarland.

Constant, Benjamin. (1819) 1988. The Liberty of the Ancients Compared with that of the Moderns. In: *Constant: Political Writings*, ed. Biancamaria Fontana, pp. 309–328. Cambridge: Cambridge University Press.

De Ruggiero, Guido. 1959. *The History of European Liberalism*, trans. R. G. Collingwood. Boston: Beacon Press.

Deneen, Patrick. 2018. *Why Liberalism Failed*. New Haven: Yale University Press.

Devletoglou, Nicos E. 1963. Montesquieu and the Wealth of Nations. *Canadian Journal of Economics and Political Science* 29 (1): 1–25.

Dewey, John. (1935) 2000. *Liberalism and Social Action*. Amherst: Prometheus Books.

Freeden, Michael. 1986. *The New Liberalism: An Ideology of Social Reform*. Oxford: Oxford University Press.

_____. 1996. *Ideologies and Political Theory*. Oxford: Oxford University Press.

_____. 2005. *Liberal Languages: Ideological Imaginations and Twentieth-Century Progressive Thought*. Princeton: Princeton University Press.

Gallie, W. B. 1955–6. Essentially Contested Concepts. *Proceedings of the Aristotelian Society* 56: 167–98.

Galston, William A. 2003. Expressive Liberty and Constitutional Democracy: The Case of Freedom of Conscience. *American Journal of Jurisprudence* 48: 149–177.

Glendon, Mary Ann. 1991. *Rights Talk: The Impoverishment of Political Discourse*. New York: Free Press.

Gottfried, Paul Edward. 1999. *After Liberalism: Mass Democracy in the Managerial State*. Princeton: Princeton University Press.

Gray, John. 2000. *The Two Faces of Liberalism*. New York: New Press.

Gregory, Brad S. 2012. *The Unintended Reformation: How A Religious Revolution Secularized Society*. Cambridge, MA: Belknap Press.

Hirschman, Albert O. 1970. *Exit, Voice, and Loyalty: Responses to Decline in Firms, Organizations, and States*. Cambridge, MA: Harvard University Press.

Hobhouse, Leonard Trelawny. (1911) 1994. *Liberalism*. In: *Hobhouse: Liberalism and Other Writings*, ed. James Meadowcroft, pp. 1–120. Cambridge: Cambridge University Press.

Holton, Sandra. 2002. John Bright, Radical Politics, and the Ethos of Quakerism. *Albion: A Quarterly Journal Concerned with British Studies* 34 (4): 584–605.

Huxley, Julian. 1957. Transhumanism. In: *New Bottles for New Wine: Essays by Julian Huxley*. London: Chatto & Windus.

Kaplan, Benjamin J. 2007. *Divided by Faith: Religious Conflict and the Practice of Toleration in Early Modern Europe*. Cambridge, MA: Harvard University Press.

Katznelson, Ira. 2013. *Fear Itself: The New Deal and the Origins of Our Time*. New York: W. W. Norton.

Kraynak, Robert P. 1980. John Locke: From Absolutism to Toleration. *American Political Science Review* 74 (1): 53–69.

Laski, Harold J. 1936. *The Rise of Liberalism: The Philosophy of a Business Civilization*. New York: Harper & Brothers.

Lawler, Peter. 2005. *Stuck with Virtue: The American Individual and Our Biological Future*. Wilmington: ISI Books.

Lilla, Mark. 2017. *The Once and Future Liberal: After Identity Politics*. New York: Harper Collins.

Lowi, Theodore J. 1969. *The End of Liberalism: Ideology, Policy, and the Crisis of Public Authority*. New York: Norton.

Machiavelli, Niccolò. 1985. *The Prince*, trans. Harvey Mansfield, Jr. Chicago: University of Chicago Press.

Mill, John Stuart. (1859) 2002. On Liberty. In: *J.S. Mill, On Liberty and Other Writings*, ed. Stefan Collini. Cambridge: Cambridge University Press.

Mises, Ludwig Von. (1927) 2005. *Liberalism*. Indianapolis: Liberty Fund Press.

Ozment, Stephen. 2003. Martin Luther on Religious Liberty. In: *Religious Liberty in Western Thought*, eds. Noel B. Reynolds and W. Cole Durham, Jr, pp. 75–82. Grand Rapids: Eerdmans.

Pocock, J. G. A. 1975. *The Machiavellian Moment: Florentine Political Thought and the Atlantic Republican Tradition*. Princeton: Princeton University Press.

Rawls, John. 1971. *A Theory of Justice*. Cambridge, MA: Belknap Press.

_____. 1993. *Political Liberalism*. New York: Columbia University Press.

_____. 2001. *Justice as Fairness: A Restatement*, ed. Erin Kelly. Cambridge, MA: Belknap Press.

Remer, Gary. 1994. Dialogues of Toleration: Erasmus and Bodin. *Review of Politics* 56 (2): 305–336.

Rosenblatt, Helena. 2018. *The Lost History of Liberalism: From Ancient Rome to the Twenty-first Century*. Princeton: Princeton University Press.
Rousseau, Jean Jacques. (1762) 1978. On the Social Contract. In: *On the Social Contract: with Geneva Manuscript and Political Economy*, trans. Judith Masters, ed. Roger Masters. New York: St. Martin's Press.
Skinner, Quentin. 1998. *Liberty before Liberalism*. Cambridge: Cambridge University Press.
Voegelin, Eric. 1974. Liberalism and Its History, trans. Mary Algozin and Keith Algozin. *Review of Politics* 36 (4): 504–520.
Weber, Max. (1904–05) 2011. *The Protestant Ethic and the Spirit of Capitalism*, trans. Stephen Kalberg. Oxford: Oxford University Press.
Westler, Brandon. 2015. Between Tradition and Revolution: The Curious Case of Francisco Martínez Marina, the Cádiz Constitution, and Spanish Liberalism. *Journal of the History of Ideas* 76 (3): 393–416.
Wolfe, Alan. 2010. *The Future of Liberalism*. New York: Vintage Books.
Wolffe, John. 2005. Lord Palmerston and Religion: A Reappraisal. *English Historical Review* 120 (488): 907–936.

# Liberalism for the Twenty-First Century: From Markets to Civil Society, from Economics to Human Beings

Gus diZerega

While liberalism has no single founder, its core values can be reduced to two: the individual is society's fundamental moral unit, and all individuals are equally so. Early liberal thought consisted of two major streams, the earliest was rooted in Lockean individualism, and the second arose independently, beginning during the Scottish Enlightenment. To contrast it with the individualist tradition in all its forms, I will term it "evolutionary liberalism." No single figure or work is as central to it as John Locke, and its pattern of development has been quite different. Rather than being a primarily philosophical or theological doctrine applied to social reality, it resembles an ongoing scientific research program, developing and elaborating over the years, even into the present time.

The Lockean tradition emphasized individuals as independent units, whereas the evolutionary tradition emphasized individuals as inextricably rooted within their societies. To put the point most simply, Lockean individualism held the social whole was the sum of the actions of the individuals who composed its parts. Lockean ethics were prior to the actual

G. diZerega (✉)
Independent Scholar, Taos, NM, USA



D. F. Hardwick, L. Marsh (eds.), *Reclaiming Liberalism*, Palgrave Studies in Classical Liberalism, https://doi.org/10.1007/978-3-030-28760-3_6

circumstances of human life. The evolutionary alternative argued the whole is more than the sum of its parts because the nature of the parts was intimately entwined with the social whole to which they both contributed and were shaped. Its ethical foundation emerged from the logic of social relationships rather than transcendent rules.

## The Individualist Tradition

John Locke's defense of individual rights, private property, and of making government subordinate to the people, reflected his times. Rights came from God, property was originally held by all in common as God's gift, but could be privatized by mixing labor with unowned property, so long as "as much and as good" remained for others. This normally happened because private property was more productive than common property. Locke wrote when agriculture dominated England, and, ideally, each person could own a small farm, providing independence from arbitrary authority. What authority that was needed could arise from a common commitment to general rules ending the "inconveniences" of a stateless world.

Today, hardly anyone would describe themselves as a Lockean in this sense. But much ink has been spilled and considerable thought devoted to developing an alternative to Locke's God for establishing a strong theory of individual rights. Among those associated with classical liberal and libertarian traditions Robert Nozick is a recent exemplar (Nozick 2001). From a more activist approach to government as enforcer of rights, one could mention the work of John Rawls (1999). There are many others.

## An Evolutionary Tradition

Along with Enlightenment thinkers in general, men of the Scottish Enlightenment rejected viewing social order reflecting the will of God. But unlike most other Enlightenment thinkers, they were equally skeptical of reason's ability to play a Godly role in improving social conditions. Consequently, they rejected social contract theory, whether in its liberal Lockean form, or the illiberal arguments of Hobbes and Rousseau.

Men like David Hume, Adam Ferguson, Adam Smith and others argued social order arose through piecemeal change by independent actors. Over time coherent customs and mores developed and survived without anyone's deliberate intention to create them. Evolutionary processes created unanticipated cultural patterns which might perform important social functions not immediately obvious to onlookers. In developing this perspective, the Scotts constructed a profound critique of the Enlightenment's over-confident rationalism.

Pursued in one direction, this mistrust of rationalism and appreciation for the role of spontaneously arisen social institutions became a foundation for conservative thought rooted in Edmund Burke. Don't mess with what is not obviously broken, because it is probably linked with the rest of society in ways we do not understand. While there was truth in this insight, as F. A. Hayek noted, its weakness was that "by its very nature it cannot offer an alternative to the direction in which we are moving (Hayek 1960, p. 398)."

But this evolutionary approach also had profoundly liberal implications, because the adaptive process it identified was most effective when people were free to act independently within a framework of basic procedural rules applying to all equally. With appropriate rules, distributed knowledge circulating within a network of relationships was more effective at handling complexity than top down direction. This insight provided a powerful support for the liberal ideal of individual equality under the law *without* requiring a strong theory of rights.

If we think of Lockean liberalism as encouraging people to *construct* a liberal order, the Scottish approach encouraged them to cu*ltivate* it. In place of a mechanistic approach rooted in a Newtonian outlook, they offered what we would now call an ecological one.

## Liberalism, Evolution, and Darwin

Two important continental liberals, Alexander and Wilhelm von Humboldt, played an important role in the further development of evolutionary liberalism. Wilhelm was a major German liberal theorist, and his brother, Alexander, arguably the best-known scientist of his time, as well as a friend and confidant of Thomas Jefferson.

Wilhelm shared with the Scottish Enlightenment an interest in how language developed independently of human intent, but focused on how different languages shaped the cultures and people within them (Burrow 1969, pp. xxvi–xxix). In a genuine and connected sense he was also a theorist of civil society, "[f]or the State constitution and the national community, however closely they may be interwoven, should not be confused" (Humboldt 1969, p. 131).

His brother, Alexander, applied similar insights to the natural world. Nature flourished best when organisms were able to develop in spontaneous relationship with their environment, Nature, he argued, was a web of relationships, for "[e]verything is interaction and reciprocal" (Wulf 2016, p. 103). In a comment applying Hayekian style logic to the natural world, his studies in South America, particularly of Lake Valencia and its immediate environment in what is now Venezuela, were perhaps the first modern ones emphasizing how short-sighted actions, focused only on production for profit, destroyed the foundations of long-term prosperity (Wulf 2016, pp. 63–67).[1] For Alexander Humboldt, nature gives us an image of why freedom is good because of the diversity and richness that arises when each organism is free to seek its survival.

Charles Darwin helped bring the Scottish insights together with those of the Humboldts (Richards and Ruse 2016, pp. 154, 191–93).[2] Darwin was a great admirer of Alexander as well as strongly influenced by insights in the Scottish Enlightenment. While not himself a political theorist, Darwin viewed his political views as in harmony with his scientific work. And they were consistently liberal. Darwin's personal politics were firmly in the liberal tradition. He supported the Liberal Party and its liberal policies, and was active in the international campaign against slavery. In fact, his hatred of slavery was one motivation for writing *The Descent of Man*, in which he emphasized humanity belonged to one species (Desmond and Moore 2009).

In *The Descent of Man*, Darwin showed that the moral order of human life arose through a natural moral sense as shaped by organic and cultural evolution. But this moral order did not confine itself to human beings, for there was, he argued, an intellectual and emotional continuity between humans and animals, and some animals possessed qualities akin to conscience. Recent research strongly supports Darwin, even though mainstream science, enraptured by Descartes separating mind from matter, and limiting it only to people, largely ignored his arguments for 150 years (Bekoff and Pierce 2009).

Along with opposition to slavery, another cause with which he was publicly associated was opposing the widespread use of vivisection. "You ask about my opinion on vivisection. I quite agree that it is justifiable for real investigations on physiology; but not for mere damnable and detestable curiosity. It is a subject which makes me sick with horror, so I will not say another word about it, else I shall not sleep to-night."[3]

Darwin united the moral insights arising from the Scottish Enlightenment, the Humboldtian integration of individuals and their social environment, and modern biology. The moral and intellectual virtues arose through the undirected evolution of human nature and human culture, and needed no philosophical or theological explanation (Arnhart 2010). The justification for rights was in the human flourishing they facilitated.

These various threads created the foundation for a liberalism rooted in our networks of reciprocal social and biological relationships rather than in philosophical or religious individualism. The critical shift was that individuals flourished and were freest in a society that enriched their capacities rather than simply respecting their rights.

## The Nature of Social Action

Market liberals Peter Boettke and Edward Lopez have argued Austrian economics and public choice theory comprise the two most prominent economic liberal perspectives, both rooted in "methodological individualism," which they contrast to "holism (Boettke and Lopez 2002, pp. 111–119)." They include Hayek in this group. But Hayek had long left methodological individualism behind for a more insightful approach incorporating central insights from the evolutionary tradition (Hayek 1978).[4] These connections become clear when we explore the paradox of social action.

Social scientists have long argued whether society is a human creation, compatible with methodological individualism, or humans are social products, and so are best analyzed from a more collectivist perspective. Boettke and Lopez repeat this old dichotomy. To my mind each side has made excellent criticisms of the other without convincingly defending its own position.

Peter Berger and Thomas Luckmann found a solution to this interminable debate, though in doing so they penetrated more deeply than they imagined. Berger and Luckmann argued both individualist and holistic views each caught a part of the truth, but both ultimately missed the mark. A third insight needed to be incorporated: society is an objective reality (Berger and Luckmann 1966, p. 50).

This third point enabled scientists to incorporate time and generations into understanding the social world. The young child confronts all sorts of socially mediated concepts as objective realities, and no one is able to extricate themselves completely from the mental framework that thereby arises. Parts can be questioned from within the context of the whole, but never free from all such contexts.

While Berger and Luckmann thought their analysis was ultimately compatible with methodological individualism, Paul Lewis demonstrated they accomplished a more radical transformation of our social understanding than that. Social traits are not ultimately reducible to individual actions because those actions imply pre-existing social traits. As Lewis put it, society is an emergent phenomenon and "emergence refers to the possibility that, when certain elements or parts stand in particular relations to one another, the whole that is formed has properties (including causal powers …) that are not possessed by its constituent elements taken in isolation" (Lewis 2010, p. 210).

For his part Hayek argued that even the characteristics most associated with human beings, such as our rationality, had emerged from societies where customs had arisen as the preservation of successful habits. The human mind, he wrote, "can exist only as part of another independently existing distinct structure or order, though that order persists and can develop only because millions of minds constantly absorb and modify parts of it (Hayek 1979, p. 157. See also Noë 2009, pp. 117–21 and passim)." Importantly, no individual mind absorbs it all.

Correctly understood, Berger and Luckman's model harmonized with Hayek's approach. Methodological individualism was replaced with a more nuanced view that embraced generational change, since individuals did not emerge fully formed. The old dispute of individualism or holism in some form was essentially a chicken and egg one. But both chickens and eggs developed in an evolutionary way from foundations that were neither chickens nor eggs. So did human beings and societies.

In their different ways, what Berger, Luckmann, and Hayek described is an evolutionary ecological perspective applied to culture rather than biological organisms. It integrates the Scottish, and Humboldtian, foundations of liberalism with modern biology. Biologist Gerrat Vermeij captures this insight with his observation, "Adaptation in general is the formation, and continual testing, of hypotheses about the environment" (Vermeij 2004, p. 55). Be they innovative products, new life styles, scientific hunches, political proposals, or new species, all are kinds of hypotheses subject to evaluation within the systemic contexts on which they depend for resources. Successful hypotheses flourish, failures vanish.

The case for freedom is because independent decision-making among equals within a framework generating both positive and negative feedback creates a richer environment within which people can better flourish than any alternative approach. Individual rights are justified to the degree they contribute to this outcome.

This move from right-holding individuals contracting with one another to individuals in complex relationships with other individuals, in which their very individuality as human beings arises from these relationships is in remarkable harmony with what is happening to the concept of biological and psychological individuality in biology today.

## The Biology of Community

When Lynn Margulis demonstrated the cells which make up our bodies are symbiotic combinations of organisms that once lived separately and still to some degree retain their own existence, few at the time imagined its larger implications (Margulis 1970). Evolution had always been dominated by the image of distinct organisms struggling to survive, and Margulis emphasized symbiosis was as important as competition. Conceivably more so. But no one then realized how important.

Since then, biologists have discovered that organisms *at every level* are emergent outcomes of symbiotic relations with other organisms existing at less complex levels. From individual cells to superorganisms, individuality exists as an emergent outcome of a particular level of complexity that may itself contribute to a still more complex individuality at a more inclusive level.[5] In the biological world this pattern continues beyond traditional individuals. Plant communities are linked by mycorrhizal webs enabling different organisms not only to communicate with one another, but even to provide others with nutrients when needed, even if they are of different species (Frazer 2015). Over and over scientists are discovering what were long treated as distinct organism have fuzzy boundaries and their individuality is an emergent quality. Ecosystems in fact differ from organisms in the degree of focused connection rather than the simple presence or absence of systemic agency involved. An entity has a center of action, but even this is a continuum. From its most simple to its most complex, emergent and self-organizing patterns pervade nature.

This observation holds true even for human beings (Kolata 2012). Nor is it entirely a biological phenomenon. It is also psychological.

Increasingly scientists are discovering the psychological results of different organisms coming together in a symbiotic relationship. The bacteria in our guts have been found to have significant impacts on our states of psychological well-being (O'Donnell 2015; Schmidt 2015). More recently scientists have discovered varieties of these bacteria in our brains, making more certain the linkage being discovered (Kohn 2015). But apparently these discoveries are only scratching the surface.

When mice raised in completely sterile environments are exposed to bacteria common in soil, along with other evidence of improved psychological well-being, they run mazes 15% faster. When the bacteria were then eliminated, the mice's performance drops to its previous level. Mouse + bacteria is apparently more intelligent than either alone. It is impossible to conduct such experiments ethically on human beings, but these findings raise a question about the relationships between our genetic individuality and our psychological individuality. Another even more recent finding suggests this relationship is not what we have assumed.

Toxoplasmosis is a parasitic infection by an organism that infects mice and cats sequentially to complete its normal life cycle. But mice are not attracted to cats for good reasons. However, infected mice act differently from uninfected ones. They are bolder and attracted to the smell of cat urine, but as with mountain climbers, there are no old, bold, mice. What is good for *Toxoplasma gondii* is fatal to mice.

*Toxoplasma gondii* infects people as well, but except for pregnant women and their fetuses, was long believed to have no significant impact. No longer. Evidence is now accumulating that toxoplasma also significantly influences human behavior (Flegr et al. 1996, pp. 49–54; Flegr 2013, pp. 127–133; 2007). It turns out that infected business students are more likely to focus on entrepreneurship than are uninfected ones, and that business students in general are more likely to be infected than students as a whole (Johnson et al. 2018). But what might be a mind-controlling parasite in mice is arguably a blessing for many infected people. Their collective mind of human + *Toxoplasma* apparently has capabilities lacking in either alone, such as greater tolerance for risk taking. In fact, *Toxoplasma* might even be able to influence the development of entire cultures by influencing qualities such as risk averseness.[6] Real as it certainly is, even our psychological individuality, apparently arises at least in part from relationships between different organisms.

Individuality, even apparently our own, is an emergent outcome of relationships between organisms that, when they come together, exhibit traits lacking in their component elements. *At every level* individuality appears to be an emergent process best understood in ecological and evolutionary terms.[7] The Lockean individualist tradition reflects Protestant theology and secular attempts to replicate it on rights, not science.

## The Cultural Ecosystem of Freedom

Just as a biological ecosystem arises out of networks of many different organisms, so a cultural ecosystem arises out of relations between many different organisms within its system. The evolutionary tradition's consistent interest in language, which largely links these networks, is therefore fundamental to any theory of evolutionary liberalism. At one level we see this with the concept of civil society. Rather than being a spontaneous order in Hayek's sense, civil society arises out of a number of spontaneous orders, none dominant, along with the individual plans and organizations created to further those plans (diZerega 2014).

What else might be there? Let us look again at the larger system Hayek describes where mind can arise, or what Berger and Luckmann call society as an objective reality.

In recent years some evolutionary biologists have become fascinated with the concept of a meme. First coined by Richard Dawkins, a meme is a kind of cultural gene, or in other terms, an idea or practice in its social context (Dawkins, 1989). While other cultural "bodies" can also develop a degree of individuality distinct from human beings and their intentions, I will focus here on memes (diZerega 2015).

Immersed as they are in language, cultural ecosystems exist primarily within the realm of memes. In Berger and Luckmann's terms, memes are what they describe as society as an objective reality. In Hayek's, they are a major element of what he called the larger context within which a human mind existed. Cultures are ecosystems of at least people and memes, which often take on an identity distinct from the people who comprise them.

Language changes the actions of their speakers while developing in ways not subject to individual control, and they are populated and shaped by memes. Consequently, they demonstrate qualities methodological individualism cannot adequately describe, though perspectives such as Hayek's and Berger and Luckmann's easily can.[8]

Methodological individualism encourages the false view that since society arises from individual action, economics and theories of rational choice give us an understanding of a free world. But this view is wrong.

If societies are ecosystems that shape as well as are shaped by individuals, the Scottish-Humboldtian-Hayekian emphasis on flourishing for all as the standard for a good society is more accurate. For individual flourishing to be maximized, individual freedom is a central requirement, not just abstractly, but as freedom to make as many positive choices as possible. Civil society, the network of free men and women engaged in many different spontaneous orders as well as smaller more focused networks is the image of human well-being.

Thus, the same focus on individuals as equal moral units emerges not as a gift from God or derived from abstract philosophies blind to context, but as a part of the logic of human flourishing.

## The Superiority of Evolutionary over Individualist Liberalism

Some readers might worry that a liberalism that relegates ideas about rights to a subordinate status imperils freedom. The evidence does not support this view.

It is interesting to reflect that Alexander Humboldt was a stronger defender of liberal values than were the Lockeans of his time. Unlike his friend Jefferson's ambiguities, he strongly opposed all slavery, treating Indians badly, and imperialism, even by America. The ultimate problem was not Jefferson, but the way he conceived of rights.

John Locke's famous argument for religious toleration played a constructive role in the rise of English liberty, but he drew the line with atheists. They could not be tolerated because they could not be relied upon to act morally. We know this view is not backed by experience.

More recently, Robert Nozick, another strong proponent of individual rights, supported slavery so long as someone entered it "voluntarily" (Nozick 2001, pp. 290–292). Nozick never inquired about what might lead someone to enter into such a contract, or what "owning" another might do to the owner. When one has the right to contract away everything, and context does not matter, it is not hard to imagine horrible oppressions arising in the name of respecting individual rights.

Another advocate of absolute individual rights, Murray Rothbard, rebutted Nozick. But he also argued parents could not be forced to feed their children, even if that meant their children died. Their rights came first (Rothbard 2002).

The problem with rights theories is they elevate rights *above* human beings. Rights exist at some abstract eternal level, be it God or Reason or something else, whereas human beings are always immersed in the contexts and relationships that decisively shape their lives. To paraphrase a famous comment Jesus allegedly said about the Sabbath: the evolutionary liberal argument is that rights were made for people, not people for rights (diZerega 1996).

Hume, Humboldt, Darwin, and Hayek, all derived their views from examining societies, human, and natural alike. The logic of the Scottish Enlightenment's arguments supported liberalism as particularly suited for bringing out the best within self-organizing processes. Wilhelm Humboldt argued for the role of civil society as the context within which freedom flowered. Alexander Humboldt argued liberal principles were in keeping with natural ones, that freedom enabled organisms to take advantage of opportunities around them, and that the best society was the one that enabled its members to best take advantage of such opportunities. Here he unified biology with the study of human well-being. Darwin deepened and broadened this argument, and in his own life exemplified it regarding slavery and vivisection. Hayek located the rise of freedom from within the superiority of free societies in relation to those less free. Throughout, the value of freedom moved from supporting abstract rights separate from society to creating a flourishing society good for all by maximizing opportunities for well-being. In the process, the evolutionary liberal tradition proved a better defender of what we consider human rights than any doctrine of abstract rights itself.

There is also a serious theoretical problem that explains these failures of right theories to really protect human beings. Because they treat individuals as separate from and ultimately independent of society, for each individual, freedom is freedom to choose. As many market liberals say, the science of choice is the science of freedom. If the market is "free," individuals are free. For some, selling oneself into slavery is freedom. For others letting your kids starve is the legitimate exercise of freedom. The error is connected with their adherence to methodological individualism.

But the market is one of a number of spontaneous orders arising from human choice, and these other orders privilege different values than does market exchange, which is weighted in favor of instrumental values. A free society is open to the wide range of peaceful human values, and not just those adequately encompassed by instrumental reasoning. Thus, civil society is the realm of freedom, and the market contributes to this freedom only so long as it is subordinated to this more inclusive network. Many of the problems attributed to capitalism arise from its encompassing ever larger realms of civil society and subordinating them to market values alone.

Rethinking contemporary liberalism as rooted within the traditions of the Scottish Enlightenment, German liberalism as developed by the Humboldts, Darwin's integration, and Hayek's later work, frees it from the worst problems inherited from Lockean individualistic traditions and, in the process, brings it into harmony with what we know of the rest of life. At a time when many of the world's most serious problems arise from the separation of the human world and its short-term power from the natural world and its long-term power, this foundation for liberalism is badly needed for any effective defense of freedom or long-term well-being.

## Notes

1. But Plato wrote about the problem much earlier. See *Critias* http://classics.mit.edu/Plato/critias.html
2. Informed historians who disagree on the proportional impact of each do not disagree that in both cases it was substantial.
3. Darwin letter to E. R. Lankester, *Correspondence* vol. 19, March 22, 1871. https://www.darwinproject.ac.uk/letter/DCP-LETT-7612.xml. See also Darwin and Vivisection, *The Darwin Correspondence Project,* University of Cambridge, https://www.darwinproject.ac.uk/commentary/life-sciences/darwin-and-vivisection
4. See also Caldwell (2004, p. 419), who argues the term methodological individualism "is no longer helpful and should be banished from the vocabulary, at least of those who would describe Hayek's ideas."
5. On super organisms, see in particular Wilson, 2012.
6. See *Medical News* 2006.
7. See Margulis 1992, pp. 57–66 and Gurrero 1991, pp. 50–67.
8. For more on memes see Dawkins 1989. p. 192; Dennett 2017, pp. 205–247; Pagel 2012. p. 135; and Gleick, 2011.

## References

Arnhart, L. 2010. Darwinian Liberalism. *Cato Unbound,* July 12. https://www.cato-unbound.org/2010/07/12/larry-arnhart/darwinian-liberalism

Bekoff, M. and J. Pierce. 2009. *Wild Justice: The Moral Lives of Animals.* Chicago: University of Chicago Press.

Berger P. L. and T. Luckmann. 1966. *The Social Construction of Reality: A Treatise on the Sociology of Knowledge.* New York: Knopf Doubleday.
Boettke, P. J. and E. J. Lopez. 2002. Austrian Economics and Public Choice. *The Review of Austrian Economics*, 15:2/3: 111–119.
Burrow, J. W. 1969. Introduction, Wilhelm von Humboldt, *The Limits of State Action*, W. Burrow, ed. Cambridge: Cambridge University Press 1969.
Caldwell, B. 2004. *Hayek's Challenge: An Intellectual Biography of F. A. Hayek.* Chicago: University of Chicago Press.
Can bacteria make you smarter? 2010. *Science Daily*. May 25. http://www.sciencedaily.com/releases/2010/05/100524143416.htm
Dawkins, R. 1989. *The Selfish Gene* (2 ed.). Oxford: Oxford University Press.
Dennett, D. C. 2017. *From Bacteria to Bach and Back: The Evolution of Minds.* New York: W. W. Norton.
Desmond, A. and J. Moore. 2009. *Darwin's Sacred Cause.* New York: Houghton Mifflin.
diZerega, G. 1996. Deep Ecology and Liberalism: The Greener Implications of Evolutionary Liberalism. *Review of Politics*, 58:4, Fall.
———. 2014. Paradoxes of Freedom: Civil Society, the Market, and Capitalism. *Cosmos and Taxis*, vol. 2, no. 1. https://cosmosandtaxis.files.wordpress.com/2014/12/g_dizerega.pdf
———. 2015. Not Simply Construction: Exploring the Darker Side of Taxis. *Cosmos and Taxis*, vol. 3, no. 1, 2015. https://cosmosandtaxis.files.wordpress.com/2018/03/dizerega_ct_vol5_iss3_4.pdf
Flegr, J. 2007. Effects of toxoplasma on human behavior. *PubMed.* May 33(3):757–60. http://www.ncbi.nlm.nih.gov/pubmed/17218612
———. 2013. Influence of latent *Toxoplasma* infection on human personality, physiology and morphology: pros and cons of the *Toxoplasma*–human model in studying the manipulation hypothesis. *The Journal of Experimental Biology*. 1/1/2013. 216: 127–133. http://jeb.biologists.org/content/216/1/127.full
Flegr, J., Ztkovai, S., Kodym, P., and Frynta, D. 1996. Induction of changes in human behavior by the parasitic protozoan Toxoplasma gondii. *Parasitology*, Jul., 113 (Pt 1):49–54. http://www.ncbi.nlm.nih.gov/pubmed/8710414
Frazer, J. 2015. Dying Trees Can Send Food to Neighbors of Different Species. *Scientific American*, May 9. https://blogs.scientificamerican.com/artful-amoeba/dying-trees-can-send-food-to-neighbors-of-different-species/
Gleick, J. 2011. What Defines a Meme? *Smithsonian Magazine*. May. https://www.smithsonianmag.com/arts-culture/what-defines-a-meme-1904778/
Gurrero, R. 1991. Two Plus Three Equals One: Individuals Emerge from Bacterial Communities. In: William Irwin Thompson, ed., *Gaia 2: Emergence: The New Science of Becoming*. Pp. 50–67. New York: Lindesfarne Press.

Hayek, F. A. 1960. *The Constitution of Liberty*. Chicago: Henry Regnery.
———. 1978. Coping with Ignorance. *Imprimis*, July.
———. 1979. *Law, Legislation and Liberty*, III. Chicago: University of Chicago Press.
How common 'cat parasite' gets into human brain and influences human behavior. 2012. *Science Daily*. http://www.sciencedaily.com/releases/2012/12/121206203240.htm
Humboldt, W von. 1969. *The Limits of State Action*, W. Burrow, ed. Cambridge: Cambridge University Press.
Johnson, S. K. et al. 2018. Risky business: linking *Toxoplasma gondii* infection and entrepreneurship behaviours across individuals and countries. *Proceedings of the Royal Society B: Biological Sciences*, July 25. http://rspb.royalsocietypublishing.org/content/285/1883/20180822
Kohn, D. 2015. When Gut Bacteria Change Brain Function. *The Atlantic* June 24. https://getpocket.com/explore/item/when-gut-bacteria-change-brain-function
Kolata, G. 2012. In Good Health? Thank Your 100 Trillion Bacteria. *New York Times* June 13. http://www.nytimes.com/2012/06/14/health/human-microbiome-project-decodes-our-100-trillion-good bacteria.html?pagewanted=all&_r=2&
Lewis, P. 2010. Peter Berger and His Critics: The Significance of Emergence. *Society* 47:207–13.
Margulis, L. 1970. *Origin of eukaryotic cells*. New Haven: Yale University Press.
———. 1992. Microcosmos. In: C. Barlow ed., *From Gaia to Selfish Genes: Selected Writings in the Life Sciences*, pp. 57–66. Cambridge, MA: MIT Press.
Medical News 2006. Toxoplasma may be affecting human behavior on a mass scale, August 3. https://www.news-medical.net/news/2006/08/03/19237.aspx
Noë, A. 2009. *Out of Our Heads: Why You Are Not Your Brain, and Other Lessons from the Biology of Consciousness*. New York: Hill and Wang.
Nozick, R. 2001. *Anarchy, State, and Utopia*. Hoboken: Wiley-Blackwell.
O'Donnell, E. 2015. Cryan Explains Gut Feelings, Thoughts and Behaviors. *NIH Record*, vol. LXVII, number 5. Dec. 4.
Pagel, M. 2012. *Wired for Culture: Origins of the Human Social Mind*. New York: Norton.
Rawls, J. 1999. *A Theory of Justice*. Cambridge, MA: Belknap Press.
Richards, R. J. and M. Ruse 2016. *Debating Darwin*. Chicago: University of Chicago.
Rothbard, M. N. 2002. *The Ethics of Liberty*. New York: New York University Press. https://mises.org/library/children-and-rights

Schmidt, C. 2015. Mental Health May Depend on Creatures in the Gut. *Scientific American*, March 1. https://www.scientificamerican.com/article/mental-health-may-depend-on-creatures-in-the-gut/ https://nihrecord.nih.gov/newsletters/2015/12_04_2015/story3.htm

Toxoplasma may be affecting human behavior on a mass scale. *MedicalNews*, August 3, 2006. http://www.newsmedical.net/news/2006/08/03/19237.aspx

Vermeij, G. 2004. *Nature: An Economic History*. Princeton: Princeton University Press.

Wilson, E. O. 2012. *The Social Conquest of the Earth*. New York: W. W. Norton.

Wulf, A. 2016. *The Invention of Nature: Alexander von Humboldt's New World*. New York: Vintage.

# Origins of the Rule of Law

Andrew David Irvine

## Introduction

Central to the idea of the rule of law is the requirement that even governments must be bound by law.[1] Under the rule of law, even those who have the ability to make and change the law remain subject to it. Even those who have the power to interpret and enforce the law remain governed by it. It is this feature of law, as much as the ballot box or the free press, that protects the ordinary citizen from arbitrary state power.[2]

Understood in this way, the rule of law is more than just the requirement that governments must act *according* to the law. Should a law be passed that gave a government the power to act whenever and however it wanted, such a government would not be *bound* by law. To be genuine, rule of law must place substantial, non-trivial constraints on the use of state power, just as it does with ordinary citizens. It requires not only that

A. D. Irvine (✉)
Department of Economics, Philosophy and Political Science, The University of British Columbia, Okanagan, Kelowna, BC, Canada
e-mail: andrew.irvine@ubc.ca



D. F. Hardwick, L. Marsh (eds.), *Reclaiming Liberalism*, Palgrave Studies in Classical Liberalism, https://doi.org/10.1007/978-3-030-28760-3_7

government authority be exercised in accordance with publicly disclosed and appropriately adopted procedures.[3] It also requires that genuine prohibitions exist against at least some types of state action. It is in this sense that rule *of* law differs from rule *by* law or rule *through* law.

Simply put, rule of law requires not just that all government actions find their source in law. It also requires governments to acknowledge the difference between powers granted to them in law and powers they do not have.

In 2006 in *Hamdan v. Rumsfeld*, the US Supreme Court struck down the use of military commissions established for the purpose of trying suspected terrorists at the US Navy base in Guantanamo Bay, Cuba. It was the court's conclusion that without congressional authorization the government of the day lacked the authority to initiate such trials. Even though Mr. Hamdan had confessed to working closely with Osama bin Laden, the court ruled that, "in undertaking to try Hamdan and subject him to criminal punishment, the Executive is bound to comply with the Rule of Law that prevails in this jurisdiction" (p. 72). In other words, no administration has the power to act in such cases unless it has the legal authorization to do so. This same observation was made two years earlier in *Hamdi v. Rumsfeld*. There, the court put the point even more bluntly: "We have long since made clear that a state of war is not a blank check for the President" (p. 29).

Nothing in these two decisions is new. In London in 1762, the King's Chief Messenger, a Mr. Nathan Carrington, broke into the home of the writer John Entick looking for proof of sedition. The resulting trial, *Entick v. Carrington*, focused on whether Carrington, as an agent of the Crown, had unlimited powers or whether his only powers, *qua* government agent, were those granted to him in law. The court's decision was clear: Carrington had no powers over and above those assigned to him in law. The case served as motivation for adoption of the Fourth Amendment in the United States in 1792. It also gave rise to the famous dictum, "If it is law, it will be found in our books. If it is not to be found there, it is not law."[4]

The *Entick* decision has influenced western democracy's view of government ever since. When the question of Quebec separatism arose in Canada in 1998, Canada's highest court concluded in its *Reference re Secession of Quebec* that any actions leading to the possible breakup of the country would have to take place according to the law. As the Court reminded Canadians, even though "democratic institutions necessarily accommodate a continuous process of discussion and evolution, which is reflected in the constitutional right of each participant in the federation to initiate constitutional change" (p. 150), and even if there were to be a clear referendum result requesting separation, no province could purport "to invoke a right of self-determination to dictate the terms of a proposed secession to the other parties to the federation" (p. 151).[5] Even in such dramatic circumstances, it is the rule of law that establishes how and when government action may be undertaken. It is the rule of law that gives government its power, both modest and far-reaching, and, by placing limits on this power, it is the rule of law that "provides a shield for individuals from arbitrary state action" (p. 70). Even acts of secession and other acts intended to rewrite a country's most fundamental constitutional law must proceed in accordance with the law. No act of government, let alone an act of separation, can be carried out unless it is authorized through procedures recognized in law.

Admittedly, throughout history there has been no precise, universally agreed-upon definition of the rule of law.[6] Some commentators have held that the rule of law is something purely formal, requiring only that laws be publicly and unambiguously promulgated after being created by those who have the proper authority to do so.[7] Others have held that the rule of law is something more substantive, requiring that specific social, economic or political conditions be met, for example, that certain legal rights or economic goods be guaranteed.[8] Others have held that the rule of law must be related to theories of natural law, to theories associating law with various normative concepts justified through reason.[9] Yet others have understood the rule of law as having a necessary connection to democracy.[10]

Despite these various suggestions, there remains widespread agreement in today's courts that, unlike rule through law, rule of law exists most clearly in contrast to rule by arbitrary power. As much as anything, it is this idea—that no government is all powerful, that even governments having the authority to create and enforce the law must be bound by it—that distinguishes modern constitutional democracy from other forms of government, including theocracy, totalitarianism and unrestrained mob rule.

## The Arginusae Trial

How did this idea—the idea that even governments must be bound by the law—first arise? How did we come to believe that even the most politically powerful among us are not all powerful? Like so many ideas central to the democratic ideal, it originated in ancient Greece. In a trial that today often remains overlooked, it was one man's dedication to the law that helped establish the first rudimentary distinctions between constitutional democracy and mob rule.

In 399 BCE, the philosopher Socrates was charged with believing in false gods and corrupting the young.[11] He was found guilty and sentenced to death.[12] To carry out the execution he was required to drink a cup of hemlock, a type of poison. Plato tells us he did so without hesitation (*Phaedo*, 117c), believing he had a duty to follow the law even when it happened to go against his interests (*Crito*, 45c–54e).

What is less often remembered is that seven years earlier, in 406 BCE, Socrates was involved in another important trial, one that in its day was even more famous than the trial that eventually led to his execution. This earlier trial, referred to by historians as the Arginusae trial, deserves to be remembered, not simply as a contributing factor to Socrates' guilty verdict, but as a crucial step in the development of what we now call the rule of law.

As in other Athenian trials, the *epistatês* (or presiding officer) in the Arginusae trial was chosen by lot. Plato and Xenophon both report that, as luck would have it, it was Socrates who was chosen to fill this important role.[13] It was during this trial, in the most dramatic of circumstances, that Socrates publicly insisted that even Athenian lawmakers must be bound by the law.

Just as modern law on occasion allows for impeachment and trial within some legislative bodies, Athenian law sometimes made it legal to try people in the Assembly.[14] The process was reserved for important, powerful people. It is reported that as well as being used in the Arginusae trial, the process was used on only ten other occasions.[15]

Within ancient Athens, it was ordinary adult, male citizens who exercised most of the city's political power. Of course, some men were appointed to serve as government officials, but for the most part, they were selected by lot and served relatively short terms.[16] A few officials, like generals (*stratēgoi*), were elected. Even the democratic Athenians refused to serve in military campaigns led by leaders chosen by lot. Despite such exceptions, the great majority of important decisions were made not by elected or appointed officials, but by the people (*demos*) themselves in their regular meetings of the Assembly.

Overseeing the Assembly (or *ekklēsia*) was an administrative body called the Council of 500 (or *boule*). This body had considerable but limited power. It set the Assembly's agenda and drafted the proposed motions on which the Assembly would vote, although the Assembly itself retained the power to alter these proposals and make new motions from the floor if it wanted to do so. The Council was also carefully constructed to be representative of the entire *demos*. Each year a new Council was chosen, with fifty men being selected randomly from each of the ten artificial tribes into which all Athenians were legally divided. Each tribe was composed of three *trittyes*: one from the city proper (*asty*), one from the coast (*paralia*) and one from inland (*mesogeia*). Each *trittys* in turn was composed of one or more neighbourhoods (or *demes*). The use of this artificial tribal system ensured that all citizens had a roughly equal chance of being called up for military service and that no group of citizens was ever systematically excluded from power. During Socrates' time, it was possible for someone to serve on the Council of 500 only twice.

During their term of office, each tribe's representatives took a turn serving as the Council's executive committee (or *prytany*), and each day one member of the executive committee was selected by lot to serve as *epistatês*. It was this man's job to preside over the Council that day and, if it were meeting, to preside over the Assembly as well. No man could serve in this position more than once.[17] The presiding officer had the power to recognize speakers and call the question on a motion. He took an oath promising that all appropriate rules and regulations would be followed (Xenophon, *Memorabilia*, 1.1.18).

In the Assembly over which Socrates happened to preside, eight of Athens' ten generals and two others, who also had been charged but who fled before they could be arrested, were tried together as a group. The word "general" will do as a translation for "*stratēgos*" as long as we remember that the men being tried had been in command of an army fighting at sea. That the fighting was at sea is important because the charge made against all ten men was dereliction of duty during a sea battle: they had failed to pick up shipwrecked Athenian soldiers and sailors, both living and dead, whose ships had gone down during the largest battle of the Peloponnesian War.[18]

This battle, the Battle of Arginusae, and the trial that followed it are described in detail by both Xenophon in his *Hellenica* (1.6–1.7) and Diodorus in his *History* (13.76–79 and 13.97–103). The trial is also mentioned twice by Plato. In *Gorgias*, Plato reports Socrates' role in the trial, but only as a comic aside. There he has Socrates poke fun at himself for his lack of familiarity with the duties of a presiding officer: "Last year I was elected to the Council by lot, and when our tribe was presiding and I had to call for a vote, I came in for a laugh. I didn't know how to do it" (473e–474a).

In addition to this reference in *Gorgias*, Plato also mentions the trial in Socrates' *Apology*. When Socrates is defending himself after being charged with corrupting the young, he mentions the earlier trial, but again speaks of it only briefly (32b–c). Given Plato's goal in writing the *Apology*, this makes obvious dramatic sense.[19] Even so, by relying on other ancient sources, it is possible to piece together the following more detailed series of events.

The Arginusae trial took place near the end of the decades-long Peloponnesian War, in October or November of 406 BCE. Xenophon identifies the year both by number and as the year "in which there was an eclipse of the moon one evening, and the old temple of Athena at Athens was burned, Pityas being now ephor at Sparta and Callias archon at Athens" (*Hellenica*, 1.6.1). Prior to the trial, the Battle of Arginusae had taken place on the eastern side of the Aegean Sea, just off the coast of modern-day Turkey where the Athenians had established colonies on the islands and on the mainland. Mytilene, an Athenian ally, was on the island of Lesbos.

Shortly before the battle, another significant battle had been fought at the mouth of Mytilene's harbour. Thirty Athenian ships were lost and the remaining forty were blockaded. Conon, the commander of the force bottled up at Mytilene, managed to send word back to Athens. To break the blockade, the Assembly voted to send 110 ships to Conon's aid. This was a difficult vote because the war had been going on so long that resources were running low. According to one report, to raise a fleet this large the entire Athenian treasury had to be liquidated, except for a single gold wreath.[20] Whether this report is accurate or not, it signals the depth of commitment required by the Athenians at this late stage of the war. There also were not enough able-bodied citizens available to man this many ships. Even allowing for the inclusion of many volunteers from the aristocracy, who normally would have served only in the cavalry, the city's resources were stretched to the limit. Several ships had to be manned by metics (*metoikoi* or foreign residents) and slaves (*doulos*), all of whom were promised Athenian citizenship in return for victory.[21]

When the head of the Spartan forces blockading the harbour at Mytilene got word that the Athenian fleet was approaching, he left fifty of his ships behind to sustain the blockade and sailed with 120 others to do battle against the Athenians (*Hellenica*, 1.6.26). The two fleets met off the islands of Arginusae between Lesbos and the mainland. With forty additional ships provided by their allies, the Athenian fleet numbered 150, thirty more than the Spartans (*Hellenica*, 1.6.24–26).

In the ensuing battle, the Athenians lost either twenty-five ships or twelve. Xenophon gives the first figure in his description of the fighting, but later, when describing the men who were not picked up, he says they came from twelve ships (*Hellenica*, 1.6.34, 1.7.31). Diodorus tells us that the number was twenty-five (*History*, 13.100). Perhaps twenty-five ships were lost eventually, but at the time of the recovery twelve of these ships may have remained afloat, however precariously. In any case, it was a clear Athenian victory since the Spartans lost at least sixty ships and the rest of the Spartan fleet fled once the outcome of the battle became clear.[22]

At this point, a disagreement broke out among the Athenian generals (*History*, 13.100). Some wanted to sail immediately to Mytilene to break the blockade. Others wanted to delay further fighting until those still alive were rescued, bodies were recovered and buried, and an appropriate trophy was erected. As a compromise, the eight generals who were present put forty-seven of their ships under the command of two of their captains and gave them orders to perform the appropriate actions (Xenophon, *Hellenica*, 1.6.35, 1.7.17, 1.7.30). The generals then took the rest of the Athenian fleet and sailed off to lift the blockade at Mytilene.

According to both Diodorus and Xenophon, it was as this decision was being made that a fierce storm arose and both parties were delayed (Diodorus, *History*, 13.100; Xenophon, *Hellenica*, 1.6.35–38). By the time the main fleet reached Mytilene, the blockading force had already received word of the battle's outcome and had departed. For their part, having been prevented by the storm from searching for survivors and recovering bodies, the two captains and their crews simply returned to Athens.

As far as it goes, this explanation for why the captains were prevented from following their orders may seem plausible. However, if this is what happened, why were charges brought against anyone? This is a difficult question to answer.

One possible explanation is that although there was a storm, there might still have been time before it arrived to collect more of the dead and wounded.[23] For example, Xenophon tells of a shipwrecked survivor who "had been saved by clinging on to a barrel" and who later spoke at the trial (*Hellenica*, 1.7.11). According to this man, those soldiers "who were drowning, had told him, if he got away safely, to report to the people that the generals were doing nothing to rescue the men who had fought most gallantly for their country" (*Hellenica*, 1.7.11). This is not what we would expect even a shipwrecked man to say in the midst of a storm.

A second possibility is that there may have been disagreement between the generals and the two captains about who was responsible for the death of these men.[24] This idea gains support from Diodorus, who reports that the generals and the captains turned against each other once Athenian dissatisfaction with their actions became clear (*History*, 13.101). Rather than holding fast to their explanation of why rescue was impossible, some members of both groups began to blame the other. Being at Mytilene and not being able to communicate easily from such a distance, the generals may have been unable to respond in detail to accusations made against them until after they had returned home and significant damage to their reputations already had been done.

A third explanation is that there may have been some kind of hidden, political agenda against some or all of the generals. Ancient Athens was full of this sort of thing. People regularly used the courts and the Assembly to attack each other for political and personal reasons. They fought for power, for money and over reputation. In this case, Xenophon goes so far as to claim that a man named Callixenus was bribed to put forward a case against the generals (*Hellenica*, 1.7.9). This claim is supported by Aristotle's *Constitution of Athens* where we read that in the Arginusae trial, the generals "were all condemned by a single decision, owing to the people being led astray by persons who aroused their indignation" (p. 34).

In any event, the command of the generals was suspended and they were ordered to return to Athens. Two of them preferred voluntary exile and were never heard from again (Xenophon, *Hellenica*, 1.7.2). The others returned and a proposal was made before the Council that they all should be imprisoned and handed over to the Assembly for a special trial (*Hellenica*, 1.7.1–3).[25] Accepting this, the Council organized a meeting of the Assembly and a trial was held.

In Socrates' later trial, the jury voted against Socrates and he was sentenced to death. In this earlier trial, the outcome was similar. The Assembly voted against the generals and those who had returned to Athens were executed. Unlike most other trials, this trial took more than a single day to complete. Every Athenian jury trial had to be completed before sunset. Either this rule did not apply to trials held in the Assembly or because of the complexity and importance of the trial the rule was ignored.

The main reason the trial took so long to complete is that at one point Socrates refused to let the Assembly proceed. Exactly how he did so and exactly how much of a delay he caused remains a matter of debate. What is clear is that, for some reason, Socrates believed the Assembly was acting illegally.

## Socrates as *Epistatês*

By any measure, the Athenian action at Arginusae should have been viewed as a victory. The objective of breaking the blockade had been accomplished. The Spartan fleet had been defeated and the enlarged Athenian navy had been tested and found battle ready. Even so, at the Assembly initial sentiment was clearly against the generals. Despite the storm, it was believed that a greater effort should have been made to pick up Athens' shipwrecked soldiers, both living and dead. According to Xenophon, several of the defendants were given an opportunity to speak in their own defence, but the speeches "were short, since they were not allowed to speak for the length of time permitted by law" (*Hellenica*, 1.7.5). In any case, it was emphasized that there had been a storm and the generals had left the job of recovering their shipwrecked colleagues to the two captains, both of whom were fully competent, having themselves previously served as generals. In this way, the other ships could move on to the fleet's ultimate objective of breaking the blockade. When asked whether the captains should be found guilty, the generals stuck to their story that because of the storm no one was at fault.

Sentiment now began to turn in favour of the generals and a number of citizens made offers of bail (*Hellenica*, 1.7.7). Others began to call for a vote. Seeing the tide turn in this way, several men who were opposed to the generals convinced the Assembly that no further discussions should be held that day since the coming darkness would make it difficult to get an accurate count of hands when it came time to vote (*Hellenica*, 1.7.7). The result was a delay of several days, since the Festival of Apaturia, "at which fathers and their families meet together," was to begin the following morning (*Hellenica*, 1.7.8).

Xenophon writes that it was during this festival that several conspirators "made arrangements by which a number of people, dressed in black and with hair close-shaven, should attend the Assembly, pretending to be kinsmen of those who had been lost after the battle. They also bribed Callixenus to attack the generals at the meeting of the Council" (*Hellenica*, 1.7.8–9). These arrangements appear to have been successful. When the Assembly reconvened, Callixenus brought forward the following motion:

> That, since in the previous Assembly the speeches in accusation of the generals and the speeches of the generals in their own defense have been heard, the Athenians shall now proceed to voting by tribes; that for each tribe there shall be two voting urns; that in each tribe a herald shall proclaim that whoever judges the generals guilty for not picking up the men who won the victory in the sea battle shall cast his vote in the first urn, and whoever judges them not guilty shall cast his vote in the second urn; and,

> if they are adjudged guilty, they shall be punished with death and handed over to the Eleven, and their property shall be confiscated to the state and the tenth part of it shall belong to the goddess (*Hellenica*, 1.7.9–10).

A loud, spirited debate followed, to the effect that Callixenus himself should be charged with putting forward an illegal motion since, according to a decree known as the *Decree of Cannonus*, it was required that the generals be tried individually rather than as a group (*Hellenica*, 1.7.12, 1.7.20–21 and 1.7.34).[26] In response, a majority of the crowd "shouted out that it was an intolerable thing if the people were not allowed to do what they wanted" (*Hellenica*, 1.7.12). Apparently someone even went so far as to make the extraordinary motion that anyone who wanted to vote in opposition to the will of the Assembly and who opposed Callixenus' motion should be tried and executed along with the generals (*Hellenica*, 1.7.14–15).

Despite this threat, Socrates and several other members of the Council held the view that, since Callixenus' original motion was illegal, the motion should not be put to a vote. In response, Callixenus took the rostrum and repeated the motion that anyone opposing the will of the Assembly should be executed along with the generals. Again the crowd roared its approval. Seeing this, the members of the executive committee who had spoken in favour of the law and in favour of refusing to allow Callixenus' motion to come to a vote began to lose their nerve. All except Socrates. It was at this point that Socrates refused to give his consent to allow the trial to proceed (*Hellenica*, 1.7.15).[27]

Among scholars, there are at least three views about what might have happened next. First, because it is at least plausible (and on a plain reading of Xenophon, close to certain) that on the day in question Socrates was serving as the Assembly's presiding officer, some believe his refusal to allow the Assembly to act illegally must have caused a delay of a day until, as was required by law, a new presiding officer was chosen and the vote was allowed to proceed.[28]

A second interpretation is that, despite Socrates' role as presiding officer and despite his refusal to allow the vote, the vote somehow went ahead later that same day. Perhaps Socrates changed his mind or perhaps other members of the executive committee somehow overruled him.[29]

Yet a third interpretation is that although he may have served as presiding officer earlier in the trial, by this stage Socrates was no longer in that position, if he ever had been. According to this view, he was merely a member of the fifty, so his opposition, while noted, was ineffectual.[30]

Of these three accounts, it is the first that is most likely.

Plato's version of events given in the *Apology* is largely consistent with all three interpretations. In the *Apology*, Plato has Socrates tell the jury,

> I have never held any other office in the city, but I served as a member of the Council, and our tribe Antiochis was presiding at the time when you wanted to try as a body the ten generals who had failed to pick up the survivors of the naval battle. This was illegal, as you all recognized later. I was the only member of the presiding committee to oppose your doing something contrary to the laws, and I voted against it. The orators were ready to prosecute me and take me away, and your shouts were egging them on, but I thought I should run any risk on the side of law and justice rather than join you, for fear of prison or death, when you were engaged in an unjust course (32b–c).

Socrates' less famous comment in *Gorgias*, stating that "I had to call for a vote" is much less neutral. There, Plato explicitly reports that it was Socrates' personal duty to preside over the trial and take the votes (473e–474a).

Xenophon's account is even more definitive. In his *Memorabilia* we read that

> when he was on the Council and had taken the councilor's oath by which he bound himself to give counsel in accordance with the laws, it fell to his lot to preside in the Assembly when the people wanted to condemn Thrasyllus and Erasinides and their colleagues to death by a single vote. That was illegal, and he refused the motion in spite of popular rancour and the threats of many powerful persons. It meant more to him that he should keep his oath than that he should humour the people in an unjust demand and shield himself from threats (1.1.18–19).

Later, Xenophon similarly notes that, "When chairman in the Assemblies he [Socrates] would not permit the people to record an illegal vote, but, upholding the laws, resisted a popular impulse that might even have overborne any but himself" (4.4.2).

The unknown author of yet another Greek work, *Axiochus*, makes much the same point when he has Socrates ask, "How did the ten[31] commanders recently die, when I refused to refer the question to the people? I didn't think it was proper for me to preside over a mad mob, yet on the next day the party of Theramenes and Callixenus suborned the presiding officers of the meeting and secured a condemnation against the men without a trial" (Pseudo-Plato, 368d–369a).[32]

For his part, Xenophon again agrees:

> Next some members of the presiding committee declared that they would not put the motion, since it was an illegal one, to the vote. Callixenus then mounted the platform again and put forward the same charge against them, and the crowd shouted out that, if they refused, they should be prosecuted. At this, all the members of the committee except Socrates, the son of Sophroniscus, were terrified and agreed to put the motion to the vote. Socrates said that he would do nothing at all that was contrary to the law (*Hellenica*, 1.7.14–15).

He would do nothing at all that was contrary to the law. Socrates' position is remarkable, not only for the courage it must have taken to stand up to an Assembly comprising thousands of impassioned citizens, but also for his claim that *even lawmakers* must act in accordance with the law. The implications of this idea were not widely understood in Socrates' day, though they are central to our modern understanding of the rule of law and to the connection between law and democracy more generally.[33]

When the Assembly eventually reconvened, a man named Euryptolemus, a cousin of the great general Pericles, gave a long, well-argued speech in favour of the generals (*Hellenica*, 1.7.16–33). He not only argued for their innocence but also for the view that proceeding with a single, common trial for all the generals would be illegal. He then made a motion to let each prisoner have a separate trial (1.7.23). In this way, he said, the trials "will be in accordance with the law" (1.7.25). This is important, he told the Assembly, since it was important to remember that the laws "are your own creation and it is the laws, above all, which have made you great. Abide by them and never attempt to do anything without their sanction" (1.7.29).

Initially it appeared that the Assembly, being swayed by Euryptolemus' argument, would decide in favour of giving each man a separate trial. However, following yet further discussion a vote was finally taken and a verdict of guilty was returned. All the generals in attendance were then executed. As Diodorus concludes, "these men were put to death by the eleven magistrates legally appointed for that purpose, though not only had they committed no offense against the city, they had won the greatest naval engagement ever fought by Greeks against Greeks" (*History*, 13.102).

## *Demos* Versus *Nomos*

What lessons were learned from this trial? In the short term, the Athenians realized their error and, focusing their wrath upon Callixenus, brought him to trial "on a charge of deceiving the people. Without being allowed a defense, he was pinioned and thrown into the public jail" (Diodorus *History*, 13.103). In the longer term, it appears that the trial helped reinvigorate a long-standing desire on the part of the Athenians to discover the ideal relationship between lawmakers and the law.

Many people think of Socrates' century, the fifth century, as the height of Athenian culture. It was during this century that the great dramatists were writing and Athens' great buildings were being built. There were important advances in art, history, architecture, sculpture, science and philosophy. It was during this century that the Athenians built the naval fleet that gave them their power. The Peloponnesian War, which resulted in part from this growing power, took place. There was a plague. It was a very full time. But by comparison with the fourth century, fifth-century Athens made relatively few advances in legal theory.[34] One commentator has even remarked that one might be tempted to say that there had been *no* advances in legal theory in Athens from about 460 to 410.[35]

In contrast, the decades following the Arginusae trial stand out as a period of significant legal change. The anti-democratic coups of 411 and 404 BCE appear to have been especially pivotal.[36] Following the first restoration of democracy in 411, the Athenians appointed citizen officials called *anagrapheis* (or inscribers) to compile the laws that had been left to them since the time of Solon. Initially, it was expected this would take four months. Instead, it took six years. Following the second restoration of democracy in 403, the Athenians returned to this task. As MacDowell 1978 points out, they did so because they "evidently felt that they could not simply go on as if nothing had happened" (p. 47). The events of 404 overturning democracy "had shown that the old legal code was somehow inadequate and some kind of fresh start" needed to be made (ibid.).[37] As a result, they began studying and reforming their laws with the goal of constructing what they hoped would be the ideal constitution.

One overarching issue was the relationship between the people (*demos*), especially as they were represented by votes in the Assembly, and the law (*nomos*). The question was a straightforward one: Which is sovereign over the other? The law over the people? Or the people over the law? If the former, how can the law ever bind lawmakers, those who have the power to write and rewrite the law? If the latter, how can legitimate democracy ever be distinguished from elected tyranny? A democracy, by definition, needs to be responsive to the changing desires of its citizens. Law, by definition, needs to place inviolable constraints on at least some forms of human action. There thus arises a tension between what a citizenry wants and what it can have, between a people's changing, circumstantial desires and those institutions heavy with precedent that are designed to block the whim of circumstance.[38]

It was this issue that was raised during the Arginusae trial when Euryptolemus spoke against the illegal motion put forward by Callixenus and when Socrates refused to allow the Assembly to ignore its own laws. Two thousand years later, it was exactly this same tension that political theorists such as Hobbes, Locke and Montesquieu were still struggling to resolve.[39] If lawmakers really are law *makers*, how can they ever be bound by previously adopted laws? Alternatively, if not bound by law, what guarantee do citizens have that their leaders will act in accordance with principles of fundamental justice? These questions need to be answered if democratic lawmakers are ever to be anything more than elected tyrants.[40]

In his *Leviathan* (1651), Hobbes gives six interrelated arguments against the possibility that legislators can be bound by law. In Hobbes' view, civil law (as opposed to divine law) is embodied in three types of officeholders: those having the authority to create the law (the sovereign), those having the authority to adjudicate the law (the judiciary) and those having the authority to administer the law (public ministers). As Letwin 2005 observes, "By emphasizing that the source of law must be an authorized legislator, Hobbes explains how, even though it is wholly a human artifact, law constitutes a protection, indeed the only protection, against arbitrary power" (p. 95). Even so, the question remains: Can this protection ever be absolute? In a democracy, what connections, if any, can be realized between political authority and legal accountability?

For Hobbes it is the office, not the man, that has the authority to create law.[41] The sovereign occupies this office only so long as he continues to perform his proper function, thereby fulfilling the objectives of the office. He ceases to perform this function whenever he ceases to provide the protections required to keep his people safe from harm. As Letwin explains, according to this view no sovereign can "be a tyrant exercising arbitrary power because he could not then secure 'peace' … To ensure that men may live without fear, Hobbes stressed that the sovereign's authority was to be exercised by making and maintaining stable rules. Such rules constitute the rule of law" (p. 95). But how can the citizen be confident the officeholder will fulfil his proper function? In the case of a potentially ineffective sovereign, at what point should it be concluded that the officeholder has failed to perform his duty? In the case of a potentially corrupt sovereign, at what point can it be concluded that the officeholder has become vice-ridden? In short, how can the democrat distinguish Hobbes' version of the rule of law from mere rule by law?

Undoubtedly, cases will arise in which a sovereign ceases to perform his proper function, either through inaction or corruption. In such cases, debate will arise over whether a line has been crossed, over whether the sovereign's action or inaction has been sufficient to show that the officeholder has ceased to fulfil his proper role, and therefore over whether he no longer is entitled to exercise the powers of his office.

Members of the government and public alike will also want to know whether such issues are themselves going to become a source of conflict. They will want to know whether answers to such questions can ever be based on something more than individual, subjective judgement.

In Hobbes' account, since the sovereign is not subject to legal limitation, there can be no formal method for adjudicating such debates. If so, there will always remain an element of arbitrariness about whether an officeholder has ceased to occupy his office. Letwin goes so far as to say that, about this arbitrariness "Hobbes says nothing" (p. 106). The question therefore arises: Is Hobbes mistaken to think that the sovereign can never be bound by law? Is he mistaken to identify rule of law with rule by law, regardless of how effective the law might be?

Hobbes' first argument in support of his claim that no sovereign can be bound by law is to the effect that someone who has the power to write and rewrite the law will always have the power to free himself from any law with which he disagrees. As Tamanaha 2004 summarizes, "The creator of law cannot be limited by the law for the plain reason that the law may be altered at the lawmaker's will" (p. 48). As Hobbes puts it, he who is bound only to himself is not bound:

> The Soveraign of a Commonwealth, be it an Assembly, or one Man, is not Subject to the Civill Laws. For having the power to make, and repeale Lawes, he may when he pleaseth, free himselfe from that subjection, by repealing those Lawes that trouble him, and making of new; and consequently he was free before. For he is free, that can be free when he will: Nor is it possible for any person to be bound to himselfe; because he that can bind, can release; and therefore he that is bound to himselfe only, is not bound (pt. 2, ch. 26, para. 6).

Hobbes' second argument is that being sovereign means there can exist no judge powerful enough to render judgement over the sovereign, for if there were, the sovereign would no longer be sovereign:

> Besides, if any one, or more of them, pretend a breach of the Covenant made by the Soveraigne at his Institution; ... there is in this case, no Judge to decide the controversie (2, 18, 4).

Third, if there were such a judge, the very idea of sovereignty would become incoherent, since the introduction of a judge who stands above a sovereign would be equivalent to the creation of a new sovereign. It follows that sovereignty, by definition, requires any actual sovereign to be above the law:

> But to those Lawes which the Soveraign himselfe, that is, which the Commonwealth maketh, he is not subject. … [To believe so,] because it setteth the Lawes above the Soveraign, setteth also a Judge above him, and a Power to punish him; which is to make a new Soveraign; and again for the same reason a third, to punish the second; and so continually without end, to the Confusion, and Dissolution of the Commonwealth (2, 29, 9).

Fourth, for anyone to be bound by law, that person must have given his consent to be so bound. In Hobbes' view, ordinary citizens do this whenever they leave the state of nature and enter into an agreed-upon covenant to abide by the laws of the jurisdiction in which they have chosen to reside.[42] Once they become members of a commonwealth, they effectively have agreed to accept the laws under which they live. We reiterate our acceptance of these laws whenever we decide not to abandon our homes and relocate to some other jurisdiction.[43] Even so, as Hobbes points out, this is not a covenant into which the sovereign enters. Being sovereign means being given the power to change any law at any time. Hence, according to Hobbes, the sovereign need not enter into, and cannot be bound by, any such voluntary covenant:

> Because the Right of bearing the Person of them all, is given to him they make Soveraigne, by Covenant only of one to another, and not of him to any of them; there can happen no breach of Covenant on the part of the Soveraigne (2, 18, 4).

Fifth, by entering into a covenant with the sovereign, each citizen has authorized the sovereign to act however he sees fit. To then complain of unjust action on the part of the sovereign, or of an injury caused by the sovereign, is to misjudge the original source of responsibility:

> [W]hatsoever he doth, it can be no injury to any of his Subjects; nor ought he to be by any of them accused of Injustice. For … by this Institution of a Commonwealth, every particular man is Author of all the Soveraigne

> doth; and consequently he that complaineth of injury from his Soveraigne, complaineth of that whereof he himselfe is Author. … [Thus] no man that hath Soveraigne power can justly be put to death, or otherwise in any manner by his Subjects punished. For seeing every Subject is Author of the actions of his Soveraigne; he punisheth another, for the actions committed by himselfe (2, 18, 4–5).

Finally, Hobbes observes that we honour our covenants (i.e. we obey the law) to avoid sanction. Sanctions, by definition, are penalties imposed against one's will. No person, and hence no sovereign, can act against his own will. Therefore, no sanction introduced by the sovereign can bind the sovereign. It follows that no sovereign can be bound by laws that he himself is charged with creating:

> [To the Soveraigne] is given the Right of Judicature; that is to say, of hearing and deciding all Controversies … For without the decision of Controversies, there is no protection of one Subject, against the injuries of another (2, 18, 11).

It was not until more than three decades after Hobbes raised these objections to the rule of law that Locke was able to give a convincing answer to the question of how even a sovereign can be bound by the law. In his *Two Treatises of Government* (1689), Locke addresses Hobbes' objections with his now famous theories of mixed government and separation of powers. For Locke, each branch of government—the legislature, the executive, the judiciary and the monarchy—is to be given separate, independent areas of responsibility. At the same time, by incorporating multiple political constituencies into government—the institutional mixing of citizenry, aristocracy and monarchy—it becomes more likely that no individual constituency and no single branch of government will ever be able to obtain the power needed to exercise absolute control.[44]

Locke's doctrine of the separation of powers means that although each state remains sovereign over itself, no branch of government within a state will ever become completely authoritative. It means that even those in government who have the power to write and rewrite the law will remain "subject to the Laws they have made," something that in turn provides "a new and near tie upon them, to take care, that they make them for the publick good" (*Second Treatise*, ch. 12, para. 143). At the same time, by mixing democratic, aristocratic and monarchial elements within government, no constitutionally bound government will be able to ignore its component constituencies. Because each constituency provides a check on the others, no government will devolve into the evils of anarchy, oligarchy or tyranny.

This introduction of a workable system of checks and balances not only helps solve Hobbes' logical puzzle of how a government can be both sovereign over the law and yet subservient to it, it also answers the political question of how democracies will be able to address the all-too-human temptation for rulers to "exempt themselves from Obedience to the Laws they make, and suit the Law, both in its making and execution, to their own private advantage" (12, 143).[45] Lawmakers, it turns out, will be free to write and rewrite the law, but only as permitted by law. As Locke sums up,

> *No Man in Civil Society can be exempted from the Laws of it.* For if any Man may do, what he thinks fit, and there be no Appeal on Earth, for Redress or Security against any harm he shall do; I ask, Whether he be not perfectly still in the State of Nature, and so can be *no part or Member of that Civil Society:* unless any one will say, the State of Nature and Civil Society are one and the same thing, which I have never yet found any one so great a Patron of Anarchy as to affirm (7, 94).

Locke's theories of mixed government and the separation of powers explain how one branch of government can retain the power to write and rewrite the law even as another has the power to enforce that law upon the first. His writings, along with later, related theorizing by Montesquieu and others, give constitutional clarity to the idea of democratic checks and balances. With these insights, constitutional government and the rule of law finally could be said to have been placed on sound theoretical footing. As Locke concludes, "*Absolute Monarchy,* which by some Men is counted the only Government in the World, is indeed *inconsistent with Civil Society,* and so can be no Form of Civil Government at all" (7, 90).[46]

Perhaps not surprisingly, the first rudimentary constitutional distinctions made in Athens some 2000 years earlier lacked the clarity of these insights. As Vile 1967 points out, the Athenians never foresaw Locke's idea of separation of powers:

> When we turn from the idea of distinct functions to the view that these should be entrusted to distinct groups of people, we find little to support it in Aristotle. It is true that in the Constitution of Athens, attributed to him, the impropriety was stressed of the execution by the council of a citizen who had not been tried in a law-court, but this was a matter of attributing certain tasks to the proper agency, a matter of due process, rather than the assertion of a doctrine of the separation of powers (p. 23).

Vile himself goes even further, pointing out that the guiding principle of the Athenian Constitution—that all functions of government had to be open to the direct participation of all citizens—might even be thought to be opposed to any doctrine fully akin to the modern separation of powers:

> Thus Aristotle asserted that "Whether these functions—war, justice and deliberation—belong to separate groups, or to a single group, is a matter which makes no difference to the argument. It often falls to the same persons both to serve in the army and to till the fields"; and more specifically, "The same persons, for example, may serve as soldiers, farmers and craftsmen; the same persons again, may act both as a deliberative council and a judicial court." Thus the major concern of ancient theorists of constitutionalism was to attain a balance between the various classes of society and so to emphasize that the different interests in the community, reflected in the organs of the government, should each have a part to play in the exercise of the deliberative, magisterial, and judicial functions alike. The characteristic theory of Greece and Rome was that of mixed government, not the separation of powers (p. 23).

In the late fifth century BCE, Athens already had begun asking how and when the *demos* should have the power, not only to create new laws, but to change old laws. As MacDowell 1978 points out, presumably the city concluded that a simple majority vote should never again be allowed to overturn already existing laws since this had been one of the factors contributing to the rise of the Four Hundred in 411 and the Thirty in 404 (p. 48). So what was to be done? In response to this worry, laws initially were passed to the effect that no previously adopted law could ever be altered. Laws later were passed saying when, how and by whom such laws could be altered. A special provision called the *graphē paranomōn* (literally *law suits concerning things contrary to law*) was re-instituted, or at least given a new prominence in practice, allowing for the prosecution of anyone who attempted to introduce illegal or unjust laws.[47] It was in the midst of this turmoil that the Arginusae trial was held and Socrates insisted that even lawmakers must be bound by the law.

## Justice and the Rule of Law

Was the Arginusae trial the first trial in which the rule of law was raised as a pivotal and decisive issue? Perhaps not. The connection between rule of law and Athenian democracy had been a long-standing topic of public discussion. Sophocles, Euripides and Aeschylus all discuss questions relating to the rule of law and democracy. In *Antigone*, Sophocles asks which is greater, the law of the gods or the law of man?[48] In *Suppliant Women*, Euripides asks the same question and then goes on to debate the virtues and failings of both democracy and one-man rule.[49] In *Prometheus Bound*, even Zeus is described as a tyrant because he exercises his power in accordance with no fixed law: "I know that he is savage," says Prometheus, "and his justice a thing he keeps by his own standard."[50]

Even so, few episodes would have focused Athenian attention on the question of the rule of law more forcefully than a public trial having as its defendants all of Athens' most powerful citizens, her generals. Few actions could have raised the question of whether the law is supreme over the Assembly or the Assembly supreme over the law more forcefully than Socrates' refusal to allow the Assembly to have its way at the height of this emotional and consequential trial. Prior to the Arginusae trial, the *graphē paranomōn* appears to have been used primarily (and perhaps exclusively) as a vehicle for rendering various actions *ultra vires* (beyond the powers of an office holder). Following the trial, the process appears to have begun to evolve into something much closer to the modern idea of judicial review.[51] Seven years later, in the midst of Socrates' own trial, the issue was still top of mind.

It was also following these two trials that Plato and Aristotle began writing about the rule of law. As Letwin 2005 reminds us, "No philosopher is more emphatic about the opposition between law and tyranny than Plato" (p. 21). As she also points out, it was Aristotle in turn who made the distinction between arbitrary power and the rule of law "the foundation of his analysis of the varieties of political life" (p. 21).

For Plato, a tyrant (whether an individual, an oligarchy or a mob) is a ruler who is free to do whatever he pleases. It follows that good government is not just accidentally connected to the rule of law. To be successful, any good government must be bound by law: Just as "the city has drawn up laws invented by the great lawgivers in the past" and has compelled her lawmakers "to govern and be governed by them" (*Protagoras*, 326d), the law must also bind all future lawmakers.[52] As Plato reminds his readers, tyranny has been defeated elsewhere only when "law became the lord and king of men, not men tyrants over the laws" (*Letter 8*, 354b–c). Similarly, he notes that "Where the law is subject to some other authority and has none of its own, the collapse of the state, in my view, is not far off; but if law is the master of the government and government is its slave, then the situation is full of promise and men enjoy all the blessings the gods shower on a state" (*Laws*, 715d).[53]

In his *Politics*, Aristotle reaches much the same conclusion, arguing that "he who bids the law rule may be deemed to bid God and Reason alone rule, but he who bids man rule adds an element of the beast: for desire is a wild beast, and passion perverts the minds of rulers, even when they are the best of men. The law is reason unaffected by desire" (1287a28–32). He also observes that democracies bound by the rule of law have the potential to be governed by their very best citizens. In contrast, democracies lacking the rule of law inevitably evolve into despotism (1286a32–35, 1287a19–b35).[54] As Letwin again summarizes,

> The manner of selecting the ruler or of apportioning offices was for him [Aristotle] secondary to the question: Are all public decisions subject to rules of law? Monarchy, aristocracy, and *politeia* [the city state] are all legitimate forms of government, Aristotle says, because they are all ruled by law, but a democracy, where the majority decide as they please from one moment to the next, is just as tyrannical as rule by one man without law because in both there is the same subjection to arbitrary will (p. 21).

Without the rule of law, there can be no recognizable difference between tyranny of the majority and tyranny of the despot.[55]

Aristotle's reason for taking this view was likely that he had learned from Plato what Socrates and Euryptolemus had done during the most famous trial of the previous century and how they had reminded the Athenians that, by ignoring the law, even democratically elected lawmakers would evolve into tyrants. Like Plato, Aristotle almost certainly also would have been influenced by reports of Socrates' own later trial.

Socrates might rightly be described as the most law-abiding of the Athenians.[56] Because of this, it is ironic that he was eventually executed. After the trial of 399 BCE in which he was condemned, Plato reports Socrates as saying that, even though it had been decided he was to die, it was still his duty to follow the law (*Crito*, 45c–54e, especially 51e). It is hard to imagine a more *nomocractic* or law-abiding point of view.[57]

In taking this position, Socrates was acting much as he had seven years earlier. In his earlier trial, as the voice of government, Socrates wanted to make sure Athens' government acted in accordance with the law. In his later trial, when speaking for himself, he wanted to explain to his fellow citizens why he, as a citizen, refused to disobey the law. In both cases Socrates believed that, within a democracy, procedural obedience to properly enacted laws is itself a type of justice.

Why is procedural obedience itself a type of justice? Is it not enough simply that justice be done, that the right people end up being punished, that each person's ledger be properly balanced? Why must a specific set of procedures be required to obtain this result? The answer comes in two parts. The first concerns the citizen, the second the lawmaker.

Following his later trial, Socrates explained to his life-long friend Crito that, because he had lived in a democracy all his life, he had been given every opportunity to attend the Assembly and convince his fellow citizens to change the law, had he wanted to do so (*Crito*, 51b–c and 52a).[58] Furthermore, if a person was unsuccessful in changing the law, and if he believed the law to be more advantageous elsewhere, he was free to take his family and his possessions and leave Athens (*Crito*, 51d).[59] Because he had done neither of these things, he could hardly criticize the law when it acted against his interests. In other words, laws in a democracy have much greater moral authority than laws elsewhere. It is by obeying the law that each citizen within a democracy upholds his side of a bargain, one he has freely entered into with the state.[60]

At the same time, the state must uphold its side of this agreement. As Socrates emphasized seven years earlier, it is not just the citizen who is required to abide by the law but the lawmaker as well. In 406 BCE, there was a requirement for each of the generals to be tried separately, not collectively. If that is the law, Socrates told the Assembly, then even lawmakers who disagree with the law will still be required to obey it.

Requiring even the state to obey the law may seem on the surface to be only a procedural matter. In fact, it is more. Requiring courts, police officers, public officials and governments to follow the law is itself a kind of justice.[61] Not only does this requirement make government action less arbitrary and more predictable, it makes it easier for citizens to participate in the creation and implementation of those laws that directly affect their lives. Abandoning rule by arbitrary power requires both the citizen and the lawmaker to obey the law. It is only when both sides do so that justice can be said to have been achieved.[62]

In *The Constitution of Athens*, Aristotle, with a brief phrase, explains why trying the generals collectively was also unjust in a second, more substantive (or non-procedural) sense. According to Aristotle, the generals were condemned even though some of them "had actually taken no part in the battle, and others were themselves picked up by other vessels" (34). In other words, since there were differences in what the generals deserved, it was not just (in the non-procedural sense) to try them collectively. This is no doubt true, but it is not Socrates' point. According to Socrates, even if there had been no difference in what the generals deserved, it still would not have been right to try them as a group. To do so would imply that the state is free to act contrary to the law. Requiring not only citizens but also courts, police and governments to abide by the law is what distinguishes legitimate constitutional democracy from democratic mob rule.

In his later trial, Socrates stood by his claim that citizens are required to obey the law, even when it goes against their interests. Given the enormity of the stakes, the significance of Socrates' decision not to escape execution when escape was offered to him has been recognized throughout history. Even so, there was nothing new in Socrates' adoption of this principle. Since the invention of law itself, it has been understood that laws need to be obeyed by citizens if they are to be effective. In contrast, it was in his earlier trial that Socrates made the Athenians take notice of the other half of this equation: that even lawmakers must be bound by the law.

In the great sweep of history, it has been Socrates' later trial that has been remembered more often than his first. The injustice of putting Socrates to death has rightly stood in contrast to Socrates' own law-abiding attitude. But at least initially, it was Socrates' decision to stand up to the mob during the Arginusae trial that forced his fellow citizens to begin to recognize the difference between democracies governed by the rule of law and those that are not. It was this earlier trial, together with Socrates' stubborn insistence that even lawmakers must be bound by the law, that forced the Athenians—as lawmaker and ordinary citizen alike—to continue their earlier attempts at articulating the difference between constitutional democracy and mere majority rule.[63] It is this distinction, embodied in the actions of a single man standing in front of an impassioned Assembly, that has had such importance for the history of western political thought throughout the centuries. It is this act for which Socrates especially deserves to be remembered today.[64]

## Notes

1. Classic discussions appear in Bagehot 1867, no. 7, Dicey 1885, ch. 4, Hayek 1944, ch. 6 and Vile 1967, ch. 8. More recent discussions include Tamanaha 2004 and Bellamy 2017.
2. Other features of the rule of law such as the requirement that laws must be publicly announced and publicly enforced also help achieve this end. Cf. Hayek 1944, ch. 6.
3. I am not indifferent to debate about whether the phrase "appropriately adopted procedures" includes reference to a normative element. For modern discussions of legal positivism and natural law theory, see Austin 1832, Bentham 1945, Hart 1961, Fuller 1964 and Finnis 1980. For discussion of classical authors, see Letwin 2005 and the final section of this essay.

4. This often-cited dictum differs slightly from the wording found in the original judgement, namely: "If this is law it would be found in our books, but no such law ever existed in this country" (final paragraph).
5. For discussion of a range of similar (and dissimilar) cases around the world, see McAdams 1997, Lehning 1998, Wellman 2005 and Kohen 2006.
6. Some authors are tempted to go even further. Weinrib 1987 sums up their concern by asking whether the idea of the rule of law is in fact self-contradictory: "If law inescapably implies the rule of some men over others, can a notion of the Rule of Law with its implicit contrast to the rule of men be in any sense intelligible or coherent?" (p. 59).
7. For this view Thomas Hobbes is the classic source: "Law in generall, is not Counsell, but Command; nor a Command of any man to any man; but only of him, whose Command is addressed to one formerly obliged to obey him. And as for Civill Law, it addeth only the name of the person Commanding, which is Persona Civitatis, the Person of the Commonwealth. [Hence, civil law] is to every Subject, those Rules, which the Commonwealth hath Commanded him, by Word, Writing, or other sufficient Sign of the Will, to make use of, for the Distinction of Right, and Wrong; that is to say, of what is contrary, and what is not contrary to the Rule" (*Leviathan*, pt. 2, ch. 26, para. 2–3).
8. It is this requirement that gives rise to Hutchinson and Monahan's 1987 distinction between thick and thin conceptions of the rule of law. According to Hutchinson and Monahan, the thin version "amounts to a constitutional principle of legality. It demands that government be conducted in accordance with established and performable norms; its voice remains silent or, at best, whispered on the issue of substantive policies. Rule must be by law and not discretion" (p. 101). In contrast, the thick version "incorporates the thinner one as merely one dimension of a liberal theory of justice" (ibid.). This latter conception goes back to the Greeks and Romans. It "demands that positive law embody a particular vision of social justice, structured around the moral rights and duties which citizens have against each other and the state as a whole" (p. 102). It is this ambiguity that has motivated the courts to distinguish the *rule of law* from rights guaranteed *before the law* and rights guaranteed *under the law*, and from the right of *equal protection* from the law and the right of *equal benefit* from the law.

9. It is through this normative element that law advances *eudaimonia* (human flourishing or happiness or the good life). It is also this normative element that underlies most ancient Greek law. As Plato reports, "We maintain that laws which are not established for the good of the whole state are bogus laws" (*Laws*, 715b4–5). As Aristotle adds, "The just, then, is the lawful and the equal, the unjust the unlawful and the unequal" (*Nicomachean Ethics*, 1129b1–2; cf. Aristotle's *Politics*, 1281a11–1282b12). Even so, there is no necessary connection between a normative conception of law and a normative conception of the rule of law. For Plato and Aristotle, there is no contradiction in holding that the purpose of law is to advance *eudaimonia* while the purpose of the rule of law is to protect against tyranny.
10. For a classic statement of the connection between the rule of law and democracy, see Aristotle's comment in *Politics*: "We will begin by inquiring whether it is more advantageous to be ruled by the best man or the best laws ... Now, absolute monarchy, or the arbitrary rule of a sovereign over all citizens, in a city which consists of equals, is thought by some to be quite contrary to nature ... That is why it is thought to be just that among equals everyone be ruled as well as rule, and therefore that all should have their turn ... And the rule of law, it is argued, is preferable to that of any individual" (1286a7–8, 1287a9–11, 1287a15–20).
11. Plato states the charge as follows: "Socrates is guilty of corrupting the young and of not believing in the gods in whom the city believes, but in other new spiritual things" (*Apology*, 24b). Xenophon reports essentially the same charge, telling us that Socrates was accused of "not believing in the gods worshipped by the state and with the introduction of new deities in their stead and with corruption of the young" (*Apology*, 10). Writing much later, Diogenes Laertius reports the same basic charge: "This indictment and affidavit is sworn by Meletus, the son of Meletus of Pitthos, against Socrates, the son of Sophroniscus of Alopece: Socrates is guilty of refusing to recognize the gods recognized by the state, and of introducing other new divinities. He is also guilty of corrupting the youth. The penalty demanded is death" (*Lives of Eminent Philosophers*, 2.5.40; cf. Plato, *Euthyphro*, 2c–3c). Following their defeat in the Peloponnesian War, it is likely that some Athenians would have wanted to charge Socrates with sedition, for having been the teacher of traitors such as Critias and Alcibiades. Since such a charge would have been illegal under the *Act of Amnesty* passed at the end of the war, they would

have been forced to settle for the less political and less precise charge of corruption. For a comprehensive list of sources and controversies relating to these events, see Brickhouse and Smith 2002.

12. See Plato, *Apology*, 35e–36b, 38c–39b and Xenophon, *Apology*, 31–3. For a helpful overview, see Ober 2011.
13. For example, see Plato, *Gorgias*, 473e–474a and Xenophon, *Memorabilia*, 1.1.18 and 4.4.2. Also see Pseudo-Plato, *Axiochus*, 368d–369a, MacDowell 1978, p. 188 and Hamel 2015, chap. 5, note 24.
14. The Athenians had one other form of public judgment for which there is no modern equivalent. This was ostracism. Once a year, at a specified meeting of the Assembly, a vote was held on whether to hold an ostracism. If the vote was positive, an ostracism was arranged and on a designated day the *agora* was emptied of people. Every citizen who wanted to do so could then enter the *agora* and deposit an *ostracon*, a broken piece of pottery with someone's name scratched on it. If 6000 or more *ostraca* were deposited, the person whose name was scratched on the most *ostraca* was exiled from Athens for ten years.
15. See Hansen 1975, p. 51. Hansen notes that eleven such trials took place in the almost two-century period from 495 to 322 BCE. He also notes that 86 other cases were started in the Assembly but then moved to the courts for trial.
16. For a helpful overview, see Jones 1957, pp. 99–133, 153–60.
17. For additional details, see Jones 1957, pp. 106–7.
18. See Diodorus' *History*, 13.100. For a general discussion of the importance of recovering one's war dead, see the opening remarks to Pericles' Funeral Oration, as well as the introduction leading to Pericles' speech in Thucydides, *History of the Peloponnesian War*, 2.34–2.35. Aelian also reports an Athenian law requiring anyone who discovers an unburied body to bury it (*Varia Historia*, 5.14). The more general theme of burial appears regularly throughout Greek literature, from Homer's *Iliad* in which soldiers regularly fight over the appropriate treatment of corpses, to Euripides' *Suppliant Women* in which an entire city is willing to wage war to retrieve the bodies of the dead.
19. I owe this observation to Steve Wexler.
20. For example, see Curtius 1891, p. 532.
21. For example, see Xenophon, *Hellenica*, 1.6.24 and Aristophanes, *Frogs*, 693–695. The significance of the offer of citizenship is hard to overemphasize. At the time, the normal requirement for citizenship was being the child of two legally married Athenian citizens.

22. Diodorus gives the number as seventy-seven (*History*, 13.100). Xenophon gives the number as over sixty (*Hellenica*, 1.6.35).
23. For example, this explanation is favoured in Grote 1888, ch. 64. Cf. Andrewes 1974 and Kagan 2003.
24. For example, see Andrewes 1974 and Harding 1974.
25. The issue of imprisonment is complicated for two reasons. The first is that one of the generals, Erasinides, appears to have been imprisoned on unrelated charges (apparently he was also accused of embezzling public money) and at 1.7.2 Xenophon mentions only his imprisonment. The second is that it is possible that imprisonment without bail prior to trial in the Assembly may itself have been illegal (MacDowell 1978, pp. 187–9). If so, either the imprisonment itself was against the law or the circumstances were so unusual that the regular law did not apply. The only other option is that the generals were unable to raise bail, something highly improbable.
26. For contrasting views, see Riddell 1973, p. 82, note 5 and Gish 2012, pp. 173, 182 and 183–5. See too MacDowell 1978, p. 188, as well as Lavelle 1988 and Lang 1990. In fact, there may have been several reasons for doubting the legality of the proceedings: it may have been illegal to jail the generals without bail prior to the trial; it may have been illegal to try them as a group; it may have been illegal not to allow each general a longer time in which to defend himself; it may have been illegal not to complete each trial in a single day; it may have been illegal to threaten to charge those who opposed Callixenus along with the generals. Even knowing ancient Greek law in detail, it also may be that none of these facts could be determined with certainty until the overriding issue of ultimate sovereignty (of the Assembly over the law or the law over the Assembly) was decided. Cf. Wexler and Irvine 2006.
27. Cf. Plato, *Apology*, 32b-c and Xenophon, *Memorabilia*, 1.1.18.
28. Supporting secondary opinion appears in Riddell 1973, pp. 82–4, note 7 and in Cawkwell's footnote in Xenophon, *History of My Times*, pp. 88–89. Cf. Hamel 2015, pp. 75–86. This first view squares easily with the fact that not all descriptions of the event include mention of Socrates as the presiding officer. Even so, because the trial extended over multiple days and because a new presiding officer would have been chosen each day, there is nothing mysterious about the fact that some descriptions of the trial fail to mention Socrates occupying this role. For example, anyone interested in reporting only the trial's final judgment would have no need to mention all of the presiding officers within a multi-day trial.

29. Supporting secondary opinion appears in Curtius 1891, p. 543, in Hansen 1975, p. 85 and in Gish 2012, p. 185.
30. Supporting secondary opinion appears in Riddell 1973, pp. 82–84, note 7, in a quote by George Grote.
31. This reference to the execution of ten generals is likely an error. Athens did have ten generals and at the time they were recalled, charges appear to have been filed against all ten. However, two of these men, Conon and Leon, were likely in command of the ships under siege at Mytilene. If so, and if charges were brought against them, it is not implausible that they might have been dropped early in the proceedings. This would have left only the other eight (six of whom were in attendance) to face eventual trial. The matter is further complicated by the fact that Erasinides appears to have been in charge of the ship that successfully carried news of the blockade to Athens, and so it is possible that he was both among those who were under siege at Mytilene and involved in the battle at Arginusae, although Riddell states that, by the time of the trial, one general (possibly Erasinides) was dead. (See Riddell 1973, p. 82, note 3.) It also is likely that the two generals who fled, Protomachus and Aristogenes, would have been tried and convicted in absentia, even though it is unlikely they were ever executed. In any event, it appears that charges initially were brought against all ten generals, but how many were eventually tried and then executed remains a matter of speculation. Cf. Carawan 2007, p. 20 and Lanni 2017, p. 19.
32. The fact that this report comes from an unknown author is of no special significance since, regardless of the question of authorship, the passage shows that even among authors of less prominence than Plato and Xenophon, it was generally recognized that Socrates played this central role.
33. For discussion of the modern principles under which courts may revise democratically established laws and the care which needs to be taken for a court to revisit its own decisions, see Thomson Irvine 2011.
34. I owe this observation to Steve Wexler.
35. Wilamowitz-Moellendorff 1880, p. 52. Of course this is an exaggeration. As Steve Wexler has pointed out in private communication, there was a great deal of legal activity in fifth-century Athens. (For example, see Ostwald 1986.) It is just that, in comparison to the fourth century, the legal activity of the fifth century was much less theory driven. Cf. MacDowell 1978, p. 49.

36. In 411 BCE, the short-lived oligarchy known as the Four Hundred came to power. For background discussion, see Kagan 1991. In 404 BCE, the short-lived oligarchy known as the Thirty Tyrants came to power. For background discussion, see Krentz 1982.
37. For additional, detailed, helpful discussion, see Carawan 2007.
38. For arguments against the burden of law, see the Stranger's comment in the *Statesman*, when he says that law is "like a stubborn, stupid person who refuses to allow the slightest deviation from or questioning of his own rules, even if the situation has in fact changed and it turns out to be better for someone to contravene these rules" (294b–c). I am grateful to Michael Griffin for this quotation.
39. Modern debate is connected to the classical period not only by the substance of the arguments (e.g. see Glaucon's arguments about justice in Plato's *Republic* at 357a–368c), but also by comments such as those in Montaigne 1580, where Montaigne notes that although popular government can be seen to be "the most natural and equitable" of all forms of government, he was appalled by "the inhumane injustice" exhibited at the Arginusae trial, something that made him "almost ready to vow a hatred irreconcilable against all popular rule" (1.3).
40. For a more detailed discussion of the distinction between *logos* and *nomos* and how this distinction effected Greek ideas relating to the rule of law, see Wexler and Irvine 2006 and Gish 2012, p. 183.
41. Between monarchy, aristocracy and democracy, Hobbes prefers monarchy, believing that, of the three, monarchy is the least likely to become corrupt. Even so, for Hobbes, the real test of good government lies not in whether the office of the sovereign is embodied in one person, a small group of people or a large parliament, but in whether the office holder (whether one man or many) is effective in the exercising of this sovereignty.
42. For discussion about whether a person should be bound by a covenant into which he has been coerced, see Marinoff 1994.
43. For example, see Plato, *Crito*, 52d–53e.
44. Of course nothing can guarantee this outcome. Even so, Montesquieu's famous slogan remains true: "Power should be a check on power" (1748, bk 2, s.4).
45. I owe this insight to Carl Hodge.
46. For discussion of the influence of John Locke and Baruch Spinoza on the writing of the *Declaration of Independence* and the founding of the American republic, see Stewart 2014. For a discussion of the influence of

Aristotle, see Wood 2009. For discussion of the influence of Montesquieu, see Tamanaha 2004. As noted in Lutz 1984, it was Montesquieu who was the most frequently quoted of the democratic theorists in pre-revolutionary America, surpassed only by the Bible (p. 193).

47. For example, see MacDowell 1978, p. 50. For a more detailed discussion, see Carawan 2007.
48. For example, see Sophocles, *Antigone*, 78–9, 365–83, 449–70, 675–7, 745, 1347–52.
49. For example, see Euripides, *Suppliant Women*, 298–99, 422–24.
50. Aeschylus, *Prometheus Bound*, 186–7.
51. Carawan 2007 argues convincingly for this point. He concludes that it was only "in the aftermath of the Arginousai trial" that such changes occurred (pp. 23–24).
52. An exception, for Plato, is the ideal, all-knowing ruler, the Philosopher King, presumably because he would already know how best to act in every situation. I am grateful to Jim Robinson for pointing out this exception to me.
53. Cf. Plato, *Gorgias*, 484b and *Letter 8*, 355. See too, Marcus Aurelius, *Meditations* 1.14.
54. Cf. Plato's comment that "Access to power must be confined to men who are not in love with it" (*Republic*, 521b).
55. This view is obviously incompatible with Shklar's 1987 interpretation in which Aristotle's understanding of the rule of law is unlike that of Montesquieu. For Shklar, Montesquieu's rule of law "has only one aim, to protect the ruled against the aggression of those who rule" (p. 4). In contrast, Shklar's interpretation of Aristotle suggests that the rule of law places few, if any, restrictions on those who govern, an interpretation that is not easy to make consistent with Aristotle's claim that "it is preferable for the law to rule rather than any one of the citizens, and according to this same principle, even if it be better for certain individuals to govern, they must be appointed as guardians of the laws and in subordination to them" (*Politics*, 1287a19–22). See too Shklar 1998.
56. I owe this observation to Steve Wexler.
57. Even so, Socrates' comment in *Crito* is often contrasted with his remark in the *Apology* to the effect that he would continue philosophizing even if the state forbade him from doing so, something that itself may be interpreted as showing Socrates' support for democratic principles. For further discussion, see Yonezawa 1991 and Howenstein 2009.

58. More precisely, it is the personified Laws who come to Socrates and who make the argument that, in a democracy, each citizen is given two options: either he must convince his fellow citizens to change the law when he thinks it unjust, or he must accept the law as it stands. That Socrates sees these options as being especially important in a democracy is clear from his reference to the democratic citizen's arrival at voting age in 51d. See Steadman (2006) for a defence of the claim that this speech of the Laws is itself an example of a *graphē paranomōn.* Of course, there is also a significant tradition holding that the Socrates of the *Republic* was anti-democratic. While this is not the place to reopen this debate, we can note that on a plain reading, the above passages may be interpreted as showing that the Socrates of the early dialogues was a supporter of democracy, at least in some limited form. For a more thoroughgoing defence of Socrates as democrat, see Klonoski 2014. For alternative views, see Holway 1994 and Woodruff 2011.
59. The option of leaving Athens would have been especially important for those who did not have a voice in the Assembly.
60. A possibly contrasting view is given by Plato in *Protagoras,* 319b–d.
61. In the United States, this idea is connected to what is called "due process"; in Canada the idea is connected to what are called "principles of fundamental justice"; in Great Britain, the idea is connected to what is called "natural law."
62. Cf. *Crito* 48c-d, 47e.
63. One need not equate the centuries-old doctrine of parliamentary supremacy with mob rule to find noticeable parallels in the following comment, made by the Supreme Court of Canada in its *Reference re Secession of Quebec*: "This Court has noted on several occasions that with the adoption of the Charter, the Canadian system of government was transformed to a significant extent from a system of Parliamentary supremacy to one of constitutional supremacy" (72).
64. Early drafts of this chapter were read at the University of Athens History Museum, the University of Regina and The University of British Columbia, Okanagan. I am grateful to members of all three audiences for their thoughtful comments, as well as to the organizers and sponsors of these events, including the Canadian Embassy in Athens. I am also grateful to several anonymous referees, as well as to Peter Anstey, Sylvia Berryman, Leslie Burkholder, David Camp, Michael Griffin, Phillip Harding, Thomas Heilke, Ross Hickey, Carl Hodge, Byron Kaldis, Anna

Lazou, Louis Marinoff, Christopher Martin, Barrie McCullough, Michaelis Michael, David Mirhady, Jim Robinson, Roger Shiner, Georgios Steiris and John Woods for their helpful suggestions, and to Leslie Marsh and David F. Hardwick for their unfailingly sound scholarly judgement. Finally, I especially want to thank Steve Wexler, Emeritus Professor of Law at The University of British Columbia, Vancouver. His unbounded curiosity and legal knowledge have been invaluable to me as I have worked through these issues. It is Steve who is responsible, not just for many helpful suggestions regarding the content and wording of this chapter, but for the initial idea of trying to discover the exact role Socrates played in the Arginusae trial. Like so many of his students over the years, I have benefitted immeasurably from his insight and counsel. *Ubi amica, ibi opes.*

## References

### Cases

*Entick v. Carrington*. [1765] EWHC KB J98, www.bailii.org/ew/cases/EWHC/KB/1765/J98.html

*Hamdan v. Rumsfeld*. 548 U.S. 557 (2006), www.supremecourt.gov/opinions/05pdf/05-184.pdf

*Hamdi v. Rumsfeld*. 542 U.S. 507 (2004), www.supremecourt.gov/opinions/03pdf/03-6696.pdf

*Reference re Secession of Quebec*. [1998] 2 S.C.R. 217, scc-csc.lexum.com/scc-csc/scc-csc/en/item/1643/index.do

### Classical Sources

Aelian. 1997. *Varia Historia*. Loeb Classical Library, N. G. Wilson (ed.). Cambridge, MA: Harvard University Press.

Aeschylus. 2013. *Prometheus Bound*. In: *Greek Tragedies*. David Grene and Richmond Lattimore (eds), vol. 1. Chicago: University of Chicago Press.

Aristophanes. 1979–82. *Aristophanes*. Loeb Classical Library, Benjamin Bickley Rogers (trans.), 3 vols. Cambridge, MA: Harvard University Press.

Aristotle. 1984. *The Complete Works of Aristotle*. Jonathan Barnes (ed.). Princeton: Princeton University Press.
Diodorus Siculus. 1950. *Library of History, Books 12.41–13*. Loeb Classical Library, C. H. Oldfather (trans.), vol. 5. Cambridge, MA: Harvard University Press.
Diogenes Laertius. 1972. *Lives of Eminent Philosophers*. Loeb Classical Library, R. D. Hicks (trans.), vol. 1. Cambridge, MA; London: Harvard University Press.
Euripides. 1998. *Suppliant Women, Electra, Heracles*. Loeb Classical Library, David Kovacs (trans.), vol. 3. Cambridge, MA: Harvard University Press.
Homer. 1924–25. *Iliad*. Loeb Classical Library, A. T. Murray (trans.), revised by William F. Wyatt, 2 vols. Cambridge, MA: Harvard University Press.
_____. 1919. *Odyssey*. Loeb Classical Library, A. T. Murray (trans.), revised by George E. Dimock, 2 vols. Cambridge, MA: Harvard University Press.
Marcus Aurelius. 1916. *Marcus Aurelius*. Loeb Classical Library, C. R. Haines (trans.). Cambridge, MA: Harvard University Press.
Plato. 1997. *Plato: Complete Works*. John M. Cooper and D. S. Hutchinson (eds). Indianapolis: Hackett Publishing Company.
Sophocles. 1994. *Antigone, The Women of Trachis, Philoctetes, Oedipus at Colonus*. Loeb Classical Library, Hugh Lloyd-Jones (trans.). Cambridge, MA: Harvard University Press.
Thucydides. 1943. *The History of the Peloponnesian War*. R. W. Livingstone (ed.). London, New York, Toronto: Oxford University Press.
Xenophon. 1979. *A History of My Times (Hellenica)*. Rex Warner (trans.) with an introduction and notes by George Cawkwell. Harmondsworth: Penguin Books.
Xenophon. 1923. *Memorabilia, Oeconomicus, Symposium, Apology*. Loeb Classical Library, E. C. Marchant and O. J. Todd (trans.). Cambridge, MA; London: Harvard University Press.

## Modern Sources

Andrewes, Antony. 1974. The Arginusae Trial. *Phoenix* 28: 112–22.
Austin, John. (1832) 1995. *The Province of Jurisprudence Determined*. W.E. Rumble (ed.). Cambridge: Cambridge University Press.
Bagehot, Walter. (1867) 1878. *The English Constitution*. New edn. London: C. Kegan Paul.
Bellamy, Richard. 2017. *The Rule of Law and the Separation of Powers*. London: Routledge.

Bentham, Jeremy. (1945) 1970. *Of Laws in General.* H. L. A. Hart (ed.). London: Athlone Press.

Brickhouse, Thomas C. and Nicholas D. Smith. 2002. *The Trial and Execution of Socrates: Sources and Controversies.* New York: Oxford University Press.

Carawan, Edwin. 2007. The Trial of the Arginusae Generals and the Dawn of "Judicial Review". *Dike* 10: 19–56.

Curtius, Ernst. 1891. *The History of Greece.* A. W. Ward (trans.), vol. 3. New York: Charles Scribner's Sons.

Dicey, A. V. (1885) 1959. *Introduction to the Study of the Law of the Constitution.* 10th edn. London: Macmillan.

Finnis, John. (1980) 2011. *Natural Law and Natural Rights.* 2nd edn. Oxford: Clarendon Press.

Fuller, Lon. (1964) 1969. *The Morality of Law.* Revised edn. New Haven, London: Yale University Press.

Gish, Dustin. 2012. Defending *demokratia*: Athenian Justice and the Trial of the Arginusae Generals in Xenophon's *Hellenica.* In: *Xenophon: Ethical Principles and Historical Enquiry.* Fiona Hobden and Christopher Tuplin (eds). pp. 161–212. Leiden, Boston: Brill Academic Publishers.

Grote, George. 1888. *A History of Greece.* Vol. 6. London: John Murray.

Hamel, Debra. 2015. *The Battle of Arginusae.* Baltimore: Johns Hopkins University Press.

Hansen, M. H. 1975. *Eisangêlia.* Odense: Odense University Press.

Harding, Phillip. 1974. The Theramenes Myth. *Phoenix* 28: 101–11.

Hart, H. L. A. (1961) 1994. *The Concept of Law.* 2nd edn. P. Bulloch and J. Raz (eds). Oxford: Clarendon Press.

Hayek, Friedrich A. (1944) 2007. *The Road to Serfdom.* The Collected Works of F. A. Hayek, vol. 2. Chicago: University of Chicago Press.

Hobbes, Thomas. (1651) 1985. *Leviathan.* C. B. Macpherson (ed.). London: Penguin Books.

Holway, Richard. 1994. Achilles, Socrates, and Democracy. *Political Theory* 22: 561–90.

Howenstein, Mark S. 2009. Socrates and the Moral Limits of Legal Obligation. *Law, Culture and the Humanities* 5: 55–76.

Hutchinson, Allan and Patrick Monahan. 1987. Democracy and the Rule of Law. In: *The Rule of Law.* Allan Hutchinson and Patrick Monahan (eds). pp. 97–123. Toronto, Calgary, Vancouver: Carswell.

Irvine, Thomson. 2011. Changing Course or Trimming Sails? The Supreme Court Reconsiders. In: *Public Law at the McLachlin Court.* David A. Wright and Adam M. Dodek (eds). pp. 9–37. Toronto: Irwin Law.

Jones, A. H. M. 1957. *Athenian Democracy*. Baltimore: The Johns Hopkins University Press.
Kagan, Donald. 1991. *The Fall of the Athenian Empire*. Ithaca: Cornell University Press.
_____. 2003. *The Peloponnesian War*. New York: Viking.
Klonoski, Richard J. 2014. Plato's Invisible Hero of Democracy: Socrates in the *Republic* and *Crito*. *Agathos* 5: 7–20.
Kohen, Marcelo G. 2006. *Secession: International Law Perspectives*. Cambridge: Cambridge University Press.
Krentz, Peter. 1982. *The Thirty at Athens*. Ithaca: Cornell University Press.
Lang, Mabel L. 1990. Illegal Execution in Ancient Athens. *Proceedings of the American Philosophical Society* 134: 24–29.
Lanni, Adriaan. 2017. Collective Sanctions in Classical Athens. In: *Ancient Law, Ancient Society*. Dennis P. Kehoe and Thomas A. J. McGinn (eds). pp. 9–31. Ann Arbor: University of Michigan Press.
Lavelle, B. M. 1988. *Adikia*, the Decree of Kannonus, and the Trial of the Generals. *Classica et Mediaevalia* 39: 19–41.
Lehning, Percy. 1998. *Theories of Secession*. London: Routledge.
Letwin, Shirley. 2005. *On the History of the Idea of Law*. New York: Cambridge University Press.
Locke, John. (1689) 1989. *The Two Treatises of Civil Government*. Richard Aschcraft (ed.). London: Routledge.
Lutz, Donald S. 1984. The Relative Influence of European Writers on Late Eighteenth-Century American Political Thought. *American Political Science Review* 78: 189–97.
MacDowell, Douglas M. 1978. *The Law in Classical Athens*. Ithaca: Cornell University Press.
Marinoff, Louis. 1994. Hobbes, Spinoza, Kant, Highway Robbery and Game Theory. *Australasian Journal of Philosophy* 72: 445–62.
McAdams, A. James. 1997. *Transitional Justice and the Rule of Law in New Democracies*. Notre Dame, London: University of Notre Dame Press.
Montaigne, Michel de. (1580) 1978. Nos affections s'emportent au delà de nous. In: *Les essais de Michel de Montaigne*. Pierre Villey and V.-L. Saulnier (eds). Paris: Presses universitaires de France.
Montesquieu, Baron. (1748) 1977. *De l'esprit des loix*. Trans. as *The Spirit of Laws*. David Wallace Carrithers (ed.). Berkeley: University of California Press.
Ober, Josiah. 2011. Socrates and Democratic Athens. In: *The Cambridge Companion to Socrates*. Donald R. Morrison (ed.). pp. 138–78. Cambridge: Cambridge University Press.

Ostwald, Martin. 1986. *From Popular Sovereignty to the Sovereignty of Law.* Berkeley: University of California Press.
Riddell, James. 1973. *The Apology of Plato.* New York: Arno Press.
Shklar, Judith N. 1987. Political Theory and the Rule of Law. In: *The Rule of Law.* Allan Hutchinson and Patrick Monahan (eds). pp. 1–16. Toronto, Calgary, Vancouver: Carswell.
_____. 1998. *Political Thought and Political Thinkers.* Stanley Hoffman (ed.). Chicago, London: University of Chicago Press.
Steadman, Geoffrey D. 2006. The Unity of Plato's 'Crito'. *The Classical Journal* 101: 361–82.
Stewart, Matthew. 2014. *Nature's God: The Heretical Origins of the American Republic.* New York, London: W. W. Norton & Co.
Tamanaha, Brian Z. 2004. *On the Rule of Law.* Cambridge: Cambridge University Press.
Vile, M. J. C. 1967. *Constitutionalism and the Separation of Powers.* Oxford: Clarendon Press.
Wellman, Christopher Heath. 2005. *A Theory of Secession.* Cambridge: Cambridge University Press.
Weinrib, Ernest. 1987. The Intelligibility of the Rule of Law. In: *The Rule of Law.* Allan Hutchinson and Patrick Monahan (eds). pp. 59–84. Toronto, Calgary, Vancouver: Carswell.
Wexler, Steve and Andrew David Irvine. 2006. Aristotle on the Rule of Law. *Polis* 23: 116–38.
Wilamowitz-Moellendorff, Ulrich von. 1880. Exkurse, Die Herrschaft des Gesetzes. *Philol. Unters.* 1.
Wood, Gordon S. 2009. *Empire of Liberty.* Oxford: Oxford University Press.
Woodruff, Paul. 2011. Socrates and the New Learning. In: *The Cambridge Companion to Socrates.* Donald R. Morrison (ed.). pp. 104–6. Cambridge: Cambridge University Press.
Yonezawa, S. 1991. Socrates' Two Concepts of the Polis. *History of Political Thought* 12: 565–76.

# Burke's Liberalism: Prejudice, Habit, Affections, and the Remaking of the Social Contract

Lauren K. Hall

Despite liberalism's spread over the past two centuries and its success in spreading greater openness, increasing levels of toleration, wider access to platforms for free speech, free trade, and ever-growing prosperity, the theory that has given modern civilization its most characteristic qualities is under increasing fire. The rise of populist movements in the United States and Europe demonstrates that the victory of liberalism's principles was never complete, and that the End of History proclaimed by Fukuyama in 1992 was merely another chapter in an ongoing conversation about political values (Fukuyama 2012). To some degree, liberalism's very successes opened the door for a reaction against liberal principles, revealing that liberalism's apparent dominance was one in which electoral successes hid deeper and abiding distrust. In one sense, the tensions that have most recently emerged have existed within liberal theory itself, because liberal theory is a way of responding to, though not permanently solving, the

L. K. Hall (✉)
Department of Political Science, Rochester Institute of Technology, Rochester, NY, USA
e-mail: lxhgpt@rit.edu



D. F. Hardwick, L. Marsh (eds.), *Reclaiming Liberalism*, Palgrave Studies in Classical Liberalism, https://doi.org/10.1007/978-3-030-28760-3_8

conflicts between the individual and the community to which that individual belongs. The vacillation between individual and the community plays out in the works of various liberal philosophers, each of whom moves the needle in one direction or another, correcting for what he or she sees as the deficiencies of those who came before.

While the nature of liberalism's imperfect solution to the balance between individual and community is itself one source of tension, a further source of conflict is the way liberalism has been incorporated into or paired with ideologies that threaten to undermine or challenge liberal principles in foundational ways. The politics of identity that resulted from the incorporation of progressive concerns about diversity into the contemporary liberal platform created fault lines where group identity clashes with the universality of human experience that was the traditional foundation of individual rights. On the right, neoconservatism, or the spreading of liberal democratic principles abroad, fostered a growth of the state that is in many ways inconsistent with liberalism's commitment to limited government and individual freedom. As a result of these and other internal and external tensions, liberalism has been pushed to its extremes in ways that fundamentally damage its ability to balance human ends.

Liberalism was, at least at the beginning, fundamentally a moderate ideological position, despite its revolutionary connections. This moderate positioning is seen most clearly in Madison's exhortation in Federalist 51 that the goal of liberal constitutionalism is to "first enable the government to control the governed; and in the next place oblige it to control itself"(*Federalist Papers* 2013). Madison's commentary reflects on both human nature and human governance. The combination of a self-centered and willful rationality alongside natural sociality requires unique political institutions that both support and channel the full needs of human life. Everything about human nature is a mixed bag, so to speak, and the fullest expression of human abilities requires the tightest controls to prevent exploitation and violence. The human ability for language, as Aristotle notes, is a source of both agreement and dissension, that which makes humans both capable of the greatest gifts and the worst harms. Human individuality, human sociality, and human ingenuity can lead individuals and groups to either freedom or bondage, depending on how they are expressed and in what context. The mixed character of human nature therefore requires a moderate or balanced attitude toward government, one that preserves individual rights while at the same time protecting the communities that make preservation of those rights possible. The equilibrium between individual rights and social orders and between various kinds of political and moral ends requires constant recalibration.

While the theoretical solution liberalism offers was somewhat clear in the abstract, the political answer to this problem took many years of growth and development and experimentation, resulting in a series of internal constitutional checks to create what proponents hoped would support internal recalibration between individual and community, rather than relying on constant public or elite input. The hallmarks of liberal constitutionalism—separation of powers, checks and balances, freedom of speech and the press, toleration, and various criminal justice protections and protection of private property—developed not as discrete innovations, but instead as the development over many years of attempting to balance the claims of individuals alongside those of the communities to which they belong, harnessing the best of human nature while controlling its worst impulses.

This control, of course, is always limited and never perfectly precise. It is no accident then that what most criticisms of modern liberalism have in common is a belief that a particular aspect of liberal commitments has become unbalanced, whether because it has become unhinged from the whole, forgotten or subsumed by other commitments, or because it itself has been raised up as the sole good for which all other goods must be sacrificed. Conservative liberals reject the egalitarian ethos of progressive liberals as rejecting religious freedom, property rights, and individual dignity. Once-liberal populists reject the commitment to free trade that ignores the way in which humans are bound to and identify with their local communities and ways of life. Progressive liberals reject the way in which capitalism and, in particular, crony capitalism, privileges the strong at the expense of the vulnerable. Each of these criticisms suggests that liberalism has become unbalanced as different goals and principles—equality, freedom, homogeneity—have come to dominate others, creating a disequilibrium that is difficult to correct in the moment as much as it may tend to be corrected over time.

## Contemporary Critics of Liberalism

Current criticisms of liberalism come from both political directions, though they share in common concerns about how liberalism's emphasis on individual rights undermines community. Critics from both the right and the left argue that the liberal emphasis on individual success and self-interest leads to an economic system in which everyone pursues their own self-interest at the expense of the common good. While concerns about cronyism come from both sides of the political aisle, one major concern of the left is the way rising levels of inequality undermine or even make true community impossible and undermine the democratic process. The term "neoliberalism," used now primarily by critics of free market capitalism, is used not only to describe the effects of free market economics on vulnerable populations, but also to critique the way in which capitalism has become entwined in existing power structures. The result, critics contend, is an oligarchic structure that privileges the rich at the expense of the poor and centralizes power (Jones 2014).[1] The broad contention of these critics is that liberalism's emphasis on the self-interest of individuals occurs at the expense of the community as a whole, particularly as rising levels of inequality leads to marginalization that cannot be solved through purely market forces alone.

Thomas Piketty's influential book *Capital in the 21st Century* exemplifies this critique of liberalism at least insofar as liberalism is linked to capitalist economic policies and relatively limited regulation of the economy. Piketty's work is primarily descriptive, but the normative thrust of his work is that the economic trends he claims exist show that free market liberalism is leading to greater levels of inequality, greater levels of political and economic corruption, and increasing levels of consumerism that isolates individuals from themselves and each other.[2] While Piketty argues that capitalism contains forces that could conceivably lessen inequality, the forces that support inequality "are potentially threatening to democratic societies and to the values of social justice on which they are based," and he characterizes the results of growing inequality as "potentially terrifying" (Piketty and Goldhammer 2017, p. 571). Piketty's critique, like many from those on the left, takes a substantive view of human rights and makes the claim that liberalism is torn between its ostensible commitment to human dignity and the free-market principles that undergird its economic policy. As a result, Piketty argues that the inequality that liberal capitalism fosters ultimately undermines the individualism that it claims to protect.

Concerns about the effects of liberalism also arise on the right. Tocqueville is perhaps the most famous observer of the isolating individualism and the relentless pursuit of equality that combine in a dynamic, industrializing, market society that undermines community and, ultimately, human happiness. Tocqueville initially distinguishes between selfishness and individualism, though ends by arguing that "individualism at first dries up only the source of public virtues; but in the long term it attacks and destroys all the others and will finally be absorbed in selfishness" (Tocqueville and Mansfield 2012, 483). While Tocqueville locates the salve to individualism in the free institutions that pull individuals back into the community, such a solution requires that individuals maintain an active public life, something that market economies, with their mobility and frenetic pace of life, make difficult. Liberalism, and in particular the combination of the quest for equality alongside the demands of commercial life, leads to a restlessness that has the potential to undermine free institutions and the social superstructure on which those institutions rely.[3]

Conservative critics like Nisbet, Putnam, and, most recently, Patrick Deneen, have built on Tocqueville's criticism, arguing that the isolation inherent in the combined economic and social systems that liberalism fosters undermines community and destroys the pillars of society such as the family and faith (Nisbet 2014; Putnam 2007; Deneen 2018). Patrick Deneen's 2018 *Why Liberalism Failed* follows in this tradition, arguing that it is precisely this commitment to individual freedom and self-interest that ultimately unravels the community norms on which liberalism ultimately relies. Liberalism, according to Deneen, frustrates all of its goals, partly because it is ultimately impossible to base a society on self-interest. By failing to recognize and protect the communities on which individuals rely for full flourishing, liberalism undermines its own foundation, setting the stage for a solipsistic individualism where individuals are cut off from the communities—religious, familial, neighborly—that both protect individual value and make such value meaningful. This solipsism is linked to what Deneen argues is "liberalism's great failing and ultimate weakness: its incapacity to foster self-governance" (Deneen 2018, p. 83). As a result of this failure, Deneen argues that, "A political philosophy that was launched to foster greater equity, defend a pluralistic tapestry of different cultures and beliefs, protect human dignity, and, of course, expand liberty, in practice generates titanic inequality, enforces uniformity and homogeneity, fosters material and spiritual degradation, and undermines freedom" (Deneen 2018, p. 3). Cut off from communities, religious organizations, and other communal endeavors, individuals rule themselves and ultimately, in the heat of consumeristic glories, forget how to rule themselves at all.

## Liberalism's Philosophical Commitments

The criticisms from the right and left share in common a fear that liberalism's emphasis on the individual erodes the foundation for true community. It is not merely individualism, but instead the deeper philosophic beliefs that undergird that individualism that have the potential to erode community norms and values. The Enlightenment beliefs in individual rationality, the primacy of consent that stems from that rationality, and the sufficiency of self-interest for creating order combine to create the broader commitment to individualism that characterizes liberal thought. Yet, in isolation or at their extremes, each of these commitments erodes the pillars on which communities rely, namely, sub-rational traditions and norms, sub-rational obedience to (most) authority, and concern for community wellbeing that requires more than mere self-interest for its activation. In each case, the extreme in either direction leads to either a subsuming of the individual or the undermining of community.

Perhaps the primary commitment, stemming from liberalism's Enlightenment roots, is a commitment to individual rationality, on which all other liberal commitments are built. The idea that individuals are rationally capable of determining their own life course is the justification for everything from consent to limited government. It is also the foundational rejection of the divine right to rule. If all humans are equally rational and, of course, equally fallible in their rationality, no one has a right to rule anyone else without that person's rational consent, at least where the most profound and foundational questions are concerned. Crucially, this rationality is also the source of our natural rights, the abilities, and powers that it would be *irrational* to give to anyone else absolutely.

Despite its intuitive attraction, this assumption of rationality was actually a direct attack on at least two traditional understandings of human community up to that point. Communities, particularly communities with a set of shared values, usually assumed a kind of pre-rational agreement that cannot, at least not completely, be assessed rationally. The clearest example of this is the way faith communities are organized. While traditional Judeo-Christian religion takes seriously human rational capacities, it nevertheless also emphasizes the felt and lived experience of faith as something fundamentally non-rational, something that one can generally not reason oneself into, Anselm's proofs notwithstanding. Religion requires that humans take a leap of faith, the leap coming precisely because humans cannot link every point of faith into a bridge for reason to walk over. Abraham's offering of Isaac was not a rational sacrifice, but one of trust. While reason is a defining characteristic of human beings, it is not the primary way humans are linked to other human beings. The new liberal focus on reason, in contrast, assumes in part that the only legitimate bond between human beings is that of rational consent.

The second area in which rationality challenges community stems from liberalism's attitude toward the traditions and norms that tied communities together. Many of these norms and traditions are religiously based, but many are simply the way the community discovered how to live together over time. Some are nearly universal across human societies, such as prohibitions against murder and incest, while others are much more parochial and local, such as the way to navigate a village street, or acceptable uses of a public square. In both the universal and the local, while such traditions and norms typically could be explained using reason in a post hoc fashion, the reason tradition works as an ordering mechanism is precisely because most people do not require such rational explanations before they follow the rules. Farmers who question every inherited and seemingly irrational lesson about farming would very likely starve to death. Liberalism changed the attitude toward tradition from one of a general trust in inherited wisdom to a belief that all traditions, norms, and values under the microscope of human reason, in part because they support existing power structures.

The final commitment of liberalism is that a foundation of natural rights, based on individual rationality and motivated by self-interest, is enough to create order in society. On this understanding, individuals following their self-interest, protecting their own rights to life, liberty and property and refraining from violating the rights of others, creates an order out of which communities emerge. Adam Smith's famous invisible hand is merely one iteration of this spontaneous order tradition. As Smith formulates it, "[i]t is not from the benevolence of the butcher, the brewer, or the baker that we expect our dinner, but from their regard to their own interest. We address ourselves, not to their humanity but to their self-love, and never talk to them of our own necessities but of their advantages" (Smith 1982, pp. 26–27). Smith here is of course speaking primarily about economic order, not of broader political or social order, but the point has been expanded by various libertarian and related thinkers who make the argument that all order can be rooted in self-interest alone (see for example, Ayn Rand's work).

What these later libertarians fail to recognize and what critics fail to see in Smith's work as well is that self-interest cannot alone be the primary driving force of all human society. Smith's *Theory of Moral Sentiments* provides a counter to self-interest in the form of sympathy, a point Smith scholars have long recognized but broader cultural criticisms have not. Even Smith does not claim that all order in society can be based on self-interest, largely because the narrowest form of self-interest leaves out family, friends, and the truly dependent. Whatever the complete reading of Smith, the characterization of his work—as well as that of Locke and other early liberals—as being based purely in self-interest seems to support the broader contention that liberal thought cannot make room for other-regarding or community-oriented feelings like charity, love, or self-sacrifice. That communities often need these feelings is a major criticism from both the left and right, with the distinction that the left argues that government should be fulfilling these virtues while the right argues that religious communities can fill the gap. In both cases, alternatives to individual self-interest are required to assist with common goals and protect the vulnerable in society.

At the same time, viewing liberalism not as a theory separable from time and place but instead as a corrective to the past emphasis on the community can help clarify liberalism's substantive principles. Liberalism's attack on traditional understandings of community was rooted in real concerns about how individuals were subsumed by communities in harmful ways. At least at the beginning, liberalism was a corrective to the disequilibrium between the community and the state. At the time Locke and other early liberal writers were crafting their theories, the overwhelming power in society rested with the community. Individuals in most European societies in the 1600s had little freedom to do what the community disapproved of, most obviously to dissent in religion or politics, areas where disagreement was particularly important but also particularly dangerous. Nowhere in Locke, as radical as he seems, does he claim communities are not important, only that communities must be judged on the basis of whether individuals can consent to them rationally.

As the early liberals recognized, sub-rational traditions and norms, sub-rational obedience to authority, and sacrificing the individual to the community could be (and were) pushed to extremes of their own. The world that liberalism was born into was one where received wisdom was always the most efficient and the most just, representing in some ways a calcification of norms and values that made innovation of various kinds, whether scientific, political, or moral, extremely difficult. Liberal thinkers looked at the world of the sixteenth and seventeenth centuries and found it difficult to justify why some people, merely by luck of their birth, should have access to a different justice system, a different property system, and a place in society wholly cut off from those of others. Placing traditions and systems of power under the microscope of human reason drew attention to disparities and injustice that had long been simply taken for granted. It also identified clear barriers to economic and political progress that could change the lives of millions of individuals for the better, though also undermining existing power structures at the same time. The liberal insistence on consent challenged the power of absolute monarchs who placed a stagnant understanding of community ahead of the well-being of the people themselves. The insistence on individual rationality was a corrective to the belief that the individual could access no wisdom other than that filtered through the church or the king. The insistence on self-interest was a response to the belief that individuals can and should sacrifice everything to the will and caprice of barons, or monarchs, or Popes.

Early liberalism, then, rather than being a theory unto itself, is perhaps best understood as a corrective to this imbalance. At the same time, correctives always run the risk of swinging the pendulum too far in the other direction and, whether fairly or not, liberalism's insistence on the primacy of the rational and self-interested individual was in many ways a challenge to what makes communities successful. What both liberalism and more traditional forms of community require is a recognition that individuals need communities and communities are made up of individuals. Neither individual nor community has any meaning, any protection, or any possibility of flourishing without the other. In the case of liberalism, by attacking the bedrock of human community through an attack on traditions and faith, it was perhaps inevitable that the pendulum would swing too far in the other direction and that liberalism would end up undermining the communities that make liberal life possible and worthwhile. At the same time, it seems reasonable that if one goal of liberalism is serve as a corrective to previous collectivist approaches, to balance collective needs with individual goals and interests, a reasonable task would be to find a way to guide the pendulum back into the middle where, even if the equilibrium is an unstable one, society can at least get closer to the goal of balancing individual rights or interests against the needs of the communities to which they belong.

What all these critiques have in common is the belief that the web of principles that stem from the emphasis on individual rationality—the rational critique of tradition and values, the emphasis on rational consent rather than habitual obedience, and the emphasis on self-interest over sacrificial other-regarding behavior—all undermine liberalism itself when pushed to their most extreme. For most critics of liberalism, these commitments undermine liberalism precisely because they are not compatible with the demands of communities, which rely heavily on sub-rational norms, values, and affections that guide and soften individual rationality and make it compatible with community needs. According to critics, liberalism has been so successful in establishing rational, consenting groups of self-interested individuals that it has begun to (or has succeeded in) destroying itself by undermining the very communities on which it relies for its success. But this destruction is the result, not of the failure of any particular principle itself, but in the imbalance that has occurred over time.

## Burke and Affectionate Liberalism

If, as I claim, the current moment is less a wholesale rejection of liberal values and more a rejection of an imbalance in the various values that liberalism claims to support, it seems possible that what is needed is a rebalanced liberalism, one that returns to its roots as the protector of both individuals and their communities and the fulcrum or balance of competing human values. The obvious though difficult solution to this problem is to find a way to pull the pendulum of individual-community relations back into a kind of center, one where individual rationality is paired with respect and affection for community traditions, where voluntary consent is paired with habitual obedience to the laws, and where self-interest is countered with affection for the community as a whole.

Perhaps surprisingly, one of the main thinkers who offers a version of a moderate and balanced liberalism is a thinker who many do not consider "liberal" in the traditional sense at all, Edmund Burke. While often lumped into the broadly "conservative" camp, much of Burke's work centers around the desire to moderate and balance the liberal commitments to freedom and self-interest against the needs of the communities to which those individuals belong. At the same time, the very moderation inherent in Burke's work may make him unattractive to idealists of all stripes, who believe the solution to these balancing problems is a rejection of one or more of liberalism's commitments or a wholesale rejection of liberalism itself. He will therefore likely continue to be something of a theoretical outsider—his very moderation of principle preventing his acceptance by any one side. Still, his work has important implications for understanding the perils and pitfalls facing modern liberalism today.

Burke's work is particularly illuminating because, unlike liberal theorists like Locke and Smith before him, Burke is a political practitioner. Unable to simply dictate liberal principles in the abstract, Burke must find a way to apply those principles to the complexities of modern commerce, imperial governance, colonial revolts, and religious conflict. It is not enough for Burke to simply claim natural rights for a particular constituency, but as a statesman he must filter those rights through the particular social and political reality in a prudential way. He makes this explicit when he argues that "as the liberties and the restrictions vary with times and circumstances, and admit of infinite modifications, they cannot be settled upon any abstract rule" (Burke 2014, p. 152). Instead, governance requires "a deep knowledge of human nature and human necessities, and of the things which facilitate or obstruct the various ends which are to be pursued by the mechanism of civil institutions" (ibid.). Perhaps because of Burke's suspicion of the applicability of abstract rights to governance, Burke is often considered more of a conservative than a true liberal, though his allegiance to standard liberal principles like natural rights is clear in his work. At the same time, he explicitly rejects any ability to apply these abstract principles directly to political affairs.

Burke's historical position is also relevant in that he is writing at a time when liberal principles are being pushed to their most extreme, most obviously in the case of the French Revolution. The French Revolution's emphasis on rationality in particular—as the grounding for natural rights and the legitimacy of all government—is a focus of much of Burke's criticism. In response, he lays out an alternative, distinctly British, form of liberalism that balances individual and community through the intermediaries of tradition and the affections. Burke's response to that revolution is in some ways the clearest example we have of a liberal thinker attempting to pull liberal principles back into a kind of moderate position, one that recognizes the various ways in which rational consent fails to protect individuals within a broader social order.[4] Burke's very criticisms of that revolution provide an outline or framework for a more balanced liberalism, even as some critics argue he pulls too far in the direction of collectivism.

In general, Burke's criticisms of the French revolution reflect his criticisms of the extremes of liberal thought broadly. His criticisms are not of the validity of the principles of rationality, consent, and self-interest themselves, but instead of the way those principles are applied in undiluted ways to society. As an alternative to jettisoning the principles themselves, Burke offers a kind of filter to each, preserving the ways individuals are protected within communities and providing a more robust understanding of how communities protect individuals against both the depredations of other individuals but also against the isolation of self-interested existence. In Burke's alternative liberalism, prejudice acts as a counterweight to rationality, habit as a counter to consent, and affection as a counter to self-interest. In each case, he does not reject the importance of rationality or consent or self-interest. Rather, he believes each is necessary but not sufficient to protect both individuals and the communities they inhabit. The balance Burke attempts to strike is an unstable one, requiring constant balancing, guiding, and rebalancing, in part through the act of statesmanship. As such, his thought is less a systemic point-by-point answer to liberal extremism, but is instead the laying out of a system of integrated values that creates a complex whole. At the root of his project is the balance between the individual and the community or the description and protection of the "civil social man."

Perhaps the most obvious way in which Burke pulls the liberal tradition into a kind of center is his focus on the affections as the primary way in which individuals are bound to their communities. Burke rejects the social contract theorists who rely on rational consent as the foundation for political communities, arguing that the real way in which people consent to government is through the affections built by habit over years of belonging to and participating in a community. It is not so much that rationality plays no role in Burke's understanding of how one consents to rule, but instead that rationality requires the softening supplement of affection in order for it to be compatible with community life. As Burke notes when comparing the English to the French, "we have not yet been completely embowelled of our natural entrails; we still feel within us, and we cherish and cultivate, those inbred sentiments which are the faithful guardians, the active monitors of our duty, the true supporters of all liberal and manly morals" (Burke 2014, p. 181). Liberalism, according to Burke, requires sentiment as much as rationality, because it is sentiment that links us to the community and links our rights with our duties.

The most dangerous position, for both individuals and the communities they are parts of, is that where the only thing binding people to their communities is mere rational agreement that can be withdrawn at any time.

The bare principle of rational consent, Burke argues, means that, according to the French, "there needs no principle of attachment, except a sense of present conveniency, to any constitution of the state" (Burke 2014, p. 183). The danger of such an approach is that without the binding force of sentiments, change will come too often and too quickly. The stability of constitutions is what allows them to successfully guide and structure government while providing a framework for predictable individual decision making. Constitutions cannot and should not be remade every year. The contract theorists "think that government may vary like modes of dress, and with as little ill effect" (ibid.). Yet, according to Burke, the emphasis on consent alone, without the softening and mitigating influence of sentiment, undermines the stability that constitutions need to be effective. Without sentiments, reason can nitpick any decent constitution, leading to continual calls for not just reform but revolution. As Burke laments, "It has been the misfortune, not as these gentlemen think it, the glory, of this age, that every thing is to be discussed" (Burke 2014, p. 187).

The other limitation of individual rationality is that it is time bound in a way broader social wisdom is not. Burke argues that the English are "are afraid to put men to live and trade each on his own private stock of reason; because we suspect that this stock in each man is small, and that the individuals would do better to avail themselves of the general bank and capital of nations, and of ages." It is less that Burke believes men are fundamentally irrational, but that what rationality they possess is ultimately linked most closely with the affairs that concern them directly. In areas of complex social import, where the needs and interests of many individuals mesh, trusting the inherited wisdom of ages in the form of common law or inherited traditions is a safer option than the ingenuity of any single person.

This view of the relationship between sentiment and reason relates in crucial ways to the role rights play in Burke's theory. These sentiments are the foundation for a more robust rights doctrine, one that represents the way in which the rights individuals have are softened by affections to the community and the duties those affections support. While Burke clearly argues that natural rights exist, he is much more hesitant about the role such rights play in the actual practice of government. While individuals have rights in the state of nature, those rights do not extend, while in civil society, to the ability to question every individual act of government. In agreement with Locke, Burke says the "civil social man"—the man outside the state of nature—gives up the right to "judge for himself, and to assert his own cause. He abdicates all right to be his own governor" (Burke 2014, p. 151). Burke does not, of course, mean that individuals have no rights in society, but that the shape of the rights they have are determined in large part by the society in which they live.

Moreover, the "civil social rights" of men in society are, as the name suggests, more social than the individualistic rights of the state of nature. These civil social rights include the right to property, to nourish one's offspring and, crucially for liberals, "Whatever each man can separately do, without trespassing upon others, he has a right to do for himself" (Burke 2014, p. 150). Rights in society, the rights of our "second nature," include the right to live by law and under a system of justice, the right to the "fruits of their industry," the right to inherit from their parents and pass that inheritance on to their children, "instruction in life, and to consolation in death" (ibid.). These socialized rights extend from natural rights, but are softened and socialized because, by necessity, rights in society must find a balance between the rights of individuals and the needs of communities themselves. Rights must be made compatible with community need. Such an approach is completely compatible with individualism, because "[i]f civil society be made for the advantage of man, all the advantages for which it is made become his right" (ibid.). The rights of man in society become the best way to uphold the broader goal of human flourishing, a goal that recognizes the importance of community for the happiness of individuals.

The sociality of men on Burke's understanding is not a forced or artificial one. Society is not created by an act of consent, but instead consent reflects the existence of these societies and the way they support individual well-being. The societies that Burke thinks are most tightly linked to his conception of consent are those that start at the bottom, with the natural affections of individuals for family, friends, and neighbors. As Burke's famous line goes, "To be attached to the subdivision, to love the little platoon we belong to in society, is the first principle (the germ as it were) of public affections" (Burke 2014, p. 136). For Burke, attachment to our government begins not at the rational top-down level of consent, but instead in the bottom-up affections that begin in our families and neighborhoods and filter upward. Individuals still consent to government and governments that harm individuals and their little platoons are likely to lose the affectionate attachment that makes truly rational consent possible. But without those affections any understanding of individual rights will be shallow and, in fact, dangerous, because such hollowed out rights threaten the roots of the communities that secure our rights and make them meaningful. The French, by "reasoning without prejudice, [...] leave not one stone upon another in the fabric of human society" (Burke and Ritchie 1997, p. 166).

The attachment to our little platoon is linked to the prejudice or the preference for one's own and for the past that Burke believes contains its own form of wisdom. It is also the only real source of motion in society, providing the motivation that reason alone lacks. As he notes, "[P]rejudice, with its reason, has a motive to give action to that reason, and an affection which will give it permanence" (Burke 2014, p. 182). The affections individuals have for their small platoons provide both the motivation for action and the permanence that links people's reason to their communities. Prejudice, far from being simply a negative trait, is in fact the quintessential human trait, one that provides the motivation for consent that reason alone lacks. While rational consent might be *reasonable* to provide to many different communities in many different circumstances, reason alone lacks the motive or reason to explain why consent makes sense to *this* particular community at *this* particular time. It is prejudice, the love of one's own, that provides the motivation, the linkage to a particular community, that logic alone cannot. Without prejudice, humans have no reason to settle on one particular community, a settling that is necessary for human survival and flourishing. Such settling is also absolutely necessary for the growth of precisely the institutions that protect individual rights over the long-term, such as rule of law, separation of powers, and federalism precisely because such institutions cannot be created, ad hoc, in the moment, but only result from the growth of norms and customs over time.

Burke's social contract is therefore based in a kind of historical empiricism, while Locke's more logical account is not. While Locke based his view of consent on what rational individuals would consent to as a way to uncover limits on government, Burke bases his view of consent on what passionate and reasonable humans actually need to both consent to government and to flourish. Consent for Burke cannot be simply the rational consent of Locke's theory because such consent is incompatible with community itself. Burke recognizes what Locke's account, rooted as it was in an earlier reaction to absolutism, did not, namely that human beings are equal parts rational and passionate and that consent and the communities such consent creates will require both reason and affection to inspire their creation and secure their permanence. For Burke, rather than starting at the level of logical principles, consent requires knowledge of the particulars of a community, gleaned over generations and linked to the way people have lived together and died together in that community over time. Affection roots individuals to a particular community over time, providing the stability that is required to secure the growth of the institutions that support and sustain rights. As Burke argues, "The science of constructing a commonwealth, or renovating it, or reforming it, is, like every other experimental science, not to be taught a priori" (Burke 2014).

One final and crucial reason Burke's corrective of liberal rationality is so important is that it is only through the affections that rights can become safe for the communities that secure them. The complexity of society—the various needs, rights, and interests to be held in the balance—requires that rights be "reflected" off the safer medium of the affections, which serves the goal of binding rights and duties together. As Burke notes, "the primitive rights of men undergo such a variety of refractions and reflections, that it becomes absurd to talk of them as if they continued in the simplicity of their original direction. The nature of man is intricate; the objects of society are of the greatest possible complexity" (Burke 2014, p. 153). The reflections of the rights off the affections serve the dual purpose for Burke of binding individuals to a particular community while at the same time binding rights and duties together.

## The Intergenerational Compact

As part of his larger argument about the limitations of individual rationality, Burke believes adherence to tradition and to the wisdom of the past provide a necessary corrective and supplement for individual reason. Because the ends of society go beyond a particular generation and because those ends encompass much more depth and breadth than any one human mind can understand or encapsulate, Burke believed that the wisdom of the ages could provide access to the means and ends of society that individuals themselves lack. The access points for this wisdom are prejudice, habit, and affection, which in a sense build up consent over many generations while linking rights to duties and tradition.

Burke makes this alternative to the state of nature clear when he offers the intergenerational compact as a replacement for (or correction of) traditional contract theory. Because "the ends of such a partnership cannot be obtained in many generations, it becomes a partnership not only between those who are living, but between those who are living, those who are dead, and those who are to be born" (Burke 2014, p. 193). Burke's intergenerational compact is, to a certain degree, symbolic, since it is not clear how one could have a contract with a dead person in any real sense, but symbolism has deep political relevance for Burke. That individuals believe themselves bound in some sense by the goals and ends of those who have passed and by the needs and wants of those who are to come is the crucial piece, not that such a contract be enforceable in any legal sense. For Burke, the intergenerational compact is, like the affections one has for one's own, a way of reminding individuals of their connection to others, of the limits of their reason, and of the limits of their ability to enact radical changes without harming the overall superstructure of norms and values on which society rests.

That individual reason must occasionally (or often) be sacrificed to or subsumed under the traditions and needs of the community is not in fact the illiberal sacrifice that it seems at first. Burke is not a mere reactionary, arguing that the community is above the individual. Instead, he argues that the worth of individuals is best recognized and best protected within a broader community tradition like that of Britain, where rights and duties grew alongside each other over centuries and where the kinks were worked out through a gradual process of adaptation and give and take. The appeal to tradition and history supports the respect for oneself as an individual enmeshed in a community, one with a connection to family, friends, neighbors, a way of life, traditions and values, all of which are both part of but also separate from the concept of naked, rational, self-interest.

Central to the practical nature of Burke's approach is that he does not believe he is asking humans to do anything that they do not already do naturally. His argument is both descriptive and prescriptive. The sacrifice of individual reason to the traditions and mores of the group is not only natural but is, in most cases, not seen as a sacrifice at all. It is, on Burke's account, the isolated individual of the social contract theorist who is unnatural. According to Burke, humans naturally view society in intergenerational terms. They are happy, under most circumstances, to be bound by the norms and values of past generations and they naturally look to the past for advice and counsel on how to behave in the present. The intergenerational compact is the way of nature, according to Burke, precisely because the individual's "stock of reason" is so small: "We are afraid to put men to live and trade each on his own private stock of reason, because we suspect that this stock of each man is small, and that the individuals do better to avail themselves of the general bank and capital of nations and of ages … Prejudice renders a man's virtue his habit, and not a series of unconnected acts. Through just prejudice, his duty becomes part of his nature" (Burke 2014, p. 182). This "second nature" is the result of the habitual obedience to a community framed by affectionate attachment where the limits of each person's individual reason is supplemented by the wisdom of generations.

Overall, Burke's reinterpretation of nature is concerned with rediscovering what he terms the "civil social man" for liberal theory. Burke's civil social man has a specific nature, but this nature only develops fully within a supportive political community. The civil social man is not just a socialized version of the man in the state of nature, but is in fact a rejection of that man as incomplete, a caricature of human nature, missing the crucial sentiments, affections, prejudices, and attachments that make political life possible. On Burke's account, the natural rights theory of Locke is incomplete because "the restraints on men, as well as their liberties, are to be reckoned among their rights" (Burke 2014, p. 152). In this sense, Burke sees himself as offering a corrective to the liberal view of human nature, one that more accurately reflects the way human attachments form and the relevance of those attachments to political communities broadly. This view does not undermine liberalism, but instead provides a supplement or a corrective to what Burke believes threatens to become not only an isolating individualism, but a rationalistic approach to political community that has the potential to undermine political community itself.

## Burke on Revolution

While many scholars have linked Burke to conservatism or even a reactionary rejection of all change, he explicitly rejects the idea that political stability requires the subsuming of the individual completely to the needs of the community. This is particularly true in his discussion of revolution, even as he decries the French Revolution as being both unnecessary in its ends and cruel in its means. Throughout his criticism of the French, Burke never argues that revolution is never required, nor does he believe that all resistance to community dictates is illegitimate. His concern is that constant appeals to the power or necessity of revolution have the potential to undermine the foundation of government itself. He notes, "I never liked this continual talk of resistance and revolution, or the practice of making the extreme medicine of the constitution its daily bread. It renders the habit of society dangerously valetudinary: it is taking periodical doses of mercury sublimate, and swallowing down repeated provocative of cantharides to our love of liberty" (Burke 2014, p. 155).

For Burke, constant appeals to revolution do two things. First, such constant calls make society "valetudinary" in that such calls emphasize the negative aspects of a state while undermining or casting doubt on the many ways that a given society is, in fact, functioning and healthy. It teaches citizens that the glass is politically half empty rather than half full. This tendency to criticize the state undermines the affections, habits, and mores that are the grounding for any kind of voluntary obedience. It also, in Burke's view, leads to a preference for revolution over reform. This preference for revolution and resistance is the "mercury sublimate" that, while it might work as medicine for the very ill constitution, may make a generally healthy society sick and unstable. From a purely practical perspective, revolution, of course, is much riskier than reform, and revolutionaries are, historically, more likely to end up in a worse place than they started. Burke sees most revolution as the equivalent of recommending brain surgery for a cold.

Burke's rejection of revolution does not, however, stem from a rejection of individual rights. Revolution may be necessary, particularly when a current government has rejected the traditions and ways of the people themselves. Burke's criteria for revolution do not require that an individual support the community of the moment against the traditions of the past. On Burke's account, the community is the most likely to be just when it adheres to longstanding beliefs and values. It is most likely to be unjust when it brings forth new innovative ideas about how to organize and structure civil society. The individual can and should resist the latter and use the former to defend himself and his rights against the tyranny of the present community. This leads us to Burke's broader position on revolution, one which takes the position that revolution is and always must be a matter, not of choice, but of necessity: revolution "is the first and supreme necessity only, a necessity that is not chosen but chooses, a necessity paramount to deliberation, that admits no discussion, and demands no evidence, which alone can justify a resort to anarchy" (Burke 2014, p. 193). Revolution cannot be the result of rational deliberation, but must, like the right of self-defense from which it extends, derive from the immediate and instinctive needs of the moment.

Burke's theory of revolution, like his theory of liberalism broadly, is that the act of revolution cannot rest on the reason of individual men in their individual capacities. The act of revolution must be borne by necessity, a necessity that drives men forward to protect their inherited rights against an attempt to destroy them and their community itself. Revolution therefore does not destroy a community, but is a defense of the grounding of that community itself, a defense of the principles, rights, and prejudices that made that community unique and worth protecting. In so doing, revolution protects individuals themselves, both in the practical sense by protecting them, as long as possible, from the death and destruction that revolution itself brings, but also protects individuals by recognizing the complex suite of ends for which society exists. It is in this way that Burke distinguishes between the Glorious Revolution of the British, a revolution to protect the community, and the French Revolution, a revolution that destroys the foundation of community itself.

As a statesman, Burke does not provide a consistent or rigorous theory of revolution itself. At the same time, few liberal thinkers of his era offered anything like a consistent theory of revolution. For most liberal theorists, revolutionary justifications are by their very nature post hoc. Adam Smith, for example, in response in part to the French Revolution, argues that "it often requires, perhaps, the highest effort of political wisdom to determine when a real patriot ought to support and endeavour to re-establish the authority of the old system, and when he ought to give way to the more daring, but often dangerous spirit of innovation" (Smith 1976, p. 232). Burke's appeal to necessity is echoed in the American Declaration of Independence, where Jefferson appeals continually to "necessity," arguing that the colonists were "impelled" to separate. For Jefferson and the other colonists, at least rhetorically, the revolution was not in fact the choice of men in their rational capacities so much as the forced choice of those defending their lives and liberties from tyranny. In this sense then Burke's theory, or lack thereof, of revolution falls squarely within the liberal tradition, one in which revolution is recognized as sometimes necessary and even desirable, but always fraught. Any theory of revolution then will depend heavily on the political wisdom of those in the moment who are the best able to determine what will be won and what will be lost.

## Burke's Solution for Liberalism's Ills

Pulling these various strands back together, Burke's criticism of the extremes of liberalism relies on the triad of prejudice, habit, and the affections to counter in various ways the limitations of reason, consent, and self-interest. Using these concepts, Burke offers an alternative to an isolated individualism in the form of a social individualism, the state of nature in the form of an intergenerational compact, and to revolution in the form of affectionate reform. Burke's solution to the problems inherent in extremist liberalism is not to offer another idealized world, but in fact to reflect in practical terms on a liberalism that is based not only on human nature but on how humans behave in the real world. It also, crucially, is linked to a set of institutional supports that help support this moderate liberalism.

The second half of the *Reflections*, often overlooked, provides a discussion of the various institutional structures that Burke believes are necessary to support the moderate liberalism of the civil social man. Unsurprisingly, these institutions reflect British constitutionalism and represent a rejection of the radical democratization of the French. Burke's vision is broadly representative, in that people have representation by representatives of their choosing, but it also retains important "conservative" elements that act as brakes on that democratic change. He argues that limited liberal government requires both moral and institutional instruction: "…it is very expedient that, by moral instruction, [citizens] should be taught, and by their civil constitutions they should be compelled, to put many restrictions upon the immoderate exercise of [thirst for power]" (Burke and Ritchie 1997, p. 158). Both of these goals are the tasks of a "true statesman."

Such institutional brakes play two crucial roles within the liberal tradition. In the first place, they provide a buffer against democratic incursions on individual rights through institutions like independent courts, federalism, separation of powers, and checks and balances. At the same time, such institutions soften rights claims by filtering them through tradition, manners, and mores of the people, linking rights to the particular way of life of a people. By emphasizing the particularity of both democracy and rights, Burkean liberalism makes both compatible with one another at the practical level, in a way that is difficult for abstract democracy or abstract liberalism to successfully do. In this way, liberal democracy is rooted in a particular time and place and linked to the communities in which individuals live.

Law itself plays a foundational role in this understanding of an affectionate and rooted liberal democracy. In a legal and political system that links representation and rights to particular times and places, the universality of these abstract principles is moderated by the needs of distinct communities of known individuals. Moreover, a separation between the legal and the political means that the laws that affect individuals in their day to day lives are buffered to a certain extent from the more dramatic changes in party politics. Judicial independence is therefore central to this system. As might be expected, Burke's model for the social compact is English common law, not positive law. The slow accumulation of consent over time as laws are demonstrated to be just in the daily challenges of group living is a better foundation for a truly representative liberalism, Burke believes, than an abstract moment of consent. Rather than Locke's compact where the individual consents at a discrete moment to be ruled by an abstraction of the group as a whole, in the Burkean compact the individual consents and has consented over time, through voluntary obedience to law and to institutions generally.

This common law approach to consent slows change by integrating individual desires and interests into the community in a gradual way, avoiding shocks to what is already a tenuous balancing act. But perhaps most importantly, the common law approach to consent places the individual firmly within the context of a particular community and links the process of consent to a multigenerational project. The growth of common law occurs over many generations, making it possible for individuals to feel a connection not only to a present discrete moment of consent, but allowing individuals to consent many times over throughout their lives, accepting the wisdom of the past while looking forward to the future of a community full of individuals. This understanding of the social contract looks much more like the intergenerational compact Burke lays forth, one that is a "partnership in all science; a partnership in all art; a partnership in every virtue, and in all perfection" (Burke 2014, p. 193). Burkean liberalism, on these grounds, provides a theoretical (though eminently practical) justification for limiting the nationalizing and centralizing forces of modern society, particularly the growth of the power of positive law wielded by majorities.

## Conclusion

A return to a Burkean liberalism does not, of course, solve all political conflicts or eradicate the roots of all discontent. It is not a panacea, nor are its principles easily applied to cultures unfamiliar with liberal principles. Such outcomes are far too much to ask of any political or social system. What Burke's liberalism does do is help to ameliorate some of the major concerns of communitarian critics of liberalism of all stripes. It does not, however, eradicate discrimination, provide unlimited individual freedom, guarantee equal outcomes, or protect all communities in the face of growing mobility and economic change. Liberal society, like all societies, will always be imperfect. Perhaps Burkean liberalism's most obvious weakness is that it requires both citizens and the institutions of civic discourse—universities, public debates, and so on—to accept nuance. This in itself may not be realistic because it requires pushing back against the ideological devotion to absolute equality or to absolute freedom without falling into ideological traps on the other side. And despite the Burkean commitment to a more realistic understanding of human nature, in one sense at least it may be idealistic in that it challenges the part of human nature that sees obvious solutions as the best solutions and that chaffs with impatience against the slow process of reform.

Burkean liberalism does, however, provide a corrective to two of the major criticisms facing contemporary liberal societies. Burke's liberalism maintains the balance between an individualism characterized by a homogeneity of rights and an individualism rooted in the particulars of time and place. This approach avoids two extremes that many believe to characterize modern society: the first being the isolating individualism of modern liberalism, where individuals as homogenous and isolated beings are stripped of what gives them actual meaning and import as individuals and the second being the fragmented attitude of identity politics, where differences between groups prevent any kind of cohesive community at all. Burkean liberalism supports political pluralism, complete with prejudice in the form of a preference for one's own, but without the insistence on group identity that fragments even the healthiest communities. Burke's vision supports a diverse, pluralistic community that emphasizes harmony rather than conformity. It recognizes limitations on agreement and avoids the need to either fragment or homogenize in order to achieve liberal and communal goals.

In essence, Burke's liberalism is an ideology for the non-ideological. It is a rejection of systems and the "man of system" (as Adam Smith would call him). Instead Burke offers a philosophy for the civil social man, the individual in society. Burke's liberalism will be an imperfect balance of perfect virtues, which is itself a reflection of humans themselves. Such a system will of course not guarantee liberal outcomes because no system can. What it will help do is moderate the forces that drive against individual freedom while attempting to balance the claims of the community and the individual. Burkean liberalism reflects and accounts for the unstable equilibrium between individual interests and the common good. For Burke, the best way to preserve that equilibrium is through the complex and pluralistic combination of individual affection, diverse institutions, and, where possible, thoughtful statesmanship.

## Notes

1. Neoliberalism here has a pejorative connotation.
2. Piketty's work has been criticized in a variety of contexts for his interpretation of the economic data.
3. Interestingly, Tocqueville links this restiveness to industrial crises—depressions and recessions—precisely because everyone is involved in commerce and are therefore more vulnerable to economic shocks.
4. Other examples include Montesquieu and Tocqueville, though their arguments are more subtle and therefore more open to both confusion and mischaracterization.

## References

Burke, Edmund. 2014. *Reflections on the Revolution in France*. Indianapolis: Liberty Fund Inc. http://qut.eblib.com.au/patron/FullRecord.aspx?p=3327294

Burke, Edmund (and Daniel E. Ritchie). 1997. *Further Reflections on the Revolution in France*. Indianapolis: Liberty Fund.

Deneen, Patrick J. 2018. *Why Liberalism Failed*. New Haven: Yale University Press.

*Federalist Papers*. 2013. Place of publication not identified: Stonewell Press.

Fukuyama, Francis. 2012. *The End of History and the Last Man*. London: Hamish Hamilton.

Jones, Daniel Stedman. 2014. *Masters of the Universe: Hayek, Friedman, and the Birth of Neoliberal Politics*. Princeton: Princeton University Press.

Nisbet, Robert A. 2014. *The Quest for Community: A Study in the Ethics of Order and Freedom*. Wilmington: ISI Books.

Piketty, Thomas (and Arthur Goldhammer). 2017. *Capital in the Twenty-First Century*. Cambridge, MA: Belknap Press.

Putnam, Robert D. 2007. *Bowling Alone: The Collapse and Revival of American Community*. New York: Simon & Schuster.

Smith, Adam. 1976. *The Theory of Moral Sentiments: Glasgow Edition*. Indianapolis: Liberty Fund.

_____. 1982. *An Inquiry Into the Nature and Causes of the Wealth of Nations, Volume 1*. Vol. 1 edition. Indianapolis: Liberty Fund.

Tocqueville, Alexis de (and Harvey Claflin Mansfield). 2012. *Democracy in America*. Chicago: University of Chicago Press.

# Democratic Peace Theory, Montesquieu, and Public Choice

Sarah M. Burns and Chad Van Schoelandt

In Immanuel Kant's *Perpetual Peace*, he claimed the only legitimate form of government is republican, as it derives "the constitution … from the idea of the original compact" (Kant 2016, p. 121). Along with this remarkably bold assertion in 1795, he claimed that all states should become republican in order to ensure the dignity of all human beings. More intoxicating still, if this occurred, it would foster peaceful relations among all the countries of the globe. That is, democratic political institutions on the domestic scale promote international peace. After many decades as a respected theory, it became the foundation for the creation of the UN and the Universal Declaration of Human Rights. This document would serve as a blueprint for Western powers to determine when and where to

S. M. Burns (✉)
Department of Political Science, Rochester Institute of Technology, Rochester, NY, USA
e-mail: smbgsm@rit.edu

C. Van Schoelandt
Department of Philosophy, Tulane University, New Orleans, LA, USA
e-mail: cvanscho@tulane.edu



D. F. Hardwick, L. Marsh (eds.), *Reclaiming Liberalism*, Palgrave Studies in Classical Liberalism, https://doi.org/10.1007/978-3-030-28760-3_9

send peacekeepers or their military to enforce human rights norms in the developing world—all with the hope of spreading democracy around the world.

While Western countries have championed the Kantian idea that democracy promotes peaceful relations among states, this view faces a number of important theoretical challenges. Among the challenges is that theorists disagree about the mechanism through which democracy could promote peace. One might look, for instance, for a link between the domestic democratic institutional norms and general constraints on the use of force, or, alternatively, for ways that democratic institutions tend to reduce citizens' desires for war, or that within democracies war becomes socially unacceptable. As Levy explains, while there is agreement "that democracies rarely if ever fight each other," there is no "agreement as to how best to explain this strong empirical regularity" (Levy 2002, p. 359).

We would emphasize that the incapacity to discern a clear mechanism for democratic peace theory has also come at a time when the spread of democracy has diminished (Dobson 2013). In recent decades, democratization has stagnated and many developed democracy states have turned to an exclusionary form of nationalism. Simultaneously, the world has experienced a rise in stable authoritarian regimes developing large and powerful militaries. Given the state of world politics today and the incapacity to discern the source of democratic peace, it is important to look elsewhere.

The difficulty uncovering how democracy promotes peaceful relations and the data on conflicts have led scholars to start decoupling the different systems that are typically linked within Western societies. This, in turn, led to the development of capitalist peace theory—the modern version of *doux commerce*—according to which the free market system and economic integration, rather than the democratic political system, explains the expansion of peaceful relations among states.[1] Put another way, this theory posits that economic liberalization has the greatest capacity to reduce the likelihood of interstate conflict.

Capitalist peace theory has the added benefit of circumventing the dangerous combination of philosophical traditions housed in democratic peace theory. The democracy-based theory posits that people in diverse nations around the world will see the benefits of a liberal political system, understood as a system with free elections, checks and balances, the protection of liberties, and the rule of law among other core elements. This assumption is based in part on the evolutionary view of human nature created by Hegel. According to Hegel's theory of societal development, we reached the "end of history" in the battle of Jena in 1806. At this point, thanks to Napoleon's empire, enlightenment thought spread throughout Europe. Importantly, the spread of enlightenment marks the final step of human development. For Hegel, human nature has fundamentally *changed*. At the highest level, namely developed European states, citizens were now capable of accepting the form of government associated with the end of history. After Hegel, however, this concept linked up with the Kantian ideals of a peaceful democratic world, reiterated over several decades.

When Woodrow Wilson entered World War I, he claimed the United States needed to make the world "safe for democracy" and they would fight to "vindicate the principles of peace and justice" with the other "free and self-government peoples of the world" to advance those principles (Wilson 1979). At the close of the war, Wilson then attempted to create the League of Nations to prevent glory-seeking militarism from winning out over these principles. He failed, in part because European powers were not inclined to give up the glory of their imperial holdings. The growing momentum for recognizing autonomy reached a zenith in WWII. As early as the Atlantic Charter, Winston Churchill and Franklin Roosevelt mutually pledged to "respect the right of all peoples to choose the form of government under which they will live" in order to attempt to lay the groundwork for a world of free choice for all people (Churchill and Roosevelt 1941).

By the close of the war, liberal democracy and communism stood as the two clear winners. Ideologically, the end of WWII represents a moment when liberal democracy and communism collectively beat glory-seeking imperialism and fascism. In many minds, these two metanarratives were the only two remaining forms of legitimate government. For the West and her allies,[2] we see the joining of the Kantian ideal of a democratic peace with Hegel's concept of human evolution, while the USSR upheld Marx's version of Hegel's philosophy with a similarly dangerous pull toward forcing other regimes to accept the "final" form of government. Both systems claimed to be *the* final form of government: they need only battle with each other for the title. With the close of the Cold War, as Francis Fukuyama explains, "[t]he triumph of the West, of the Western *idea*, is evident ... in the total exhaustion of viable systematic alternatives to Western liberalism" (Fukuyama 1989, p. 3). According to him, we had *finally* reached the end of history. It was only a matter of time before all states became democratic. Despite a variety of setbacks in a variety of countries in the twenty-first century, Western states continue to attempt to promote democratization founding their foreign policy on the combination of Kant's theory of peace and Hegel's theory of human evolution.

The coupling of these two theories is deeply problematic, however. If democratic peace theorists push democratization, this can cause the creation of illiberal democracies. Some states will simply have de facto one-party rule and joining that party will be necessary for anyone seeking access to power or privilege in that country. Other states have elected leaders that consolidate power and imprison or kill those who oppose their leadership (Zakaria 1997). When developed democracies attempt to convince or offer aid to those who will become democratic, there are often unforeseen consequences that leave these people no more free and the state on a road that leads away from development. In situations like this, it is unclear what the developed countries should do. Should they send peacekeepers or soldiers to enforce the new democratic norms? In the case of peacekeepers, many studies have shown that domestic audiences do not have the appetite for long occupations that do not directly relate to national security (Jentleson and Britton 1998; Eichenberg 2005). In the case of the military, as Russett explains, "[t]he model of 'fight them, beat them, and make them democratic' is irrevocably flawed as a basis for contemporary action" (Russett 1994, pp. 135–36).

The problem for democratic peace theory is therefore two-fold. If they promote the creation of new democracies and those democracies become oppressive, the theory has failed so they should intervene whether through diplomacy, peacekeepers, or military action. It is likely that diplomacy will only be successful in a few instances and the other two levels have significant costs for leaders. Furthermore, as Pickering and Peceny's (2006) study shows, whenever the United States, the United Kingdom, France, and the UN intervened, there was either no political liberalization or no democratization. Only the UN's "blue helmet" initiatives have born democratic fruit. In other words, democracy enthusiasts have tended to assume everyone will want and accept liberal democratic institutions. There is an underlying Hegelian/Kantian assumption that once a society reaches a certain stage of development, they will *want* liberal democracy and accept that it is the only legitimate form of government. When they come upon those who reject or abuse it, there is little they can do to correct this issue. They cannot force anyone to be free.

To find a different route for peaceful international interactions, this chapter will move away from the combination of the Kantian and Hegelian models and reach back to the classical liberal period where there is a more fixed understanding of human nature and human limitations. The chapter will focus largely on the theories of Montesquieu. The primary aim of this chapter is to explicate and build upon what was then called *doux commerce*, namely the softening impact of international trade. Importantly, we argue that Montesquieu provides insights for contemporary research on the conditions of international peace as well as the benefits of market societies. To this end, the chapter proceeds as follows. Section "Limits of the Theory" discusses the limitations of the theory. The next section addresses the classical liberal understanding of the impact of commerce on morals, with special emphasis on explaining Montesquieu's particular version of the theory. Section "Commerce: The Future and the Past" turns to Montesquieu's views concerning the need to separate commercial from political power and his appeal to eighteenth-century European leaders to shift focus from war to commerce. Section "A Contemporary Research Agenda for Montesquieu's Capitalist Peace Theory" discusses how Montesquieu's capitalist peace theory may be recast in terms of the recent methodology of public choice theory. This modernization highlights the potential for ongoing development and refinement of Montesquieu's insights, as well as suggests an important challenge for his theory.

## Limits of the Theory

We want to note a few of the limits of capitalist peace theory as we understand it.

First, there is a background assumption of a modern state structure. We will remain completely agnostic on whether or not the capitalist peace theory should or could extend to other forms of social organization.

Second, capitalist peace theory is closely related to questions about morality in a commercial society. Several classical liberal theorists like Hume, Montesquieu, and Smith saw the shift toward a proto-capitalist system of economics as a move that would foster important virtues—albeit one's anathema to the Christian understanding of virtue that requires renouncing worldly desires. In this chapter, we are explicitly siding with the perspective offered by classical liberalism while simultaneously recognizing its limitations for the improvement of the human condition.

Unlike democratic peace theory, commercialization does not offer a panacea for all of society's problems.[3] Within markets, some people may become more selfish, model themselves on the wealthy rather than the noble, engage in morally harmful commodification, including human beings, or fail to realize certain communal values in their relations.[4] In other words, there are recognized limitations on the capacity to "cure" all social ills. Moreover, with these theorists, we would claim that *asserting* the existence of such a panacea, as Kant does, creates a dangerous theoretical foundation for world leaders. If leaders have the sense that there is perfect solution, they can fool themselves into thinking they need only apply sufficient pressure to create that perfect world. Just as the USSR pushed too hard to create an ideal communist state and spread their ideology in the name of international peace, Western powers have pushed too hard to spread their ideology in order to achieve the same goal. We would claim that these goals are and should be seen as unattainable. Therefore, while we make claims about the moral benefit of commercialization, the theory espoused in this chapter is really only about peace, and we are emphasizing here international peace. One may hold that capitalism promotes peace while, or perhaps through, promoting morality generally, but one could also hold that though capitalism promotes peace it simultaneously undermines other aspects of morality.

Third, capitalist peace theory employs models, at least implicitly, and every model simplifies. We are discussing models as ways of gaining insight into phenomena by focusing on some details, while leaving out or simplifying others. Montesquieu, of course, considered historic cases in great detail, but the aim of theorizing is to discern a common structure within diverse particular cases. This means, however, that other variables are left out, and in a particular case these other variables may be of utmost importance. In other words, the theory cannot and does not guarantee that war will never break out. Instead, it asserts that the likelihood of war is diminished through commercialization. Despite that limitation, we think it is extremely valuable and important to gain insight into the general tendencies of social institutions, including those of market economies and of democratic political systems.

## New Capitalist Man?

We want to highlight what we call the "new capitalist man" theory, as espoused by some classical liberals. This name is inspired by the concept of the new communist man as found in Trotsky (1924, chap. 8). On this view, market societies tend to inculcate certain values and capacities in their members. Though market advocates have diverse views about the exact effects markets have, it is clear that many held that markets promote values conducive to international peace.[5]

Smith argues that if our self-interest is properly directed, it will cause positive relations between people. Among the effects that Smith saw in markets was a decline of martial virtues.[6] In a different vein, Mandeville argues that the traditional Christian virtues have a negative impact on society, while what are typically seen as vices spur change and innovation. In Mandeville's view, then, market societies depend on people with a particular type of character to prosper, but that is a character of greed and gluttony. Whether or not private vices can promote public benefit, the central thing we wish to emphasize is that Mandeville is among the theorists who seem to take these character traits as highly variable and an important driver of social action.

The view that markets make people more moral and virtuous has contemporary defenders as well. For instance, recent work by economic historian Deirdre McCloskey (2007; 2011; 2016) on the development of market societies provides significant grounds for thinking that markets come with significant changes to the values of agents. According to McCloskey, central to the great expansion of markets, and with them wealth, was a shift in ideas and values. People came to respect, rather than despise, merchants and entrepreneurs. In other words, people came to respect, rather than despise, wealth creation. This came as a product of a substantial shift in how people thought one should live and what constituted a good character in an increasingly bourgeois society oriented toward stability rather than seeking glory through war. Likewise, Ginny Choi, Ryan Langrill, and Virgil Storr argue that markets provide valuable moral training to agents in them.[7] The activity of markets, they argue, trains people to relate to others in morally valuable ways, and, importantly, this seems especially so regarding strangers and people who are significantly different from them.

There is also experimental support for belief that there is such a transformation of the members of market societies (Henrich et al. 2004; Gintis 2012; Cf. Zak 2008). For instance, anthropologists and economists have done experimental division games with members of diverse societies. These studies include societies with limited or no significant market exposure. One of the key findings is that there is a strong connection between market societies and equal divisions, even in anonymous one-shot interactions in which one agent could get away with taking unequal divisions. Equal division in such anonymous interactions seems to be unique to people in market societies. Markets thus seem to bring with them a preference for fairness and an expanded circle of moral concern outside of family, clan, and close acquaintances. There may be other significant ways in which commercial life inculcates peace-promoting preferences or trains market actors to be moral and virtuous. We must note that markets might highly correlate with certain sorts of moral commitments or virtues because markets depend upon them, even if markets do not tend to promote them per se (cf. Rose 2011; Schwab and Ostrom 2008).

Thanks to modern research, we think it is safe to conclude that the classical liberal position on the relationship between morals and commercialization has been born out. As people shift their focus to commercial interactions, they become less truculent and more open-minded. This shift, however, does not demonstrate that the glory-seeking desires and xenophobia have gone away completely. This change is at the margins, a matter of degree, and in the relative balance of motivations, rather than the creation of an entirely different kind of person with a different set of foundational motives. Instead, as Montesquieu explains, the increased interaction between states will lead societies to have fewer prejudices against others, making people who trade with one another less inclined to fight for both psychological and financial reasons. This does not mean, however, that commerce has no downside.

Like other classical liberals, Montesquieu balances the deadening effects of commerce as well as recognizing that tribalism remains as does a dangerous thirst for glory among those with political power. Trade therefore is not a panacea in his work, it is a means to temper and balance these elements of human nature. For these reasons, he provides a clearer image of the benefits of capitalist peace as well as its limitations for "curing" humans of these traits.

## *Doux Commerce* and Nature

Montesquieu's theory of *doux commerce* comes out of his understanding of the fundamental ills inherent in man's own nature. He begins *The Spirit of the Laws* with a deceptively short discussion of the state of nature. His objective here is to counter the Hobbesian account of the state of nature as "nasty, brutish, and short" (Hobbes 1982, XIII.9). Hobbes presents an asocial man who must create society due to the need to protect himself and his things from the violence in the state of nature. For Montesquieu, the war-like qualities of man came about *after* the creation of society. In the state of nature, humans are timid and fearful of each other and the danger that they perceive surrounds them. In the state of nature, "invariable laws" govern man. Unfortunately, due to man's intelligence, "he constantly violates the laws god has established and changes those he himself establishes." Furthermore, "[a]s a feeling creature, he falls subject to a thousand passions." The "invariable laws" of nature cannot control us due to our fallibility. If we remained in the state of nature, we would be constantly led astray by our foolish reasoning and our passions. Man needs philosophers to provide moral laws and legislators to "return him to his duties." Without these guides channeling his reason and emotions, humans would be constantly subject to their flaws (I.1).

As time progresses—an important element for Montesquieu—the sense of mutual fear and the "pleasure one animal feels at the approach of an animal of its own kind" would cause humans to interact. Finally, the attraction between the sexes would cause them to become more attached to each other. As they gain more intelligence, they would have a second reason to feel a bond. Montesquieu further dissents from Hobbes, saying that people are *naturally* social, which causes them to be drawn into society (I.2). He wants to overcome what he sees to be a dangerous assertion made by theorists like Hobbes. If we are naturally asocial, it is only out of fear or force that people will come into society. If instead we are naturally social, there is a compulsion toward socializing that must be channeled effectively to ensure that people treat each other with dignity.

When poorly channeled, once humans develop society, this activates the war-like element of human nature. As Montesquieu explains, "[a]s soon as men are in society, they lose their feeling of weakness; the equality that was among them ceases, and the state of war begins" (I.3). Now people begin to have a feeling of tribalism, wanting to prove the superiority of their society by attempting to conquer neighboring cities. If this continues, they may develop a law of nations that allows for atrocities against their fellow man—be it slaughtering them or enslaving them. Montesquieu hopes to show that this law of nations is antiquated and has no place in the modern, developed world.

According to a humane understanding of the law of nations, the *purpose* of war is to conquer neighboring cities and maintain them, not to pillage or destroy. Importantly, we see that he provides a means for states to justify military action, demonstrating that he does not think there will ever be a perfectly peaceful future. He merely hopes for a future with less violence and more recognition of human dignity. According to his law of nations, a conqueror has to "make amends for the part of evils he has done" by providing a positive benefit if he is ever to repay the debt incurred to "human nature" (IX.4). Montesquieu wants to combat the understanding of international law that allows imperialists to act cruelly toward those they conquer. He sees too clearly by observing Spanish imperialism that the cruelty of human nature can still facilitate this in the modern world. Leaders can break the law of nations as outlined by Montesquieu, just as man can break the laws of nature due to foolish reasoning or passions. He says this of the Spanish conquistadors:

> What good could the Spanish not have done the Mexicans? They had a gentle religion to give them; they brought them a raging superstition. They could have set the slaves free, and they made freemen slaves. They could have made clear to them that human sacrifice was an abuse; instead they exterminated them. I would never finish if I wanted to tell all the good things they did not do, and all the evil ones they did (IX.4).

The people they found there were unworthy of their respect and humanity because the Spanish saw themselves as superior to them; they too suffered from the prejudices that lead one people to seek to dominate or destroy another.[8] They based this on an inhumane understanding of the right of conquerors and their desire to spread Christianity. They thought conquerors have "a right … of killing" (X.3).[9] They decimated the native populations in order to subjugate the rest. Moreover, they saw enslavement as the quickest way to convert the native populations to Christianity. They never had any respect for local customs, culture, or human life.

The capacity for men to fight with other societies and leaders to abuse those they conquer stems from the last element of human nature. Human adaptability has benefits and drawbacks. Thanks to our "flexible" nature, we can "adapt … in society to the thoughts and impressions of others." We are as capable of "knowing [our] own nature when it is shown to [us]" as we are of "losing even the feeling of it when it is concealed from [us]" (xliii). It is this flexibility, according to Montesquieu, that can lead us toward more gentle forms of interactions or allow us to engage in crimes against humanity. It comes down to the institutions and how those institutions channel human nature. It is this flexibility that causes him to see the expansion of trade as a means to diminish harmful prejudices and change mores to create more pacific relations among states. He thinks the institutions associated with free markets channel human nature in the most positive way.

## Curing Destructive Prejudices

Montesquieu says he would be the happiest of mortals if he "could make it so that men were able to cure themselves of their prejudices" (xliv). According to his analysis of history, this is exactly what happens when trade occurs between different states:

> Commerce cures destructive prejudices … [it] has spread knowledge of the mores of all nations everywhere; they have been compared to each other, and good things have resulted from this" (XX.1).

In contrast to the early truculent societies, once people have experienced a variety of cultures, they become less attached to the view that their institutions are the best or the only legitimate one. This comes through the breaking down of the "pure mores" used in ancient society to make citizens devote themselves entirely to their state. If one dies to preserve the best system of government, one's death is justified. If, conversely, one simply thinks well of one's institution but has experienced a diversity of ways of life, it is harder for leaders to convince their people to provide this last full measure of devotion.

As these interactions continue, nations develop a dependence on the trade carried out between them. For Montesquieu, this makes them less inclined to go to war as they will lose the goods previously supplied by their now-enemy. As this relation becomes firmer, there is a concomitant shift in mores associated with *doux commerce*. As commercial states increase their interaction, in principle, it will cause people to experience fewer prejudices toward other societies as well as diminishing tribalism.

For Montesquieu, differences between people stem from differences of climate, geography, local cultures, and a host of other elements. He does not believe these differences create unbridgeable divides among different societies. Instead, he hopes to demonstrate that we all appeal to the same basic ideals and we simply access the truth about how human beings should live through the prism of our particular culture thanks to the flexibility of our being (Howse 2006, p. 5). As we communicate with each other, we begin to develop a fuller picture of how societies work and through that knowledge begin to see how societies *should* work. This knowledge "makes men gentle"; they are more humane because, "only prejudice causes [humanity] to be renounced" (XV.3).

## Changing Mores

As commerce expands, there is a larger store of goods that can move from society to society. We see here a classical liberal understanding of economics. In contrast to mercantilism that sees trade as a zero-sum game, Montesquieu sees the capacity of trade to expand the economy and grow economies internationally. Europe's international trade has led to an increase in trade among European states, besides expanding wealth within most trading states (XIX.21).[10] This, in turn, has caused people to develop a different spirit. They develop a feeling for "exact justice" opposing both "banditry" and the austere "moral virtues" that make one avoid talking about self-interest. As commerce expands both domestically and internationally, "there will be more consumption, more things on which the arts can be exercised, more men employed, more means of acquiring power." With more wealth also comes the capacity to buy more resources that can be used or distributed collectively. The state develops the ability to "give the necessary things to a greater number of its subjects" (XX.23). This further increases stability as the people are less likely to revolt due to droughts or other unforeseen disasters.

Montesquieu thinks this will appeal to states internationally, even those reluctant to open up to other societies, due to the obvious benefits of trade. Moreover, the fact that trade is carried out by individuals cuts against the worst habits of leaders who generally wish to channel wealth into an arms buildup. It shifts the peoples' and the leaders' focus because wealth, to everyone, is at least somewhat important. If the capacity to engage with this market is the source of wealth, then everyone will focus on trying to do it well. Leaders will be less likely to use violence insofar as violence will reduce access to wealth and they see the benefits of encouraging wealth production over warmongering. The people will find war less appealing because they are more interconnected and finding the interconnectedness so profitable, they do not want to risk that relationship by engaging in conflict. Instead, they are much more likely to use arbitration.

## Commerce: The Future and the Past

Montesquieu hopes to use the theory of *doux commerce* to address the "new disease" spreading across Europe. Thanks to the increase in money flowing in from trade, "[w]e are poor with the wealth and commerce of the whole universe." As he explains, glory-hungry kings have taken their larger state coffers and used them to increase troops. As one state does this, it "redoubles in strength and necessarily becomes contagious" and "nothing is gained thereby but the common ruin" (XIII.17).

Montesquieu has diagnosed the problem that plagued Europe for centuries. This is the problem of connecting political power with money or access to capital. Kings will always want to use money to increase their power. Furthermore, [i]f left unchecked, or if they acquire despotic power, leaders will eventually exploit those engaged in commerce in order to increase their coffers, for "it has eternally been observed that any man who has power is led to abuse it; he continues until he finds limits" (XI.3). This is what occurred during the middle ages when leaders had relatively unchecked powers. Due to this abuse, merchants eventually created "letters of exchange" which made goods "invisible," giving merchants the ability to bring their goods "everywhere and leave no trace anywhere." It is therefore "the avarice of princes" that slowly over time led to a method for keeping commerce safe from it (XXI.20). This opened up the opportunity to uncouple the dangerous combination of glory-hungry leaders and an exploitable rich population. This makes it harder—harder, not impossible—for leaders to bankrupt the state in an effort to increase their glory by increasing their territory.

The problem resurfaced, however, as commerce exploded. As modern European leaders and their neighbors had more money due to the steadily increasing international trade, leaders somehow mistook that as an opportunity to expand their territory, falling victim to the glory-seeking through conquest that has led leaders astray for millennia. As Montesquieu says "it is not unheard of for states to mortgage their lands even during peace and … ruin themselves" (XIII.18). He ominously claims that if states carry out wars for the "arbitrary principl[e]" of "glory … tides of blood will inundate the earth" (X.2). In the eighteenth century, they could no longer do this by exploiting individuals so they engage in these actions by levying higher and higher taxes. This creates a vicious cycle of crippling the newly emerging capitalist markets across Europe in the name of the glory of the king. Montesquieu hopes to convince leaders and advisors that they should channel these desires toward freeing commerce (with the concomitant benefits of increasing peaceful relations), which would increase the prestige and wealth that they ultimately seek.

Montesquieu wants to show that these European leaders can compete against each other in the realm of commerce, just as they had fought against each other in war. He tries to turn their minds toward commercial competition by connecting power and prosperity, since "wealth is power" they ultimately fight each other for more wealth (Larrère 2000, p. 337). He wants to counter those who look back to the example of Ancient Rome in the hopes of repeating their capacity to dominate such a large swath of territory.[11] To further this point, he claims the Roman model is inimitable.

In *Reflections on Universal Monarchy*, he says previous conquerors, like the Romans, would sack a town and use the spoils to pay for the military. Today, that model is no longer viable for moral and practical reasons. Morally, the "law of man" has changed; people feel horrified by "such barbarism" making it necessary to conserve the city or state that they conquer. Practically, this law now "ruins … those who have the greater advantage." When leaders send their military to defeat another state, they have to "send a part of their treasure to provide for [the army's] subsistence." This "enriches the state that [the leader] started to conquer" and may even cause the enemy to come after the invading state. Beyond these problems, due to the size and luxurious tastes of the armed forces in

Europe at the time, "a people who [make war] will infallibly exhaust themselves" (Montesquieu 1951, RMU, I, 18–19). Altogether, Montesquieu hopes to paint a picture that would start channeling the desire for power toward increasing commercial activity without using those funds to perpetuate unnecessarily large militaries.

When we turn to modern states, we see a similar problem that can be addressed through similar means. Large states like the United States, China, and Russia have spent huge portions of their GDP to maintain their militaries, as have smaller economies like Saudi Arabia and Brazil. As large developed nations move toward more protectionist policies, this could also spark an increase in military spending as states move from a cooperative posture to a more hostile one. Furthermore, just as in Montesquieu's time, the world presently has fairly fixed borders and while the American military is arguably unmatched, there are a number of growing military powers acting increasingly hostile to the international order created by Western countries, which may increase the likelihood of conflict. Furthermore, this movement demonstrates that history is not over and we have not evolved past human nature as understood by classical liberals. People are just as capable of losing their humanity today as they were then; leaders are just as capable of thinking they should seek glory through war. As these things have not changed, Montesquieu's advice remains salient.

## A Contemporary Research Agenda for Montesquieu's Capitalist Peace Theory

Up to this point, we have mostly maintained a historical perspective on Montesquieu to clarify his view on the relations of commerce and peace. We believe, however, that Montesquieu's theory is of more than purely historic interest and that his proposed mechanisms of peace warrant further investigation. To push forward that investigation, this closing section will consider how to clarify the mechanisms of peace in terms of modeling the political agents. There are, it seems, models implicit in Montesquieu's own discussions, and we will be considering one path of elaborating those models and illuminating their mechanisms.

As we noted in the introduction, a central problem for the democratic peace hypothesis regarded determining the mechanism through which democracy could promote peace. Capitalist peace theory faces the same issue. It seems that two broad approaches are open to the theorist.[12] She may, for instance, take a broadly sociological approach and focus on the way that markets may change the values or preferences of individuals. Though we would not discount this as an important possibility, our discussion of Montesquieu suggests a few limits on this approach. First and foremost, Montesquieu highlights that the plasticity of human nature is limited. It seems that many drives, including those of glory-seeking and a significant degree of tribalism, are deeply entrenched and should be expected to remain despite changes in social institutions.[13] To be clear, we do grant that some degree of change in values is possible, but we think it is unlikely to be of sufficient magnitude to explain the data on international conflict. While we may see marginal moves in the direction of the "new capitalist man," he is not a new and permanent fixture. Instead, he is forever capable of losing his sense of humanity and falling victim to prejudices that will cause him to fight against men in other states.

Treating fundamental values or motives as fixed, of course, does not mean that behavior is fixed. Instead, it means that we must look elsewhere to find the explanation for differences in behavior and outcomes. One may take an essentially economic approach and consider how rational agents respond to different institutions and incentives in pursuing their ends. In elaborating a capitalist peace theory in the tradition of Montesquieu, one may employ a model of individual agents as rational utility maximizers.[14] It will be important to keep clear, however, that this is not a model of individuals as all narrowly self-interested or as specifically wealth maximizing. Current researchers must consider, as Montesquieu does, that people have a diverse set of values and motives, including some that regard self-interest and wealth, but also a variety of other motives, like for glory, social approval, and concern for loved ones. Each of these can be accounted for in a person's utility function, for they regard the ends that the agent pursues and help us understand the costs that they face in making choices. Humans remain the same, but they follow the Smithian drives for barter and trade or the Hobbesian drives for pillage and plunder depending upon their options.

## Institutional Environments and Mores

It becomes centrally important to consider the effects of the institutional environments in which people make their choices. Institutions change the alternatives that people have available, as well as the costs of those alternatives. Though the importance of institutions in this regard is well known, it may still help to consider a simple example. It is clear that different institutional arrangements can dramatically affect the use of natural resources. A fish population treated as a common pool resource from which anyone can draw as they see fit is liable to be tragically driven to total extinction from overfishing.[15] That same fish population under certain forms of private property (e.g., if they are in a privately owned lake) is likely to face only a sustainable level of fishing and remain vibrant into the future.[16] The difference, of course, is not that people in private property institutions have fundamentally different values than people in common pool resource regimes. These people do not need to be any different in terms of selfishness, altruism, shortsightedness, or environmental consciousness. Instead, the different institutional rules make different actions available to people and change their incentives. Under a common pool regime, the incentives are for each person to extract resources as intensely as she can while she can, while the private property regime allows the owner to exclude others and thus enables her to manage the resource as she sees fit into the indefinite future.[17]

While formal political institutions are often salient, Montesquieu insightfully points to the importance of mores.[18] In particular, as discussed above, he argued that market societies bring about different mores and this provides an important area for ongoing research. Contemporary work makes clear that informal social norms can be extremely effective for controlling behavior.[19] The effectiveness of social norms is often independent of, and can even work contrary to, formal legal systems (Ellickson 1994). We would emphasize that social norms can control behavior without changing anyone's underlying values. Individuals may still have the same desires, yet will behave differently when facing social norms. For instance, social norms can get people to divide resources in an equal way, even if they do not have a particular taste for equality or particularly altruistic concerns (Bicchieri 2006, chap. 3). Social norms in a commercial society cause people to have a sense of "exact justice" (XX.2). Social norms are sufficiently powerful that they can maintain compliance even for individuals that dislike like the norm, and in some conditions even if the norm is extremely unpopular in the society (Bicchieri 2006, chap. 5; cf. Kuran 1997).

A central finding is, as Montesquieu suggests, that the mores of a society can significantly affect the behavior of the members of that society and channel them into different activities without requiring any changes of fundamental motivations. This may include constraining individuals from acting on some motives altogether, but will often be realized through norms preventing the most destructive behaviors and letting those same motives be realized in other activities. As Montesquieu highlights, members of commercial society may still pursue glory, but when war is prohibited or will not yield a profit-through-conquest, they will seek glory in competitions for wealth.

Montesquieu's capitalist peace theory requires that markets have significant systematic tendencies in how they change social mores, and the evidence seems to support this. We mentioned above that empirical research has found that people in market societies, and only in market societies, tend to select fair division in experimental one-shot games with strangers (Henrich et al. 2004; Gintis 2012). People from across the globe engage in the same sort of fair dealing as long as they are in a market-based society, even though they are from very different cultures, practice different religions, live under different types of political regimes, and are democraphically diverse. We would add here that the behavior in these situations seems to be best explained by norms or mores, rather than different forms of human nature constituted by different underlying values or motivations. It seems, then, that markets systematically generate, or at least are accompanied by, certain sorts of mores.

Elaborating the capitalist peace theory along the lines that Montesquieu has laid down requires much additional work in understanding the relations of markets, mores, and peace. Further research is needed, for instance, to establish the other effects that markets have on mores, including what sorts of mores they tend to generate and to undermine. It will also be necessary to formulate an account of how these changes in mores specifically impact matters of war and peace. One would want, for instance, to know exactly what market mores are promoting international peace. It is possible that the fairness norms make members of market societies less likely to favor war over resources, and particularly to help members of different market societies to find mutually agreeable compromises instead of going to war with each other. It may be, however, as some of Montesquieu's remarks suggest, that it is more a matter of markets helping to eliminate mores that tend to cause avoidable conflicts.[20]

## Incentives and Individuals

More basic than mores, we believe that Montesquieu points to the need to consider the way that commerce affects the incentives individuals face. Again, underlying motivations may be fairly stable, but people will behave very differently when confronting different options and payoffs. In elaborating Montesquieu's understanding of capitalist peace theory, it seems that one would want to consider how commerce presents people with different incentives that diminish the likelihood of seeking glory through war. Roughly, capitalist peace theory needs to bring out how commerce makes war costlier, at least in terms of opportunity costs. We want to first consider this in terms of ordinary individual decisions, then turn to the more complex and central case of political decisions.

We have already noted that we think it best to model people as having stable motivations, including glory-seeking. One source of glory comes from the actions of the individual herself. She gets glory, for instance, if she personally goes off to fight the enemy and returns to be honored for her heroism (perhaps with a hero's funeral). If a person, Alice, is considering whether or not to personally pursue the glories of war, she must decide in light of her other available options. If Alice lives in a non-market society, she is likely to have few options and the wealth she can expect to gain is very limited. Market societies, however, tend to generate tremendous amounts of wealth and provide dramatically higher standards of living for large swaths of the population. Among the benefits is even increased life expectancy. Thus, if Alice lives in a market society, her range of options will be expanded and the benefits of some of those options will be increased. On the other hand, it seems plausible to model the value of the glory as essentially fixed.[21] So, market society may systematically change the payoffs for Alice such that the opportunity costs of going to war are higher, and thus she will be less likely to pursue the glories of war. She still desires that glory, but will not be willing to pay the costs in terms of her life prospects. Put simply, market societies offer vastly greater opportunities for wealth and longevity, and this can outweigh the benefits of the glories of war.

It is important to note that people do not need to stop seeking glory per se for capitalism to promote peace. In light of the costs of war and the opportunities of commerce, people may also pursue alternative sources of personal glory. The desire for glory may be realized in forms of competition, risk, and achievement other than war, and market societies tend to make those other forms preferable. For instance, Alice may pursue glory through athletic competition or taking entrepreneurial risk. These other paths may provide Alice ample glory without requiring as much sacrifice of the wealth and material benefits made possible in markets. One route for elaboration of a capitalist peace theory would involve further specification and empirical study of these substitutes for the glories of war, including the ways that a society's mores also effect these options.

## Incentives, Politics, and Public Choice

Of course, we have been considering merely the choices of individuals here, but the primary focus of capitalist peace theory is international conflict. We need to consider more directly how commerce affects the incentives of members of society and decisions about war. The fact that fewer people would want to personally fight in a war does not on its own guarantee that there will be fewer international conflicts. Capitalist peace theory must consider the complex issues involved in collective decision-making. Here, we believe that it is especially useful to consider the methodology of public choice that applies economic models to political decisions. More specifically, as Randall G. Holcombe emphasizes, public choice takes account of the incentives and information of different agents within particular institutions for political decision making to analyze "the way the political decision-making process actually works rather than how it might, in theory, ideally work" (2016, p. xi; cf. pp. 3 and 10). Here, as elsewhere, we cannot develop a full capitalist peace theory, but we want to indicate some areas for future ongoing research in light of Montesquieu's insights.

We considered personal glory above, but people also seem to seek glory of an impersonal, collective, or associational kind. They get a kind of glory from what has been accomplished by their side, even when not performed by them personally. One way to think about this associational glory is as a sort of public good. It is a good insofar as glory-seekers would be willing to pay at least some price to bring it about. If the good is produced, however, these glory-based benefits are equally enjoyed by each member of society whether or not she personally pays any of the costs of the war.[22] We would add, parallel to personal glory, that this good seems to be of fairly fixed value insofar as the development and expansion of markets does not increase the glory-based benefits of war. That is, the members of capitalist society do not feel *more* glorious when they go to war than members of a non-capitalist society.

On this model, while the benefits of war in terms of glory are fixed, the costs are not fixed. As discussed above, market societies expand the range of alternatives available to their members, including opportunities for wealth and various aspects of wellbeing. Going to war has not only an obvious financial cost, but also means forgoing these other opportunities. The members of a society at war are, in addition to the direct taxes, losing the profit they would have gained from the commercial use of these resources. Furthermore, they lose potential trading partners abroad when the foreigners are killed or trade impeded during the war.[23] This means a reduction in markets for both imports and exports. People in non-market societies may not face as high of costs in this regard since they have fewer economic opportunities and they have fewer trade relations to disrupt. As such, in commercial societies the glories of war can become too costly to be worth producing as a public good. War seems to become a worse policy for such societies, but this does not alone settle what the policy will actually be.

If the society has not only markets, but also democratic political institutions (as is often the case), then voters have significant reason to reject the pursuit of war for glory, and to instead favor alternative policies.

Those alternatives can include the production of other public goods; lower taxes so they have the resources to privately invest; or various policies that are equally costly in financial terms but less disruptive of trade. To be more precise, we might expect that for a particular potential conflict there will be individuals in society that prefer to avoid the conflict in order to invest the resources in other ways and avoid disruption of their own market activities (including access to customers or suppliers). Overall, then, one might expect that markets will tend to increase the incentives, and democratic will, for maintaining international peace.

While this theory seems plausible in many ways, we want to note an important limitation or challenge it would need to meet. In particular, it faces a serious problem when we focus on the heterogeneity of market participants, and we want to close this section by considering the impact of war profiteers on the above considerations. Though it may be the case that wars are costly overall as they use up or destroy resources that could be profitably invested in commercial enterprises, there are some industries that gain economic benefit from war. This includes most obviously those directly engaging in the war efforts, like the military personnel and military contractors, as well as the industries that supply weapons and tools of war. Furthermore, besides the military industries themselves, there are companies that will expect to benefit from war, such as the companies that will be contracted for rebuilding efforts after the conflict, or those who may gain particular access to the plunder of war. Not everyone can be a war profiteer, for though the benefits can ripple out, they must stop somewhere. Someone is paying these costs. Some individuals may gain more in selling war-related goods than those individuals lose in the war or in their taxes, but some other individuals are net taxpayers for conflict.[24] Nevertheless, war is frequently profitable for some.

In some circumstances, those who would profit from a war may be a rather small minority. This, however, does not ensure that they will not get their preferred policy. Public choice theory reminds us that democratic political systems will often produce policies favored by concentrated special interest groups, particularly so in cases with concentrated benefits and widely dispersed costs (Becker 1983; Mitchell and Munger 1991). A problem for capitalist peace theory, then, is that those who work and invest in a war industry may be a small minority who would reap tremendous benefits from a conflict and thus have tremendous incentive to lobby, campaign, and use political capital to bring about war. If their numbers are small, the diverse war profiteers will be well positioned to overcome collective action problems.[25] The costs of war, however, may be spread widely across all the other members of society, and even those costs may be extremely uncertain to the individuals. The people paying the costs of war, in terms of financing and disruption of trade opportunities, may be great in number, but each will have little personal stake to motivate political action. Moreover, because of their large numbers, those that pay the costs of war face a collective action problem and are individually incentivized to try to be free-riders upon each other's efforts.

War profiteers present a problem for Montesquieu because their pursuit of profit leads them to support, rather than oppose, war. Profit and glory, therefore, are not always in tension. Though this is a serious problem, we believe that it amounts only to a limitation on how much commerce can pacify a society. This problem brings out that the commercial society will not ensure *everyone* has incentives to promote peace. Be that as it may, most merchants end up paying for the benefits accruing to the profiteers, and so commercial societies still create a substantial class of individuals who must see wars as unduly costly in terms of profit opportunities. Thus, we can see how commercial societies can generate peace through the amplification of opportunities for profit at the expense of glory through the changing opportunities and costs faced by agents even if those agents maintain essentially the same fundamental motivations.

## Conclusion

Montesquieu understands that European states at his time face a choice. The flexibility of human nature allows leaders, both moral and political, to guide citizens toward different ends. Furthermore, institutions channel those leaders. Falling victim to man's worst qualities, this can cause deep tribalism that pits states against others and likely devolves into war. From this war, it is possible that a state will adhere to a more "barbarous" understanding of the law of nations and enslave or kill those who lose. Knowing this to be the worst of man, and always imbedded in his nature, Montesquieu attempts to develop a theory that would channel the desires of individuals and leaders away from these destructive ends. Through international trade, individuals would come in contact with other societies and other customs. This softens their attitudes toward others by showing them to be equally worthy of dignity and respect despite their differences. Beyond softening destructive prejudices, it also increases the incentive to maintain the peace, as trade is always interrupted by war—with the noted exception of the war profiteer. For leaders, it channels their desire toward increasing their wealth in order to obtain glory rather than attempting to engage in conflict for the same end. Montesquieu thinks this shift will appeal to a sufficient number of people and leaders internationally to move the world toward more peaceful relations.

This will not change immediately, nor will it solve all of the world's problems. It is, however, less expensive and more profitable for obvious reasons. It will decrease the frequency of regime change from external invasion. It will decrease the likelihood of regime change from internal corruption because territorial expansion always causes internal corruption. He does not, however, think this presents a panacea. Human nature remains difficult to tame and institutions remain fallible. For this reason, Montesquieu's theory presents a very practical solution for the very reason that it does not suggest there is an easy or permanent way to solve the problem of human nature and war. Most importantly, it is more humane.

> In these new commercialized societies, the various peoples of the world would swap new technologies and basic scientific and cultural skills as readily as they would swap foodstuffs. These would not be empires of conquest, but "empires of liberty" (Pagden 1998, p. 49).

As we've tried to bring out, Montesquieu's views are not a mere curiosity of history, like the antiquated science of phlogiston or the labor theory of economic value. Instead, Montesquieu provides valuable insights and foundations for ongoing research that is deeply important for contemporary problems. This includes consideration of the way that markets influence the social norms or mores within a society, including generating of peace-promoting norms and undermining norms that tend toward violent conflict. It also includes a focus on how markets can incentivize glory-seeking individuals to pursue glory through means other than war or simply accept less glory in exchange for the tremendous benefits of commerce. Lastly, we highlighted that there is important work to be done in the development of capitalist peace theory to account for the real operation of political institutions in light of the diverse, and conflicting, incentives for different members of a commercial society. These are rich areas for ongoing research building upon Montesquieu's insights about the value of capitalism and the institutions of peaceful cooperation.

## Notes

1. Other sources of peace are of course possible and worth investigating. For instance, George Orwell (2002) argued that the modern technology and tactics of war, particularly use of area bombings that kill large numbers of civilians, spreads the burdens of war to a greater cross-section of the population, potentially helping maintain peace.
2. During the Cold War, both the United States and the USSR attempted to bring developing countries over to liberal democracy or communism, respectively. In many instances, both willingly accepted dictators who simply pledged to side with liberal democracy against communism or vice versa. For this reason, it would be false to say that Western powers only allied themselves with other liberal democracies just as the communists accepted fellow travelers without always requiring a devotion to the communist philosophy.
3. Deirdre McCloskey (2006) writes: "In a fallen world the bourgeois life is not perfect. But it's better than an available alternative."
4. Marx argued that market relations alienate people from each other. Along the same lines, G. A. Cohen (2009, p. 39) argues that markets are antithetical to community. Cf Archer (2016) and Steiner (2014) for elaboration of Cohen's argument, and Brennan (2014) and Van Schoelandt (2014) for objections to it. A closely related set of debates regards whether or not markets in particular sorts of goods (rather than markets in general) tend to corrupt people or relationships. Sandel (2013) and Satz (2010) each argue that certain markets are morally

problematic, while Brennan and Jaworski (2015) argue that there is nothing specially corrupting about markets in any good that it is morally permissible to give away outside of markets.

5. Of course, not every theorist who holds that markets fundamentally change the character of their participants hold that these changes are positive. For instance, Rousseau saw the focus on commerce as a deadening element, one that caused endless psychological damage to modern man. Marx goes one step further, claiming that capitalism actually *causes* violence between both individuals and states.
6. Smith's views on the relation of markets to international peace are complex. For insightful discussion, see Paganelli and Schumacher (2018).
7. See Choi and Storr (2017), Storr and Langrill (2012), Storr (2009), and Storr (2018).
8. It was a combination of unreasonable rules—the natives had supposedly committed a crime because they put food in baskets—and scorn for their religion (XV.III-IV). This is partially due to Spanish morals. Montesquieu says they, like the Romans, are arrogant. Spanish arrogance has caused "laziness, poverty, the abandonment of everything, and the destruction of the nations that chance has let fall into their hands as well as their own nation" (XIX.9).
9. This is incorrect, however, because once a conquest is complete the offensive state no longer has "a case of natural defense and of his own preservation" (X.3).
10. Engaging in trade does not guarantee prosperity. In particular, states with bad domestic policies may not gain the benefits of commerce (see Larrère 2000, p. 352). Montesquieu gives the example of Poland, saying that due to the fact that a few lords possess a large quantity of land, they exploit the workers and send the best grain abroad. For that reason, Montesquieu claims that the Polish people would actually be *better off* if they did not engage in international trade because the bad institutions have caused a concentration of wealth that has channeled the interests of the lords toward exploitation (XX.23).
11. Both Spain and France looked to Rome as an ideal, Spain an ideal empire, France as a conqueror of Europe.
12. Compare Elster (1989, p. 99).
13. Buchanan and Powell (2018, chaps. 4–6) discuss many of the difficulties for cosmopolitan and inclusive moral systems, though they remain optimistic and defend the possibility of progress being made in these areas.

14. For an introduction and discussion of rationality and utility theory, see Gaus (2008, chaps. 1–2).
15. For the classic discussion of the tragedy of the commons, see Hardin (1968).
16. Privatization is not the only, or even always the best, option for sustaining resources. For centrally important discussion of the issues, including particularly the potential for institutions of self-governance, see Ostrom (1990).
17. Classical liberals will highlight the fact that this property regime must include a considerable degree of stability and must restrict the state. Immediate consumption and a lack of investment should be expected if property rights are not clear and secure against state predation. Cf. Baumol (1990) and de Soto (2003).
18. It is worth noting that the overall political system seems particularly salient to most people, and that may be part of the attraction of democratic peace theory. We will only note here that *if* democratic institutions are a factor in promoting peace, it also appears that markets promote, and seem to be close to a necessary condition for, democratic institutions. Cf. Friedman (2002, chap. 1), Gaus (2011, sec. 24.2), Hayek (2007).
19. On social norms and their social importance, see Boettke et al. (2008), Brennan et al. (2013), Bicchieri (2006), Bicchieri (2017), Mackie et al. (2014), Mackie (1996).
20. Perhaps systems of social norms based on honor are among those that increase violent conflict and are displaced by markets. On the relation of honor norms and violence within a society, see Thrasher and Handfield (2018).
21. We are here suggesting a useful simplification, rather than claiming that the glories of war are in fact fixed across people or cultures. As noted earlier in this chapter, we agree with many classical liberals that markets may in fact tend to reduce this motivation, though only marginally and never completely. In any case, if market societies affect the value of the glories of war, one may further refine the capitalist peace theory to account for this effect. We think it is illuminating, however, to hold the value of glory fixed in order to highlight other changes in incentives.
22. Technically, we might want to say that it is a quasi-public good, rather than a true public good, insofar as the costs of producing it may be higher than the benefits for members of society. It would maintain some

core public good features, since if the glory is produced it is non-rivalrous and non-excludable for members of the society, though it is somewhat perverse to treat it as a good when its production entails more costs than it is worth. For discussion of public goods and consideration of war from a different theoretic angle, see Van Schoelandt (2018).

23. One might expect, as Montesquieu's account suggests, that the incentives to avoid conflict will be stronger with regard to trading partners. Capitalist peace theory may thus predict that peace will be most promoted between market societies that have high levels of trade with each other.
24. On this, see the classic Bastiat (1995, sec. 2)
25. For the classic discussion of the role of group size is collective action, see Olson (1971, chap. II).

## References


Archer, Alfred. 2016. Community, Pluralism and Individualistic Pursuits: A Defence of Why Not Socialism? *Social Theory and Practice* 42 (1): 57–73.

Bastiat, Frédéric. 1995. What Is Seen and What Is Not Seen. In: *Selected Essays on Political Economy*, translated by Seymour Cain. Irvington-on-Hudson: The Foundation for Economic Education, Inc.

Baumol, William J. 1990. Entrepreneurship: Productive, Unproductive, and Destructive. *Journal of Political Economy* 98 (5): 893–921.

Becker, Gary S. 1983. A Theory of Competition Among Pressure Groups for Political Influence. *The Quarterly Journal of Economics* 98 (3): 371–400. https://doi.org/10.2307/1886017.

Bicchieri, Cristina. 2006. *The Grammar of Society: The Nature and Dynamics of Social Norms*. Cambridge: Cambridge University Press.

______. 2017. *Norms in the Wild: How to Diagnose, Measure and Change Social Norms*. Oxford: Oxford University Press.

Boettke, Peter J., Christopher J. Coyne, and Peter T. Leeson. 2008. Institutional Stickiness and the New Development Economics. *American Journal of Economics and Sociology* 67 (2): 331–58.https://doi.org/10.2307/27739707.

Brennan, Geoffrey, Lina Eriksson, Robert E. Goodin, and Nicholas Southwood. 2013. *Explaining Norms*. New York: Oxford University Press.

Brennan, Jason. 2014. *Why Not Capitalism?* 1st edition. New York; London: Routledge.

Brennan, Jason F., and Peter Jaworski. 2015. *Markets without Limits: Moral Virtues and Commercial Interests*. 1 edition. New York; London: Routledge.

Buchanan, Allen, and Russell Powell. 2018. *The Evolution of Moral Progress: A Biocultural Theory*. New York: Oxford University Press.

Choi, Seung Ginny, and Virgil Henry Storr. 2017. Markets as Moral Training Grounds. *Annual Proceedings of the Wealth and Well-Being of Nations* IX: 129–46.

Churchill, Winston, and Franklin Roosevelt. 1941. Atlantic Charter. The Avalon Project.

Cohen, G. A. 2009. *Why Not Socialism?* Princeton: Princeton University Press.

Dobson, William J. 2013. *The Dictator's Learning Curve: Inside the Global Battle for Democracy*. Reprint edition. New York: Anchor.

Eichenberg, Richard C. 2005. Victory Has Many Friends: U.S. Public Opinion and the Use of Military Force, 1981–2005. *International Security* 30 (1): 140–77.

Ellickson, Robert. 1994. *Order Without Law: How Neighbors Settle Disputes*. Cambridge, MA: Harvard University Press.

Elster, Jon. 1989. Social Norms and Economic Theory. *The Journal of Economic Perspectives* 3 (4): 99–117.

Friedman, Milton. 2002. *Capitalism and Freedom*. Fortieth Anniversary Edition. Chicago: University of Chicago Press.

Fukuyama, Francis. 1989. The End of History? *The National Interest*, no. 16: 3–18.

Gaus, Gerald. 2008. *On Philosophy, Politics, and Economics*. Belmont: Thompson Wadsworth.

———. 2011. *The Order of Public Reason: A Theory of Freedom and Morality in a Diverse and Bounded World*. New York: Cambridge University Press.

Gintis, Herbert. 2012. Response: Giving Economists Their Due. *Boston Review*, no. May/June. http://www.bostonreview.net/BR37.3/ndf_herbert_gintis_markets_morals.php

Hardin, Garrett. 1968. The Tragedy of the Commons. *Science* 162 (3859): 1243–48. https://doi.org/10.1126/science.162.3859.1243.

Hayek, F. A. 2007. *The Road to Serfdom*. Edited by Bruce Caldwell. Vol. 2. The Collected Works of F. A. Hayek. Chicago: University of Chicago Press.

Henrich, Joseph, Robert Boyd, Samuel Bowles, Colin Camerer, Ernst Fehr, and Herbert Gintis, eds. 2004. *Foundations of Human Sociality: Economic Experiments and Ethnographic Evidence from Fifteen Small-Scale Societies*. 1st edition. Oxford and New York: Oxford University Press.

Hobbes, Thomas. 1982. *Leviathan*. Harmondsworth: Penguin.

Holcombe, Randall G. 2016. *Advanced Introduction to Public Choice*. Cheltenham; Northampton, MA: Edward Elgar.

Howse, Robert. 2006. Montesquieu on Commerce, Conquest, War, and Peace. *Brooklyn Journal of International Law* 31: 1–16.

Jentleson, Bruce W., and Rebecca L. Britton. 1998. Still Pretty Prudent: Post-Cold War American Public Opinion on the Use of Military Force. *Journal of Conflict Resolution* 42 (4): 395–417. https://doi.org/10.1177/0022002798042004001.

Kant, Immanuel. 2016. *Perpetual Peace: A Philosophical Essay*. Translated by Mary Campbell Smith. Project Gutenberg. https://www.gutenberg.org/files/50922/50922-h/50922-h.htm#Page_117

Kuran, Timur. 1997. *Private Truths, Public Lies: The Social Consequences of Preference Falsification*. Cambridge, MA: Harvard University Press.

Larrère, Catherine. 2000. Montesquieu on Economics and Commerce. In: *Montesquieu's Science of Politics*, edited by David W. Carrithers, Michael A. Mosher, and Paul A. Rahe. Lanham: Rowman & Littlefield Publishers.

Levy, Jack S. 2002. War and Peace. In: *Handbook of International Relations*, edited by Walter Carlsnaes, Thomas Risse, and Beth A. Simmons, pp. 350–68. London: Safe.

Mackie, Gerry. 1996. Ending Footbinding and Infibulation: A Convention Account. *American Sociological Review* 61 (6): 999–1017. https://doi.org/10.2307/2096305.

Mackie, Gerry, Francesca Moneti, Elaine Denny, and Holly Shakya. 2014. What Are Social Norms? How Are They Measured? UNICEF/UCSD Center on Global Justice.

McCloskey, Deirdre N. 2006. Bourgeois Virtues? Cato Institute. 2006. https://www.cato.org/policy-report/mayjune-2006/bourgeois-virtues

_____. 2007. *The Bourgeois Virtues: Ethics for an Age of Commerce*. 1st edition. Chicago: University Of Chicago Press.

_____. 2011. *Bourgeois Dignity: Why Economics Can't Explain the Modern World*. Chicago; Bristol: University of Chicago Press.

_____. 2016. *Bourgeois Equality: How Ideas, Not Capital or Institutions, Enriched the World*. Chicago; London: University Of Chicago Press.

Mitchell, William C., and Michael C. Munger. 1991. Economic Models of Interest Groups: An Introductory Survey. *American Journal of Political Science* 35 (2): 512–46. https://doi.org/10.2307/2111373.

Montesquieu, Charles-Louis de Secondat. 1951. *Oeuvres Complètes, Tome II*. Paris: Gallimard.

Olson, Mancur. 1971. *The Logic of Collective Action: Public Goods and the Theory of Groups*. Revised edition. Cambridge, MA.: Harvard University Press.
Orwell, George. 2002. As I Please 25. In: *Essays*, edited by John Carey, Second Printing edition, pp. 602–5. New York: Everyman's Library.
Ostrom, Elinor. 1990. *Governing the Commons: The Evolution of Institutions for Collective Action*. Cambridge: Cambridge University Press.
Paganelli, Maria Pia, and Reinhard Schumacher. 2018. Do Not Take Peace for Granted: Adam Smith's Warning on the Relation between Commerce and War. *Cambridge Journal of Economics* Volume 43, Issue 3: 785–797.
Pagden, Anthony. 1998. *Lords of All the World: Ideologies of Empire in Spain, Britain and France c.1500-c.1800*. New Haven: Yale University Press.
Pickering, Jeffrey, and Mark Peceny. 2006. Forging Democracy at Gunpoint. *International Studies Quarterly* 50 (3): 539–59.
Rose, David C. 2011. *The Moral Foundation of Economic Behavior*. New York: Oxford University Press.
Russett, Bruce. 1994. *Grasping the Democratic Peace*. Reprint edition. Princeton: Princeton University Press.
Sandel, Michael J. 2013. *What Money Can't Buy: The Moral Limits of Markets*. Reprint edition. New York: Farrar, Straus and Giroux.
Satz, Debra. 2010. *Why Some Things Should Not Be for Sale: The Moral Limits of Markets*. Oxford University Press.
Schwab, David, and Elinor Ostrom. 2008. The Vital Role of Norms and Rules in Maintaining Open Public and Private Economies. In: *Moral Markets: The Critical Role of Values in the Economy*, edited by Paul J. Zak, pp. 204–27. Princeton: Princeton University Press.
Soto, Hernando De. 2003. *The Mystery of Capital: Why Capitalism Triumphs in the West and Fails Everywhere Else*. Reprint edition. New York: Basic Books.
Steiner, Hillel. 2014. Greed and Fear. *Politics, Philosophy and Economics* 13 (2): 140–150.
Storr, Virgil Henry. 2009. Why the Market? Markets as Social and Moral Spaces. *Journal of Markets & Morality* 12 (2): 277–96.
_____. 2018. The Impartial Spectator and the Moral Teachings of Markets. In: *Oxford Handbook of Freedom*, edited by David Schmidtz and Carmen Pavel, pp. 456–72. New York: Oxford University Press.
Storr, Virgil, and Ryan Langrill. 2012. The Moral Meanings of Markets. *Journal of Markets and Morality* 15 (2): 347–62.
Thrasher, John, and Toby Handfield. 2018. Honor and Violence. *Human Nature* 29 (4): 371–389.

Trotsky, Leon. 1924. *Literature and Revolution (8. Revolutionary and Socialist Art)*. Translated by Rose Strunsky. https://www.marxists.org/archive/trotsky/1924/lit_revo/ch08.htm

Van Schoelandt, Chad. 2014. Markets, Community, and Pluralism. *Philosophical Quarterly* 64 (254): 144–151.

______. 2018. A Public Reason Approach to Religious Exemptions. In: *Philosophy and Public Policy*, edited by Andrew I. Cohen. Lanham: Rowman & Littlefield International.

Wilson, Woodrow. 1979. An Appeal to the American People, 18 August 1914. In: *The Papers of Woodrow Wilson*, 30:427. Princeton: Princeton University Press. http://rotunda.upress.virginia.edu/founders/WILS-01-30-02-0427

Zak, Paul J., ed. 2008. *Moral Markets: The Critical Role of Values in the Economy*. Princeton: Princeton University Press.

Zakaria, Fareed. 1997. The Rise of Illiberal Democracy. *Foreign Affairs* 76 (6): 22–43. https://doi.org/10.2307/20048274.

# "China's Hayek" and the Horrors of Totalitarianism: The Liberal Lessons in Gu Zhun's Thought

Chor-yung Cheung

## Liberalism in Modern China

Modern liberalism was first systematically introduced to China in the late nineteenth century when China's national survival was threatened by the imperialist powers. Yan Fu is regarded by many as the first Chinese liberal who translated the classical works of Smith, Mill, Montesquieu, among others, in the 1890s and 1900s into Chinese (Schwartz 1964; Huang 2008). Leading constitutionalist reformers of the late Qing dynasty and early republican period like Liang Qichao (Chang 1971) also helped spread many of the ideas of liberal constitutionalism to the Chinese intelligentsia. The challenge of imperialism to China then went far beyond military defeats, political upheavals and the need for institutional reforms. The Chinese intellectuals found that the Chinese tradition alone was far from adequate to help respond to the challenge brought by the sudden

C.-y. Cheung (✉)
Department of Public Policy City, University of Hong Kong,
Kowloon Tong, China
e-mail: scccy@cityu.edu.hk



D. F. Hardwick, L. Marsh (eds.), *Reclaiming Liberalism*, Palgrave Studies in Classical Liberalism, https://doi.org/10.1007/978-3-030-28760-3_10

intrusion of the need for modernization in China, and Western political ideologies, liberalism included, were regarded as the kind of new knowledge essential for China's transformation into the modern world.

While the pre-1949 Chinese liberals were neither the most revolutionary nor profound in responding to this crisis, modern liberalism nevertheless was one leading political ideology at that time that helped shape the national development of China. For example, John Dewey's Chinese disciple Hu Shih (Grieder 1970), the leading Chinese liberal since the early twentieth century until his death in Taiwan in 1962, was the one who started modern China's new literary movement, in which he succeeded in replacing the use of classical Chinese with the vernacular language in Chinese writing. His advocacy of scientific method and human rights at that time also contributed to the demand for democracy and science in the patriotic May-fourth Movement of 1919 (Chou 1960) and beyond.

Although the 1911 republican revolution managed to overthrow the Qing dynasty, the subsequent political chaos in the warlord period and the failure of the republican government under the Chinese Nationalist Party to modernize China and to drive out foreign invasions turned many Chinese disillusioned with the republican regime. The revolutionary alternative provided by the Chinese Communist Party and the successful example of the soviet experience in Russia at that time, particularly when the capitalist West suffered from the Great Depression of 1929, looked increasingly attractive to many Chinese. Intellectually, the belief in the superiority of scientific reasoning since the May-fourth also brought scientism to China (Kwok 1965; Lin 1979, p. 69), which not only helped promote a total critique of the Chinese culture, but also indirectly helped create a widespread support for radical politics in the name of scientific socialism or Marxism, leading to the eventual success of Mao Zedong's Communist revolution in 1949 and the establishment of the People's Republic of China.

Mao of course was no friend of liberalism. In his essay "Combat Liberalism" (Mao 1961, pp. 31–33) written in 1937, Mao denounced liberalism as opportunistic, arguing that the liberal ideology was rooted in petty bourgeoisie's selfishness and always placed personal interest above the interest of the revolution. He called for the elimination of liberalism in the ranks of the revolution. Not unexpectedly, therefore, in Mao's China, liberalism was not only denounced, but also disappeared from public discussion because of the above reasons. But ironically, one could argue that the seeds of the revival of liberal thinking in Communist China were sowed soon after it had launched its first five-year plan (1953–1957). These seeds were further developed during Mao's heyday of totalitarian rule in the Cultural Revolution. One leading thinker in this liberal revival was a veteran Communist revolutionary named Gu Zhun, who is now being credited by many present-day Chinese liberals as the first mainland Chinese economist who openly advocated the necessity of market reform under Communist China in the second half of 1950s (Wu 2005, in Luo ed. 2017, p. 184; Bottelier 2018, p. 132), which was ahead of Deng Xiaoping's post-Mao opening up of China in 1978 for more than 20 years.[1]

## From "Venture Communist" to "China's Hayek"

Gu Zhun (1915–1974) was born in Shanghai, China's most economically developed city before the Communist takeover. He started to apprentice as an accountant since the age of 12 under the mentorship of the then Harvard trained accountant Pan Xulun. Gu was a successful young professional at that time and authored several widely circulated textbooks on accounting. Upon Pan's recommendation, Gu became a professor of economics at the Shanghai College of Commerce. However, he chose to join the Chinese Communist Party when he was 20 because the Nationalist regime failed to resist Japan's invasions to China. Before Gu became a Communist, he was radicalized through his contact with the young printers of the Shanghai Commercial Press during his liaison with them for his books' publication. These printers, according to an historian of Shanghai at Berkeley, "were among the most radical of Shanghai's organized workers" (Yeh 2007, p. 199). Gu was also influenced by one former senior schoolmate at Chinese Society for Vocational Education who joined the then Communist and unionist infiltrated Labor University, where Gu picked up Western radical political thought like anarchism and the idea of capitalist exploitation of the laborers. It was from about that time that Gu gradually started to embrace the idea of violent revolution in China and regarded his professional accounting work to serve the capitalists in Shanghai as a kind of disgrace (Gu 2002, pp. 15–20; Yeh 2007, p. 199).

Late in 1934, because of his radical ideas and political activities, Gu was forced to flee from his home from possible persecution to Shanghai's foreign concessions where the Chinese government did not have jurisdiction. At around the same time, Gu formed the Society for Progress with his former classmates of Chinese Society for Vocational Education and his young associates in the accounting profession, and the Society eventually became a spontaneous Marxism-Leninism cell under the Chinese Communist Party. After joining the Chinese Communist Party, Gu became a leading cadre in the Shanghai and East China region. He, however, needed to flee again in 1940, this time out of Shanghai and went finally to Yanan, the revolutionary base of the Chinese Communist Party, in 1943. In April 1949, Gu returned to Shanghai triumphantly with the People's Liberation Army. He was tasked with the responsibility of taking over the financial and taxation departments of the municipal government of post-civil war Shanghai (Gu 2002, pp. 65–149; Yeh 2007, pp. 200–204).

Although Gu Zhun's time wielding at the helm of taxation and public finance of liberated Shanghai was far from long (1949–1952), his excellent professional knowledge, his good old-boy network with Shanghai's accounting and finance elites who had been working with him and his mentor, together with his pragmatic strategies helped him not only come up with creative policies and measures to implement a smooth takeover, but also restore Shanghai's war-torn economy and fill up the coffers of the nation by increased tax revenues soon after the civil war. By March 1951, tax receipts in Shanghai, through Gu's insistence on the implementation of his specialist system of taxing on the profit on capital, had already swelled to almost 11 times their level of 1950. When compared with the ideologically more orthodox bottom-up democratic assessment method as advocated by some other cadres, Gu's system appeared to be less politically correct by indirectly allowing the capitalists' profit motive to thrive in a newly created socialist state. But the success of Gu's professionally oriented system managed to provide the new state with increased and durable sources of revenue for the urgent tasks of national reconstruction and funding the war in Korea, to which the People's Republic of China was firmly committed at that time. To Gu, the democratic assessment method was arbitrary, allowing members of different trade associations to ascertain rather subjectively how to apportion their respective shares of tax payment to fulfill the state-imposed overall quota of tax revenue. Gu's taxation system eventually got the blessing of Mao and was practiced nation-wide.[2]

Christopher R. Leighton has given us an excellent account of Gu Zhun in Shanghai in 1949–1952 (Leighton 2014). It is interesting to note that Leighton calls Gu a "venture Communist". He argues that Gu confounds some general assumptions about Communist cadres, since "while he may have been a cadre, Gu Zhun was also something of an entrepreneur (of economic related ventures more than actual firms, to be sure), conversant with the language and processes of business, and accomplished at introducing novel ways to novice audiences ... Not all cadres were bent on wiping away Shanghai's [capitalist] past; taxes could be an exciting, modernizing innovation, and within the party some evangelists for economic change imagined a different sort of socialism" (ibid., p. 120).

For Leighton, Gu was never a doctrinaire Communist. To Gu, the Western-style accounting methods were a tool. While the capitalists might use it to protect profit, Communists could wield it to raise state revenues or wrest back imperialist-owned property (ibid., p. 130). Leighton further shows us that Gu was never a fan of the Soviet-style centralized command economy from day one. Instead, he and other like-minded cadres in this period pursued "a decentralized, locally based system of socialist enterprise, overseen by regional governments with budgetary independence from the central government" (ibid., p. 136), in which the locally controlled state enterprises each should implement "enterprise-type accounting" to tighten fiscal control for effective and economically efficient management as much as possible (ibid., p. 137).

Gu did not stay long enough in his leadership position in Shanghai to allow his scheme mentioned above to succeed, though Leighton regards it as having set a very early "precedent for decentralization and market socialism" for Deng's reform era (ibid., p. 136). Somewhat unexpectedly and without any pre-warning, Gu was abruptly removed from office in early 1952 during the Five Anti Campaign launched by Mao. The Campaign was to fight against the "capitalists" in the Party and on the mainland on charges of bribery, tax evasion, theft of state property and economic information. However, Gu was never accused of any substantial "capitalist" crimes in the Campaign and no specific charges were raised. The Shanghai party committee only accused him of "grave individual heroism" and "disregarded organizational discipline" (Gu 2002, pp. 209–213). While here we see many signs of an idiosyncratic Communist cadre in Gu Zhun with unorthodox views on how to pursue socialism on Chinese soil, his substantial and well-articulated departure from doctrinaire socialism came a few years later in 1957 when he first challenged the then orthodox view of the dispensability and temporality of the law of value and the price mechanism under socialism in his theoretical article "A Tentative Discussion of Commodity Production and the Law of Value under the Socialist System" (2002, pp. 77–133).[3] In the article (hereinafter called "Tentative Discussion" in this chapter), he argued that socialism could not do without the law of value, the price mechanism and using money as a circulating medium for exchange. This is because without following the law of value in economic production, there is no rational basis for socialist planning, not to say a more effective and efficient utilization and allocation of resources. This was a challenge that in many ways quite similar to Ludwig von Mises' and Friedrich von Hayek's critique of socialism in the famous socialist calculation debate in the 1920s and 1930s in the West (Hayek [1948] 1980, pp. 119–208).

## Economic Calculation and Socialist Planning

Mises is the first theorist who argues that since it is not possible to have economic calculation under socialism as understood by Marx and Engels, the system of socialist central planning is "just a system of groping about in the dark" (1963, p. 699). To Mises, socialism is a system of social cooperation without a market, in which private property is replaced by collective ownership, with the state owning all the means of production. Production is purely for use in accordance with a centralized command plan and not for exchange. Commodities under such a system will eventually be abolished since all consumption goods are only for socialized use. Money is no longer required as there is no need for any medium of exchange to be circulated, and the price mechanism is superfluous because values of the products only reflect the useful labor time for their production. Exchange value has allegedly become irrelevant.

Mises believes that under socialism, economic calculation is logically impossible since without the price mechanism and money as the medium of exchange, there is no common standard to compare the relative economic efficacy of different products, services and factors of production in a society. It is therefore unclear how socialism can make improvement to its economic performance to better serve the need of the people. To Mises, the Marxian labor theory of value is problematic not only because it is never clear if there exists any universally valid scale to define what is skilled and what is simple labor and to conduct conversion between the two, it is also because if value is defined as the amount of socially useful labor time for production, it is far from adequate since it fails to take all other non-labor factors of production into account in determining the true value of a product. "What is ultimately decisive for the solution of the problem of the feasibility of using labor as a basis of economic calculation", says Mises, "is the question whether one can assimilate different kinds of work to a common denominator without a valuation of the products by the consumer" (1981, p. 115). Mises points out that with the abolition of private property and the market, it is doubtful if the central planners can come up with a rational plan for production and distribution for all that could serve the respective preferences of the producers and consumers.

Hayek's contribution to this debate is to develop Mises' logical critique into an epistemological critique, spelling out the indispensable part plays by circumstantial knowledge (such as market participants' here and now preferences) in economic decision and social coordination and why the contextual and interactive nature of this kind of knowledge (e.g. market players' decisions are dependent on their anticipation of what other players may decide) makes central planning impossible ([1948] 1980, pp. 77–91). To Hayek, "[t]he economic problem arises…as soon as different purposes compete for the available resources" (ibid., p. 123), and it is unclear on what rational basis a central planner can rely to determine which purpose should be chosen in his plan over other competing purposes to better suit the needs and demands of the citizens.

A close examination of Gu's "Tentative Discussion" shows that he came up with similar views on this question of economic calculation, even though there is no evidence to suggest that when he wrote the article in 1956–1957, he had the privilege of having learned from Mises and Hayek in the famous socialist calculation debate of 1920s and 1930s.[4]

Gu argued that on matters like this, it was more important to empirically examine the issues involved (i.e. looking at the actual practice of state socialism we found in the USSR and China) rather than dogmatically assuming that Marxism had already solved all the economic problems under socialism once and for all. In "Tentative Discussion", Gu was not only courageous enough to point out the contradictions committed by Stalin (2002, p. 96) and the inadequacy of classical Marxist theory on this matter, he in effect advanced the thesis that without the price mechanism in the market, there was no rational basis to come up with a common yardstick to measure and compare the relative economic efficacy of different products, services and factors of production in a society. Like what Mises and Hayek had argued, Gu believed that central planning alone would not provide us with the necessary information for economic allocation, production and coordination.

Gu admitted in "Tentative Discussion" that classical Marxism argued that in theory, market exchanges among individuals would be abolished and money as a medium of exchange was therefore superfluous under socialism. Money would then be replaced by coupons which represented the useful labor time contributed by the workers concerned in productive work. Workers could use the coupons to redeem the allocated consumption products they deserved to get under a socialist economy (ibid., p. 79). However, Gu reminded us that the historical experience in Soviet Russia demonstrated that the efforts in introducing the labor coupons to replace money in the country after the October Revolution failed, and Lenin was forced to reverse this policy by 1921. Money as a medium of exchange had since been reintroduced and it remained in place in the USSR and in socialist China (ibid., p. 83). On matters like this, Gu thought that instead of being dogmatic, one should be open-minded and learn from our actual experience, since Marx and Engels were not in a position to know about all the subsequent developments that occurred in the socialist states with ready-made answers to the new problems we might encounter subsequently (ibid., p. 88).

Gu argued that money as a medium of exchange had many functions that could not be replaced by labor coupons. For example, as a general medium of exchange, money allows consumers to use it to buy different kinds of products and services since it provides a common numerical standard for exchange. Also, through savings, interests, credits, loans and other related financial tools, money can be developed into a credit system that facilitates delayed or advanced spending and investment if the people or enterprises find it desirable to do so. However, the crucial point is that money, together with the price mechanism and the law of value, provides a common standard in economic calculation to help determine what rational economic decisions should be made to enhance productivity and better distribution of resources.

Gu noted that classical Marxism did not anticipate the need of doing economic calculation under socialism. Quite the contrary, it postulated that products produced under socialism would not be converted into value since they were produced for socialized use, not for exchange (ibid., pp. 104, 108–109). However, Gu argued that if socialism aimed to increase a society's overall productivity and to improve the wellbeing of the people, we could not simply rely on a pre-determined central plan to come up with information about the relative economic efficacy of a certain product when compared with its substitutes before making the most economically rational decision for production and resource distribution. Instead, we would have to rely on economic calculation to ascertain the relative economic efficacy of the concerned product before a production and distribution decision was made. This, in effect, is the same as admitting the inevitability of the economic problem under the circumstances, a theoretical point recognized by people like Hayek, who believes that "decisions of this sort will have to be made in any conceivable kind of economic system, wherever one has to choose between alternative employments of given resources" so that the advantages deriving from the most economical use of given resources can be taken ([1948] 1980, p. 123).

Why the most economical use of given resources cannot be planned in advance? Gu's answer was that it was because the level of labor productivity changes all the time, depending on many contingent and changing factors, such as the more efficient use of given resources due to technological breakthrough, the change in the length of necessary labor time, the improved skillful use of production facilities, the reduction in management cost, variation of time in the cycle of production, the extent of using recyclable materials, so on and so forth (2002, p. 85). Gu believed that only through economic calculation could we capture this kind of dynamic information to help planners come up with a rational approach in economic planning. Gu argued that historically, it had been proven that treating the whole society or country as one accounting unit in economic calculation was not viable (ibid., p. 97). Instead, each enterprise should be treated as one separate and independent accounting unit, each possessing its own fund and balance sheet to do the calculation. Where necessary, a big enterprise should also be sub-divided into different independent sub-units for the same accounting purposes. This, in effect, amounts to suggesting that there should be decentralization in the management of enterprises, with each enterprise enjoying its autonomous status in economic calculation. This eventually was a reform measure adopted under the Deng era for the development of market socialism after the late 1970s.

Gu's idea is that the price of a product is a numerical index expressed in the form of a circulating currency that represents the value of a product. If the currency is relatively stable, the price of a product, when compared with the value of that product, is relatively more stable, though the sum total of all the prices in a society in the end must equal the sum total of the values of all the products produced in that society. If the price of a particular product in that society is higher than the value of the product concerned, it will be balanced out by the lower than value price of another product in the same society in the end. In a society's division of labor, the necessary labor spent on a particular product is not a constant, and hence the value of the product may vary from time to time as explained above. The value of that particular product is also not the same as the average useful labor time spent on all the products of the society too, and it is through this relativity in values, which ultimately are translated into the relative prices of different products in the market, that helps determine the relative economic efficacy of different products (ibid., pp. 106–111).

Gu said that the pure income in an accounting unit through the sale or transfer of products was not a pre-known data. Instead, it is through economic calculation, reflecting the changes in the unit's productivity level and the demand and supply situation in the economic process, that the enterprise concerned could come up with the actual data, which is the total income minus the cost of production (including workers' salary, expenses for resources and facilities for production, maintenance and management fees, depreciation, taxation and so on) (ibid., pp. 155–173). The same kind of product or its substitute may be produced by different accounting units, but the pure income of each of them may vary, depending on their ability to control cost and to meet new demands. If the enterprises or producers are in a position to adjust the price of the product in accordance with their productivity level and with the demand and supply situation found in the market, those with higher productivity and earn more pure income will be in a position to adjust the price of the product to facilitate more production and sales, aligning the price more with the adjusted value of the product. This in effect is bringing market competition back in to the economic process.

The dynamic nature of economic calculation and the static nature of central planning were clearly recognized by Gu in "Tentative Discussion":

> Economic calculation's ability to make adjustment helps economic planning obtain data that cannot be obtained by statistical surveys, and it is on the basis of these data that future economic planning is to be made. For example, when a society's level of consumption is raised, production of consumption materials should in parallel be expanded accordingly. However, amongst the different and diverse kinds of consumption goods, which ones should be expanded, the extent of expansion, and the proportion of expansion amongst different consumption goods are all important data that cannot be reliably found just by consumption surveys, no matter how meticulous these surveys are. Yet by observing the movements in the retail market of consumption goods, by identifying which products are very much sought after and which are not, and by looking at the price adjustments made in the sales of these products, one can detect all the changes happened in demand and supply and, in accordance with which,

> one could adjust one's production decisions. Similarly, in each production enterprise, the sales situations and the related price and profit adjustments happened to its products are important indicators telling us the degree of equilibrium achieved between product production and consumption and the changes in productivity level. Information of these kinds are all very useful for future economic planning. Society's re-production process is a continuous process and the annual production plan for the society does not come out of the blue. The information and data generated from economic calculation form one fundamental basis for economic planning. Without these, no economic planning can be made (ibid., p. 99).

While Gu mostly adopted socialist ideas and terminology in advancing his arguments for economic calculation under socialist planning in "Tentative Discussion", the logic underlying his analysis was in many respects consistent with the critique of socialist calculation as separately developed by Mises and Hayek, though Gu did not go all the way to analyze in what ways were the decentralized, independent accounting units (i.e. enterprises) different from the privately owned enterprises and how these state-owned but independent units could be autonomous and state-directed at the same time when doing economic calculation. Likewise, Gu's insistence on economic calculation did not go all the way to deny socialist planning, even though it was clear from his arguments that the two were logically rather incompatible.

The publication of "Tentative Discussion" in 1957 eventually earned Gu the honor of being regarded by many as the true "father" of socialist China's market reform (Bottelier 2018, p. 132), though its more immediate impact was that partly because of this, he was purged by the Party as a rightist (i.e. a reactionary who opposed the revolution). He was expelled from the Party in the autumn of 1957 (Gu 2002, pp. 225–250). Although Gu was not the only first generation economist (Bottelier 2018, pp. 125–138) since the establishment of the People's Republic to advocate the importance of the market in building socialism after 1949, his "Tentative Discussion" was the most critical and comprehensive theoretical treatise before the Cultural Revolution to openly examine the limits of central planning and the necessity of introducing economic calculation in China.[5]

Hayek is of the view that "the differences between socialists and non-socialists ultimately rest on purely intellectual issues capable of a scientific resolution and not on different judgments of value", and he believes that the doctrines advocated by the socialists "can be shown to be based on factually false assumptions", and the whole family of socialists thought can be "proven erroneous" (1973, p. 6). When it comes to Gu's understanding of the relationship between economic calculation and socialist planning, I think it can be said that he was closer to Hayek than to Mao and the then Chinese Communist Party. This is one reason why he is labeled by some today as "China's Hayek" (Ma 2010, in Luo ed. 2017, pp. 328–348). But the subsequent political purges against him and his experience during the Great Leap Forward and the Cultural Revolution helped convince Gu that Communist idealism was not the answer to China's modernization. Instead, liberal empiricism was what was needed if one wanted to avoid the horrors of totalitarianism.

## Famine, Politics in Command and the Horrors of Totalitarian Rule

Not long after Gu was expelled from the Party in November 1957, he was sent to labor camps for re-education. He was first sent to a camp in Hebei province (May–December 1958), and later to the remote rural area of Shangcheng (March 1959–February 1960) in Henan where he experienced one of the worst famines in human history. That was the Great Chinese Famine of 1959–1961, in which close to 30 million people were estimated to have died in the food crisis (Sen 1999, p. 181; Lin and Yang 2000, p. 145).

In November 1961, Gu managed to remove his rightist label and resumed his work in the Economic Research Institute of the Chinese Academy of Science. But he was purged as a rightist again in September 1965 before the start of the Cultural Revolution. This time, his wife divorced him and later committed suicide. His children denounced him as father and refused to see him again throughout his life.

Gu, however, did not stop reflecting on the Communist experience of China during these difficult times. Most of his critical reflections in these two re-education periods can be found in his diaries from October 1959 to January 1960 and October 1969 to September 1971 (Gu 1997, 2002), respectively, with the former chronicling how the Famine killed many of the rural peasants in Shangcheng, and the latter recording his personal suffering after having learned of his wife's suicide. These diaries also contained his analysis that the politics in command kind of revolutionary approach adopted by Mao would eventually need to give way to economic reform and opening up if China wanted to avoid further economic catastrophes and to build a strong nation.[6]

Although Gu's diaries were no systematic studies of the Communist experience of China in those periods, his analysis was sharp as his critique profound. For example, a careful reading and reconstruction of his observations there could help vindicate Amartya Sen's subsequent entitlements approach in explaining the cause of famines in modern society where both property and democratic rights are absent (Sen 1981; Zhang 1998, in Luo ed. 2017, pp. 191–212). One famous quote of Hayek is from Leon Trotsky: "in a country where the sole employer is the State, opposition means death by slow starvation" (Hayek [1944] 1972, p. 119). Gu's analysis in his diaries echoed this observation. It showed that in a country where the sole employer and power holder was the Party, and the Party upheld politics in command with a wartime economy imposed on the peasants with a view to achieving rapid industrialization in the urban cities at the expenses of the rural areas, death by slow starvation for many peasants in the countryside was probably inevitable, even though the overall food supply may still be sufficient to feed the whole population. The absolute control in this period was supplemented by ruthless political campaigns and oppression against the "class enemies", in which Gu was labeled as one of them.

In Gu's Shangcheng diary (Gu 1997, pp. 1–131), three things came out very prominently. They were, firstly, hunger, food and death by starvation. Secondly, hard labor by the rural people and those who were undergoing re-education in the labor camps even at the time of food crisis. Thirdly, Gu's reflection on the cause of the Famine and how Communist oppression inevitably led to general moral depravity, which was reminiscent of what Hannah Arendt has to say about totalitarian domination: the killing of the juridical person in man, the murder of the moral person in man, leading finally to the killing of man's individuality (Arendt 1973, pp. 437–459).

We learn from Gu's December 1959 diary entries that there were 79 members in his hard labor team, most of them were under re-education in Shangcheng (ibid., pp. 71–72). He reported that in the summer of 1959, a few team members started to look bloated because of malnutrition. This was to increase to over 40 in September and October, which later jumped to over 70 in November/December 1959 when the famine in Shangcheng sunk in and hit the population hard (ibid., pp. 47–48). Gu subsequently recorded that three members of the hard labor team died (ibid., p. 119). This, on its own, already indicated the seriousness of the famine, and we should be mindful that even under such a situation, most of them in the team (except the leading cadres who were there to enforce party rules) were required to do whole day hard labor work most of the time. Gu himself was required to engage in all day hard labor work in 190 days out of the 199 days while he was with the team in Shangcheng (ibid., p. 82).

However, when compared with the local peasantry, the situation in the hard labor team looked like "heaven" and a "safe haven". This was the case because while food was scarce, its supply had not been stopped for the team (ibid., p. 13). On the contrary, out of the 13 members in Gu's vegetable farming sub-unit in his hard labor team, there were six local members, out of which five had family members died of starvation at that time (ibid., p. 87). In his 17 December 1959 diary entry, Gu recorded that a member in another sub-unit named Huang had his wife, father, elder brother and two kids died of starvation within a matter of one and a half months. At least four local members in the hard labor team had more than one family member died of starvation (ibid., pp. 51–52, 94). In fact, there were horrendous news of cannibalism in Shangcheng as recorded in Gu's 22 December 1959 entry, in which a husband ate his wife after he had killed her, and an aunt ate her niece after the latter had passed away (ibid., p. 58).

Gu estimated that in that winter, if the then 420,000 population of Shangcheng could be reduced by 70,000 to 350,000 before local food supply was expected to improve next spring, it would be a very good thing already (ibid., p. 53). Gu observed that hunger would drive people to do whatever necessary for survival, such as cannibalism, prostituting, lying, flattering in order to get favor, falsely accusing others in return for food and so on (ibid., p. 118). In his 14 January 1960 diary entry, Gu was tormented by the fact that he stole food in order to combat hunger many of the times while he was in the hard labor team (ibid., p. 113). Gu described Shangcheng as a land full of wailing and despair (ibid., p. 74) where it was not uncommon that half of the members of an agricultural production team in the rural area died. Gu also noted that while the situation in Henan was bad, the province further south in Hubei was even worse (ibid., pp. 119, 130). That spoke volumes of the serious situation in this Famine during the Great Leap Forward.

But the situation in the urban areas was very different. Gu was allowed to leave the labor camp in Shangcheng on 28 December 1959 after having served in the hard labor team for 199 days. He, together with other released members of the team, stayed in the county town area of Shangcheng until 17 January 1960 before returning back to Beijing. Throughout these weeks, Gu no longer faced starvation. Food supply for him and his colleagues was not a problem then. They even had the opportunity of visiting a designated model village Changchunyuan south of Shangcheng. Gu found that Changchunyuan had a population of 20,000 with 20,000 acres of good quality farm land. Although it was a remote village, food supply was abundant. Unlike peasants in other rural areas who were required to help with massive infrastructural projects, such as highway and big dam construction, people in Changchunyuan were not required to do the same. A nearby village called Daquandian also enjoyed similar privilege and was relatively well off (ibid., p. 90).

Even in the badly affected areas, as we have seen above, the hard labor team was in a better situation than the ordinary peasantry in Shangcheng. Although members in the team were mostly rightists and were undergoing socialist re-education, most of them were from the big cities. The team and the labor camp were managed by the Party with relatively secure though reduced food supply. The ordinary peasants, on the contrary, did not enjoy this treatment. In addition to facing reduced supply, the peasants had to fulfill the official procurement quotas before they could have food to eat. Also, within the team, the leaders and those who were close to or favored by the leaders never had the problem of having adequate food supply.

For example, Shen Wanshan was the party secretary responsible for re-educating the members of Gu's hard labor team. Not only that he could eat whatever he wanted, he also occupied the best acre of land in the camp, which could produce high quality vegetable with members of the team helping him do many of the necessary chores in the field (ibid., p. 3). Gu described Shen as a "dictator" and "emperor", saying that while members who planted the melons in the field were thieves if they picked the melons without formal permission, Shen could pick them anytime he liked for private use. His family members could take whatever food they wished in the collective kitchen anytime, which was a forbidden area for other team members. Similarly, those who had the fortune of working in the collective kitchen or were being favored by Shen were a privileged few with their own rights (ibid., pp. 8, 37).

In his diary, Gu did not subscribe to the view that the main cause of the Famine was the sudden drop of total food supply, even though China did suffer from drought and bad harvest then (ibid., p. 58). Instead, he believed that it was the result of a centralized, tightly controlled political system imposed by the Chinese Communist Party, with the aim of speeding up China's industrialization by creating a kind of semi-military type of wartime economy to exploit a backward, massive and overpopulated rural sector in order to squeeze enough surplus for urban modernization.

Gu argued that China had long been a vast agricultural country with the peasantry living on a subsistence kind of economy. Any rapid population growth in the countryside would easily lead to overpopulation without a corresponding growth of food supply, unless there was a great improvement in agricultural productivity, which could only be achieved by agricultural mechanization in a large scale. This situation well fitted into the Malthusian trap and the related theory of population (ibid., p. 48). In order to cope with this problem, Gu believed that the Chinese Communist Party under Mao wanted to solve the problem of rural overpopulation and the need for rapid industrialization in one go by following Stalin's collectivization program of the 1930s. In the Chinese context, what was introduced was a rigid household registration system, in which there was a strict control for people's movement between the urban and rural areas and from one's registered household location to other locations. Secondly, in the rural areas, people's communes, a kind of semi-military production and labor formations, grouped all the peasants into different units, the organization of which were modeled after the military for mass mobilization to help build great infrastructural projects for the state during their off-peak agricultural seasons. According to Gu's diary, 70 million people nation-wide were organized for this purpose in 1959 to exploit the cheap and massive labor force in the rural areas for rapid modernization.

In the communes, collective kitchens were established with food rationing and consumption under tight control. When overall food supply was a problem, the collective kitchens would be hit seriously since the Party adopted a policy of favoring the urban areas in order to facilitate urban development and rapid growth in heavy industry (ibid., pp. 58–59, 86). Another serious problem for the rural areas in the Great Leap Forward was that under the euphoria of rapid transition to socialism promoted at the time, many local authorities had largely exaggerated many of their alleged production quotas in order to demonstrate their revolutionary zeal and achievement, the result of which was that local rural food supply was further diminished because of the need to fulfill the inflated quota requirements. Lin and Yang's (2000) research showed that while 1959s overall food supply dropped by 15%, China's net grain export (presumably to earn foreign currency) still continued to reach historical height. In addition, the total procurement of grain output by the central authorities also reached a peak since the quota-output ratio of 25.9% in 1958 was raised by inflated quotas to 37.7% in 1959. "As a result", Lin and Yang said, "the excessive procurement severely reduced the food supply to which rural people were entitled" (Lin and Yang 2000, pp. 143–144) during this serious food crisis.

Gu at that time did not have the benefit of having access to the relevant macro data that Lin and Yang later have in analyzing this Famine.

But what he observed in his diary was essentially confirmed by Lin and Yang's more systematic work almost 40 years later, in which they argued:

> In 1953, the central government introduced a system of Unified Procurement and Unified Sale for grain and oil-bearing crops, which brought all grain procurement and distribution under its direct control, as a way to suppress food prices...Accompanying the Unified Procurement and Unified Sale was a rigid household registration system, which deprived the rural population of the right to move to urban areas and thereby put the country-to-city migration under the government's tight control. The aim of these schemes was to extract as much agricultural surplus as possible to facilitate the heavy-industry-oriented development strategy that had resulted in an increased demand for grain and other agricultural products for urban food consumption and exports (ibid., p. 139).

Under such a central command policy, when there was a sudden drop of overall food supply, the rural areas had to bear the crux of the food crisis since they were only entitled to the residual grain. The result for this was 30 million deaths by slow starvation. Gu speculated that this perhaps was Mao's conscious policy to control the problem of overpopulation in rural China (Gu 1997, pp. 108–109). He further suggested that the accompanying political persecution campaign of the Anti-rightist Movement served the political purposes of mass mobilization against "class enemies" in a crisis situation. The official line was always that food problem was essentially an ideological, not a practical, problem (ibid., p. 97) because, as always, politics was in command to serve revolutionary cause to build socialism.

Gu's re-education experience in Shangcheng convinced him that the kind of socialism practiced by the Chinese Communist Party at that time was to centralize the whole nation's strengths for wartime-like construction so that the privileged minority could live a normal or luxurious life (ibid., p. 37). He pointed out that while the labor cost in the communes was squeezed to a bare minimum, big and small industrial enterprises in the urban areas could be built whatever the costs, with the remaining surplus going to finance the construction of the Great Hall of the People next to the Tiananmen Square of Beijing and other grand buildings for national celebrations (ibid., pp. 70–71). To Gu, such kind of political control and economic centralization was bound to produce abuse of power, grave disparity and corruption. He believed that the kind of "re-education" offered in the hard labor team would bring nothing but moral depravity (ibid., p. 107). In his 29 December 1959 diary entry, Gu mentioned about the last speech made by party secretary Shen to his team members before they were released. In Gu's view, the essential point made in Shen's speech was to warn them that when compared with the overall achievements of the Party, what the members suffered in the hard labor team—i.e. lying, hunger, death—was nothing, and they, after their release, would have to mind their words in the future if they wanted to avoid further political incorrectness (ibid., p. 76).

Gu's 1959–1960 and 1969–1971 diaries contain many entries describing how he and his fellow members in the labor camps suffered political oppression and moral depravity. But two things stand out most clearly that are close to what Arendt describes as attempts for total domination (1973, pp. 437–459) by totalitarian rule.

The first was the so-called thought exposure exercises, in which the accused were constantly required to expose their innermost "evil" thoughts to the Party and to the people in public if they wanted to have a chance for rectification. The accused were also required to participate in the thought exposure exercises against other rightists and to join criticizing and accusing the latter openly. The more actively they participated in these mutual criticisms and exposures, the more politically correct they would be as perceived by the Party (Gu 1997, pp. 15, 20, 24–25). The second was that refusal to admit guilt and even committing suicide by the accused were no escape, for these would only be regarded as proofs that they were die-hard counter-revolutionaries in life and in death. This would likely bring adverse consequences to family members or close colleagues of the accused.

In Gu's 12 November 1969 diary entry, there is a very tragic and moving description of how he received the news about his wife's death in Beijing while he was about to be sent to a labor camp in Henan for re-education. Gu's wife, as we now know, took her own life in April 1968. Gu did not learn about this piece of sad news for over one and half year. Though he had suspected that something terribly wrong must have happened to her, the Party refused to inform him about this for a long time since he was a second-time rightist. This is what was written down by Gu in his diary when the news was broken to him:

> When I learned about this fatal news, I was both surprised and not surprised. I was surprised because since she loved the children so much, how could she leave this "mother committing suicide" label to the family? I was not surprised because she had written a will in the autumn of 1965. And in May 1967, it was then clear that she was no longer strong enough to cope with all the pressure she had to face. When Yang told me about the news, I said, "Why committing suicide? She did not allow me to do that, saying that people like me committing suicide would harm people [who were related to me]. Now, why she wanted to harm people?" All I want to know now is how she died. Zhao said that they would try to find out this for me. I then went to get my portion of meal to eat [in the canteen]. After having eaten a few mouthful of rice, I was overwhelmed by my feeling of great sorrow. I buried my face down in the rice tray and burst out crying. But I still tried to restrain myself, making every effort to finish my meal. I need to stay alive (ibid., p. 160).

Gu's entry here reminds me of Arendt's acute analysis of total domination:

> Totalitarian terror achieved its most terrible triumph when it succeeded in cutting the moral person off from the individualist escape and in making the decision of conscience absolutely questionable and equivocal...when even suicide would mean the immediate murder of his own family—how is he to decide? The alternative is no longer between good and evil, but between murder and murder (1973, p. 452).

Although Gu was spared the fate of choosing between murder and murder in his case, his children no longer recognized him as father. Until his death in 1974, Gu was never to meet them again.

Gu observed that the so called thought exposure exercise was both a divide and rule tactic and a kind of political blackmail, with the former attempting to destroy one's moral self, and the latter to exert control over the accused since if the accused wanted to beg for rectification, they would need to fully cooperate in these exercises (1997, pp. 20, 40). By the same logic, Gu realized that thought exposure must start with admission of "guilt" by the accused in order to stand any chance of being accepted. The more serious the "guilt" and the more "evil" the counter-revolutionary thought and action the accused confessed, the more politically correct one might be (ibid., 24). If we remember that Gu had written over 200,000 words for self-confession (2002), we cannot say that Gu refused to participate in this morally corrupt undertaking. But what was remarkable was that he was not crashed by the attempts of total domination. He remained critical through and through to examine what had gone wrong with an idealistic revolution which he had so enthusiastically embraced when he was a young professional.

## From Revolutionary Idealism to Liberal Empiricism

Gu's post-1949 experience in Communist China had changed his outlook and political belief fundamentally, transforming him from advocating revolutionary idealism to embracing liberal empiricism. "Today", Gu wrote in 1973, "when people in the names of the martyrs have changed revolutionary idealism into conservative, reactionary authoritarianism, I am determined to embrace the most thorough kind of empiricism and pluralism and to fight against this type of authoritarianism to the end" (2013, p. 187).

Given the vicissitudes of Gu's life, he did not have the opportunity to produce systematic work on the horrors of totalitarian domination and his conversion to liberal empiricism. Some of his family members (his younger brother in particular) and colleagues nevertheless managed to keep his diaries, private correspondence, reading notes and some unpublished papers safe for publication in the 1990s, which contained many of his important, albeit fragmented, reflections on post-revolution China. When commenting on the 1990s posthumous publication of Gu's works, historian Yinghong Cheng says, "in his loneliness and having no access to the resources of Western liberal literature, Gu worked to seek answers for the questions related to Marxism and revolution…[t]he result was an unintended crossover between his thoughts and some fundamental liberal ideas...[This] showed the world the fact that even in the darkest years of intellectual suffocation, some seeds of liberal ideas still survived [in Communist China]" (2008, pp. 385–386).

In this concluding section, I am going to summarize some of the more important thoughts of Gu that can be regarded as crossovers to liberalism.

My analysis in the socialist planning section of this chapter should have made it quite clear that when Gu was still a member of the Chinese Communist Party, his idea on economic calculation and on the price mechanism, the law of value and market exchange had already put him more on the side of Mises and Hayek in the theoretical debate of socialist central planning and market reform, though Gu's discussion was very much formulated in socialist jargon. Equally important was the fact that very early on, Gu supported financial and managerial autonomy of local enterprises under a socialist state. Intellectually speaking, the remarkable thing about Gu was that he probably was the first mainland Chinese economist who dared to openly challenge some central tenets of Marxism and Stalinism in economic theory and demanded solid empirical corroboration in order to ascertain the validity of classical socialist thought. Gu was always a fighter against dogmatism.

Gu's reflection on the horrors of the labor camps and the Great Chinese Famine in his diaries not only paralleled Sen's entitlements approach in explaining famines in modern societies, it was also a damaging indictment against the deprivation of the basic rights of the people and the blindness and dangers of a top-down, pre-determined command plan for forced modernization and industrialization. Gu's reflection demonstrated the moral bankruptcy of the attempt to exert total domination over dissension, since total domination required total power, which would easily lead to total abuse of power, encourage hypocrisy, double standards and, in the end, promote corruption of the moral self.

In the last two years (1973–74) of his life, Gu and his younger brother Chen Minzhi[7] exchanged a lot of letters discussing many issues, both academic and political, of common concern. Chen subsequently edited Gu's letters to him into a book and published it under the title *From Idealism to Empiricism* (Gu 2013). In this book, Gu examined the important question of what happened after the revolution. Here Gu alluded to the main character Nora of Henrik Ibsen's famous play *A Doll House*, who decided to take control of her own fate by leaving her husband and family in pursuit of the meaning of life in the then male-dominated Norwegian society. The important question for Gu was: "what happens after Nora has left?"

Gu noted that since the seventeenth century, there had been two revolutionary traditions. One was England's Glorious Revolution and the American War of Independence, the other the 1789 and 1870 French Revolutions. Gu pointed out that the first tradition triggered the development of capitalism, while the latter, bringing two empires and five republics to France, attempted to replace capitalism with socialism without success (2013, p. 136). It was until 1917 that the revolutionary force in Russia was strong enough to smash all opposing resistance to the vanguard party by revolutionary dictatorship. One thing common to the two French Revolutions and the 1917 Revolution was that they both had an ultimate goal, which was to establish an ideal society of socialism on earth. Gu linked the origin of this "ultimate goal" tradition to Christianity, which not only postulated a divine standard of perfection and the ultimate good, but also believed that Christ was destined to return to the world and bring with Him perfection on earth. Following this tradition, the earthly revolutionaries were there to bring the ultimate good of communism on earth too. Gu argued that while to start with, most revolutionaries were democrats, in the end, for the sake of the realization of the "ultimate goal" of the revolution and the ultimate good, they invariably resorted to all necessary coercive means, including sacrificing democracy, imposing dictatorship and Stalinist tyranny to achieve heaven on earth (ibid., pp. 137–138).

While this formulation of the argument here may be crude, it can be regarded as spelling out the folly of an embryonic idea of establishing a kind of modern collective state called "enterprise association" or "teleocracy", as postulated by Oakeshott and Hayek (Oakeshott 1991; Hayek [1978] 1990).[8] Gu's reservation of this "ultimate goal" approach of the revolution is threefold. Firstly, historically speaking, not only the "ultimate goal" has never be realized, the opposite is usually the case. The following, as one example, was what Gu wrote in 1973:

> With the victory of the 1917 revolution, Lenin assured the Russian youths of that generation that communism would be realized within their life time. However many of those youths by now would have been dead. For

> those who are still alive, what they now see is that while the Soviet navy is cruising around the world, their living standard is worse than Czechoslovakia. They also witness the protests initiated by the wife of [the dissident] Andrei Sakharov and her persecution [by the Communist Party]. As for today's definition of communism, it is increasingly inconsistent with and divergent from Marx's definition in *The Communist Manifesto*—"we shall have an association, in which the free development of each is the condition for the free development of all"—to the extent that it is increasingly difficult to understand what it really means (2013, p. 138).

Gu reminded us that while Lenin promised direct democracy after the revolution and set up the soviets in the factories then, sooner rather than later, direct democracy was replaced by centralization of power. The history of the USSR and the People's Republic of China so far had both corroborated the same trend of post-revolutionary dictatorship (ibid., p. 134).

Gu's second reservation is this. At best, the idea of the "ultimate good" cannot be a fixed and static one. Since a static concept implies no further development, it is the end of human progress and is far from satisfactory. In other words, the "ultimate good" in the end is by nature a moving and slippery target that can never be achieved. The more we pursue it, the farther it will move away (ibid., p. 138). Thirdly, Gu found it doubtful if we could demonstrate a priori that the "ultimate good" postulated must be the truth and could not be challenged. Such an assumption could easily be slid into dogmatism (ibid., p. 169). The only way to prove if our judgment of the so-called ultimate good was valid, Gu argued, was to subject it to further empirical test, which must be open-ended, with different possible results and interpretations (ibid., p. 170).

For the above reasons, Gu preferred the empirical and pluralistic approach and argued that the English and American Revolutions, whatever their shortcomings, had embodied the open-ended empirical tradition of freedom and democracy, even allowing dissenting voices and political opposition to exist so long as they subscribed to a common set of procedural rules for peaceful co-existence. For this tradition of revolutions, there is no "ultimate goal" pre-determined. It only postulates a process of continuous interaction trying to make improvements (ibid.,

p. 138). While Gu's discussion here again is sketchy comparing with what Oakeshott and Hayek postulate as "civil association" or "nomocracy" in their discussion of the liberal state in their political philosophy (Oakeshott 1991; Hayek [1978] 1990), it is perhaps not unreasonable to say that what Gu preferred was clearly closer to nomocracy than teleocracy.

Not long before Gu died in December 1974, he said that even Mao accepted the fact that it was inevitable that there were rival factions in revolutionary parties. The liberals would certainly argue that if there is no institutionally accepted arrangements to resolve factional conflicts after the revolution, revolutionary dictatorship by those in power will lead to endless internal political struggles which, in the end, are self-destructive and self-defeating. To them, it is better to follow the American Revolution's example of allowing opposition factions to develop into different political parties and allow them to peacefully compete for office. Gu came to admit that there was no perfect institution as such on earth. The logic of this points to the conclusion that any system that can inherently develop a capacity of self-correction is far better than a system that leads to self-destruction, although how one can bring about this to a particular political community is a different matter.

The publication of Gu's works in the 1990s has revived much interest in liberalism in mainland China (Cheng 2008; Zhu 1999, pp. 151–170; Qian 2017, pp. 667–708, 943–1021; Luo 2017). Gu's courage, foresight and the crossovers of his ideas to some fundamental values of liberalism at a time when China was under totalitarian rule attracted a lot of attention amongst the intellectuals then. They started to reconnect China's political discourse to liberalism, a discourse that had been severed for over four decades since the Communists took over the mainland. This chapter does not have the space to explore what has happened after this revival of interest in liberalism, but it is not without ironies to say that China's present-day policy of supporting economic globalization and international free trade would not have been conceivable if there has been no liberal turn in ideology in the Communist Party's pursuit of socialism with Chinese characteristics. Gu's example, nevertheless, shows that liberalism, even under the most adverse circumstances, could still find its strengths and adherents amongst some of the most outstanding Chinese intellectuals after all.

## Notes

1. The development of modern Chinese liberalism is too big a topic for this chapter to deal with. For a critical discussion of the revival of interest in market and classical liberalism in post-war Taiwan and the Chinese mainland, please see (Cheung 2017).
2. According to (Leighton 2014, pp. 133–135), Gu's specialist system of taxation comprised the compilation of an updated and detailed list of commercial taxpayers in Shanghai, on the basis of which he ranked the taxpaying entities and companies into three tiers, from large enterprises to peddlers, with each group having different treatment in terms of taxing their profit or income. Gu instituted several control mechanisms to ensure proper tax payment, with investigation teams set up to double check the companies' vouchers and compared them with the accounts in their books. He also created tax-paying mutual aid groups for taxing small- and medium-sized capitalists. In December 1951, Chen Yun, the leading official responsible for economic policy in Beijing, opined in a central Party meeting that Gu Zhun's method was correct with Chairman Mao's endorsement.
3. The Chinese title of this article is〈試論社會主義制度下的商品生產和價值規律〉. The translation of the Chinese texts into English in this chapter is all done by the author.
4. To the best of my knowledge, there is no reference in Gu's works to indicate that he had the benefit of having read Mises and Hayek in his lifetime, although in his reading notes and diaries (Gu 1997, 2002c), we find that he had read the following non-Marxist economists from the West: Cannon, Pigou, Smith, Keynes, Sraffa, Fisher, Böhm-Bawerk, Veblen, Clark, List, Marshall and Rostow. In addition, Gu did translate Schumpeter's *Capitalism, Socialism and Democracy*, volume two of Joan Robinson's *Collected Economic Papers* and most of Mill's *Principles of Political Economy* into Chinese in the 1960s. But Gu did not manage to finish translating Mill's work due to his persecution in 1968 (Luo 2017, p. 69), and the translated works of Schumpeter and Robinson were published only posthumously after the Cultural Revolution in 1979 and 1984, respectively. In 2 January 1970 entry of his diary, Gu did mention that he had read Oskar Lange's textbook of political economy (Gu 1997, p. 179). But he did not refer to the debate on market socialism between Lange-Taylor and Hayek in the late 1930s and early 1940s there.

5. Other market-oriented first-generation economists at that time include Sun Yefang and Xue Muqiao, both were key economic advisers to Deng Xiaoping during the opening up period after the Cultural Revolution. Sun is famous for being the first Chinese mainland economist who advocated the indispensability of the law of value in socialist economy in the 1950s (Sun 1979, pp. 1–14), but Sun personally acknowledged to his colleagues and students that he was influenced by Gu while developing this idea (Zhang 1993, in Luo ed. 2017, pp. 24–25). In the 1960s, Xue put a lot of emphasis on the price mechanism for macroeconomic management under socialist planning, but Gu went beyond Xue's idea by emphasizing that the price mechanism will have to follow the law of demand and supply closely in order to function well (Gu 2002b, pp. 155–173).
6. Judging from the different writing styles of these two periods of Gu's diaries, I agree with the observation that his 1959–1960 diary was written without the fear of being discovered, while his 1969–1971 diary was written in a way that was mindful of the danger of being used for further political persecution against him. During the Cultural Revolution, Gu was forced to write over 200,000 words of confessional statements (2002a), reexamining his life's "capitalist" and "counter-revolutionary" ideas and actions and how he was prepared to "wholeheartedly" and "thoroughly" transform himself through re-education to become a new man again.
7. Unlike his brothers and sisters, Gu used his mother's maiden name as his surname in the family while his siblings all followed his father's surname.
8. Space limits prohibit me from analyzing the nature of teleocracy versus nomocracy/enterprise association versus civil association in this chapter. For my discussion on this, see Cheung (2014).

## References

Arendt, Hannah. 1973. *The Origins of Totalitarianism*. San Diego: A Harvest/HB Book.

Bottelier, Pieter. 2018. *Economic Policy Making in China (1949–2016): The Role of Economists*. Milton: Routledge.

Chang, Hao. 1971. *Liang Ch'i-ch'ao and intellectual transition in China, 1890–1907*. Cambridge, MA: Harvard University Press.

Cheng, Yinghong. 2008. Liberalism in Contemporary China: ten years after its 'resurface'. *Journal of Contemporary China*, 17(55): 383–400.
Cheung, Chor-yung. 2014. Hayek on Nomocracy and Teleocracy: A Critical Assessment. *Cosmos + Taxis: Studies in Emerging Order and Organization*, 1(2), 24–34.
_____. 2017. Oakeshott, Hayek and the Conservative Turn of Chinese Liberalism. In: *The Place of Michael Oakeshott in Contemporary Western and Non-Western Thought*, ed. Noel K. O'Sullivan, pp. 160–180. Exeter: Imprint Academic.
Chou, Tse-tsung. 1960. *The May fourth movement: intellectual revolution in modern China*. Cambridge, MA: Harvard University Press.
Grieder, Jerome B. 1970. *Hu Shih and the Chinese Renaissance: Liberalism in the Chinese Revolution, 1917–1937*. Cambridge, MA: Harvard University Press.
Gu, Zhun (顧準). 1997. *Gu Zhun Diaries* (《顧準日記》). Beijing: Economic Daily Press.
_____. 2002a. *Gu Zhun: A Self Report* (《顧準自述》). Beijing: China Youth Publishing House.
_____. 2002b. *Gu Zhun's Papers* (《顧準文稿》). Beijing: China Youth Publishing House.
_____. 2002c. *Gu Zhun's Reading Notes* (《顧準筆記》). Beijing: China Youth Publishing House.
_____. 2002d. *Gu Zhun's Diaries* (《顧準日記》). Beijing: China Youth Publishing House.
_____. 2013. *From Idealism to Empiricism* (《從理想主義到經濟主義》). Beijing: Guangming Daily Press.
Hayek, F. A. (1948) 1980. *Individualism and Economic Order*. Chicago: The University of Chicago Press.
_____. (1944) 1972. *The Road to Serfdom*. Chicago: The University of Chicago Press.
_____. 1973. *Law, Legislation and Liberty, Vol. I: Rules and Oder*. London and Henley: Routledge & Kegan Paul.
_____. (1978) 1990. *New Studies in Philosophy, Politics, Economics and History of Ideas*. Chicago: The University of Chicago Press.
Huang, Max Ko-wu. 2008. *The Meaning of Freedom: Yan Fu and the Origins of Chinese Liberalism*. Hong Kong: The Chinese University Press.
Kwok, D. W. Y. 1965. *Scientism in Chinese Thought: 1900–1950*. New Haven: Yale University Press.

Leighton, Christopher R. 2014. Venture Communist: Gu Zhun in Shanghai, 1949–1952. In: *The Capitalist Dilemma in China's Communist Revolution,* ed. Sherman Cochran, pp. 119–147. Ithaca, New York: Cornell East Asia Program.
Lin, Yu-sheng. 1979. *The Crisis of Chinese Consciousness: Radical Antitraditionalism in the May Fourth Era.* Wisconsin: The University of Wisconsin Press.
Lin, Justin Yifu, and Dennis Tao Yang. 2000. Food Availability, Entitlements and the Chinese Famine of 195961. *The Economic Journal,* 110 (Jan): 136–158.
Luo, Yinsheng ed. (羅銀勝編). 2017. *Remembering Gu Zhun* (《顧準追思錄》). Beijing: Central Compilation &Translation Press.
Ma, Tao (馬濤). 2010. China's Hayek: Comparing Gu Zhun's Thought on Market Economy (〈中國的哈耶克:顧準的市場經濟思想與比較〉). In: *Remembering Gu Zhun* (《顧準追思錄》), ed. Luo Yinsheng (羅銀勝), 2017, pp. 328–348. Beijing: Central Compilation &Translation Press.
Mao, Tse-tung. 1961. *Selected Works of Mao Tse-tung, Vol. II.* Peking: Foreign Languages Press.
Mises, Ludwig von. 1963. *Human Action: A Treatise on Economics.* Chicago: Contemporary Books. 3rd Revised Edition.
______. 1981. *Socialism: An Economic and Sociological Analysis.* Indianapolis: Liberty Classics.
Oakeshott, Michael. 1991. *On Human Conduct.* Oxford: Clarendon Press.
Qian, Liqun (錢理群). 2017. *1949–1976: Years of Vicissitudes* (《1949–1976: 歲月滄桑》). Hong Kong: City University of Hong Kong Press.
Schwartz, Benjamin I. 1964. *In Search of Wealth and Power: Yen Fu and the West.* Cambridge, MA: Belknap Press of Harvard University Press.
Sen, Amartya. 1981. Ingredients of Famine Analysis: Availability and Entitlements. *The Quarterly Journal of Economics,* August: 433–464.
______. 1999. *Development as Freedom.* Oxford: Oxford University Press.
Sun, Yefang. (孫冶方). 1979. *Some Theoretical Questions on Socialist Economics* (《社會主義經濟的若干理論問題》). Beijing: People's Press.
Wu, Jinglin (吴敬璉). 2005. The Path of Economic Studies is Far from Smooth (〈經濟學道路不平坦〉). In: *Remembering Gu Zhun* (《顧準追思錄》), ed. Luo Yinsheng (羅銀勝), 2017, pp. 183–185. Beijing: Central Compilation &Translation Press.
Yeh, Wen-hsin. 2007. *Shanghai Splendor: Economic Sentiments and the Making of Modern China, 1843–1949.* Berkeley: University of California Press.
Zhang, Shuguang (張曙光). 1998. A Thinker's Exploration under Adverse Situation: A Study of Gu Zhun's Thought (〈逆境中探索的思想家—顧準思想研究〉). In: *Remembering Gu Zhun* (《顧準追思錄》), ed. Luo Yinsheng (羅銀勝), 2017, pp. 191–212. Beijing: Central Compilation &Translation Press.

Zhang, Jinfu (張勁夫). 1993. A Piece of Important Historical Fact Related to Gu Zhun (〈關於顧準的一件重要史實〉). In: *Remembering Gu Zhun* (《顧準追思錄》), ed. Luo Yinsheng (羅銀勝), 2017, pp. 24–25. Beijing: Central Compilation & Translation Press.
Zhu, Xuequin (朱學勤). 1999. *Thinkers Missing in the History of Ideas* (《思想史上的失蹤者》). Guangzhou: Huacheng Publishing House.

# Author Index[1]

A



B



C



D



[1] Note: Page numbers followed by 'n' refer to notes.



D. F. Hardwick, L. Marsh (eds.), *Reclaiming Liberalism*, Palgrave Studies in Classical Liberalism, https://doi.org/10.1007/978-3-030-28760-3

# Subject Index[1]



[1] Note: Page numbers followed by 'n' refer to notes.



D. F. Hardwick, L. Marsh (eds.), *Reclaiming Liberalism*, Palgrave Studies in Classical Liberalism, https://doi.org/10.1007/978-3-030-28760-3

V



W

The manufacturer's authorised representative in the EU is Springer Nature Customer Service Centre GmbH, Europaplatz 3, 69115 Heidelberg, Germany. If you have any concerns regarding our products, please contact ProductSafety@springernature.com

Printed and bound by CPI Group (UK) Ltd, Croydon, CR0 4YY
05/10/2026
02228143-0005